V|D / M|A

LUTHERAN QUARTERLY BOOKS

Editor

Paul Rorem, Princeton Theological Seminary

Associate Editors

Timothy J. Wengert, The Lutheran Theological Seminary at Philadelphia and Steven Paulson, Luther Seminary, St. Paul

Lutheran Quarterly Books will advance the same aims as *Lutheran Quarterly* itself, aims repeated by Theodore G. Tappert when he was editor fifty years ago and renewed by Oliver K. Olson when he revived the publication in 1987. The original four aims continue to grace the front matter and to guide the contents of every issue, and can now also indicate the goals of *Lutheran Quarterly Books:* "to provide a forum (1) for the discussion of Christian faith and life on the basis of the Lutheran confession; (2) for the application of the principles of the Lutheran church to the changing problems of religion and society; (3) for the fostering of world Lutheranism; and (4) for the promotion of understanding between Lutherans and other Christians."

For further information, see www.lutheranquarterly.com.

The symbol and motto of *Lutheran Quarterly,* VDMA for *Verbum Domini Manet in Aeternum* (1 Peter 1:25), was adopted as a motto by Luther's sovereign, Frederick the Wise, and his successors. The original "Protestant" princes walking out of the imperial Diet of Speyer 1529, unruly peasants following Thomas Muentzer, and from 1531 to 1547 the coins, medals, flags, and guns of the Smalcaldic League all bore the most famous Reformation slogan, the first Evangelical confession: the Word of the Lord remains forever.

V|D
M|A *Lutheran Quarterly Books*

TITLES

Living by Faith: Justification and Sanctification by Oswald Bayer (2003).

Harvesting Martin Luther's Reflections on Theology, Ethics, and the Church, essays from *Lutheran Quarterly* edited by Timothy J. Wengert, with foreword by David C. Steinmetz (2004).

A More Radical Gospel: Essays on Eschatology, Authority, Atonement, and Ecumenism by Gerhard O. Forde, edited by Mark Mattes and Steven Paulson (2004).

A MORE RADICAL GOSPEL

Essays on Eschatology, Authority,
Atonement, and Ecumenism

Gerhard O. Forde

Edited by

Mark C. Mattes *&* Steven D. Paulson

WILLIAM B. EERDMANS PUBLISHING COMPANY
GRAND RAPIDS, MICHIGAN / CAMBRIDGE, U.K.

Wm. B. Eerdmans Publishing Co.
255 Jefferson Ave. S.E., Grand Rapids, Michigan 49503 /
P.O. Box 163, Cambridge CB3 9PU U.K.

Printed in the United States of America

08 07 06 05 04   7 6 5 4 3 2 1

Library of Congress Cataloging-in-Publication Data

Forde, Gerhard O.
    A more radical Gospel: essays on eschatology, authority, atonement, and
ecumenism / Gerhard O. Forde; edited by Mark C. Mattes & Steven D. Paulson.
        p.   cm.
    Includes bibliographical references.
    ISBN 0-8028-2688-1 (pbk.: alk. paper)
    1. Lutheran Church — Doctrines.   2. Theology   3. Bible.
I. Mattes, Mark C.   II. Paulson, Steven D.   III. Title.

BX8065.3.F67   2004
230'.41 — dc22

                                                                2003064343

www.eerdmans.com

Contents

Citations for Previously Published Essays   vii

Abbreviations for Frequently Used References   viii

Acknowledgments   ix

Introduction   x

ESCHATOLOGY: THE LAST WORD FIRST

Radical Lutheranism   3

The Apocalyptic No and the Eschatological Yes:
Reflections, Suspicions, Fears, and Hopes   17

Lex semper accusat? Nineteenth-Century Roots
of Our Current Dilemma   33

LEGAL AND EVANGELICAL AUTHORITY

Authority in the Church: The Lutheran Reformation   53

Scriptura sacra sui ipsius interpres: Reflections on the Question of
Scripture and Tradition   68

The Irrelevance of the Modern World for Luther   75

ATONEMENT AND JUSTIFICATION: CHRIST UNBOUND

Caught in the Act: Reflections on the Work of Christ   85

Loser Takes All: The Victory of Christ   98

In Our Place   101

Forensic Justification and the Christian Life:
Triumph or Tragedy?   114

Luther's "Ethics"   137

UNECCLESIOLOGICAL ECUMENISM

The Meaning of *Satis Est*   159

Lutheran Ecumenism: With Whom and How Much?   171

The Catholic Impasse: Reflections on Lutheran-Catholic
Dialogue Today   189

SERMONS

God's Rights: Matthew 20:1-16   203

Exsurge Domine!: Psalm 74:22-23   206

Hidden Treasure: Matthew 13:44   211

You Have Died: Colossians 2:20-3:4   215

The Day of the Lord: 2 Peter 3:8-14   218

Jesus Died for You   220

Not the Well, but the Sick: Matthew 9:10-13   223

Citations for Previously Published Essays

We gratefully acknowledge permission to reprint materials previously published in the following:

"Radical Lutheranism: Lutheran Identity in America," *Lutheran Quarterly* 1 (1987): 5-18.

"Lex Semper Accusat," *dialog* 9/4 (Autumn 1970): 265-74.

"Loser Takes All: The Victory of Christ," *Lutheran Standard* (September 2, 1975): 3-5.

"Caught in the Act: Reflections on the Work of Christ," *Word and World* 3 (1984): 22-31.

"The Meaning of Satis Est," *Lutheran Forum* 26 (1992): 14-18.

"The Catholic Impasse: Reflection on Lutheran-Catholic Dialogue Today," in *Promoting Unity: Themes in Lutheran-Catholic Dialogue Today* (1989): 67-77.

Abbreviations for Frequently Used References

CA   *The Augsburg Confession in The Book of Concord: The Confessions of the Evangelical Lutheran Church,* ed. Robert Kolb and Timothy J. Wengert (Minneapolis: Fortress, 2000).

ELCA   Evangelical Lutheran Church in America

LW   *Luther's Works* [American Edition], 55 vols. (Philadelphia: Fortress and St. Louis: Concordia, 1955-86).

WA   *Luthers Werke: Kritische Gesamtausgabe* [Schriften], 65 vols. (Weimar: H. Böhlau, 1883-1993).

Acknowledgments

The editors acknowledge with gratitude Gerhard Forde's overall assistance and work with the entire project. Throughout, he has always been courteous, gracious, and helpful in providing guidance with editing these selected lectures, essays, and sermons. In addition, he has given his trust that they would be thoughtfully and carefully handled. We have found his wise counsel and teaching to be invaluable for our ministries and hope that this volume will honor and respect his contributions for the mission and well-being of the church.

Also, we wish to thank and express appreciation to Dr. Paul Rorem of Princeton Seminary for his kind, thoughtful, and always encouraging counsel as this manuscript progressed. Finally, the editors express thanks and appreciation to Pastor Ronald R. Darge, adjunct instructor in Religion at Grand View College, for his review of their work and his accompanying recommendations which helped to shape the final version of these essays.

Introduction

For those of us who have learned theology from Gerhard Forde, the call to a more radical gospel is more than a slogan. This new collection of essays, lectures, and sermons, many previously unpublished, will make more widely available the kind of confession that has been Forde's consistent public witness concerning the preaching of law and gospel. As with many of the important theologians of the past these are occasional works, requested or demanded by the circumstances of the church at the time, yet they show the consistent themes of our Christian confession believed by everyone, everywhere, and always *(quod ubique, quod semper, quod ab omnibus creditum est)*. Many pastors and theologians have been changed and convinced by Forde simply by reading him. From the extremely popular and long-lasting texts like *Where God Meets Man* and (with James Nestingen) *Free to Be*, to his sketch of the whole of Christian dogmatics, *Theology Is for Proclamation,* Forde has communicated in clear, crisp, and almost conversational writing the freeing truth of God's word. This is never as easy as it first seems.

When Christ laid aside the bands of death, raised by the Father through the Holy Spirit, he was loosed into the world never to be bound again. Christ unbound, in what can only delight sinners and frustrate righteous doers, binds his freedom to public proclamation and thereby creates a new kingdom. A theologian constantly unpacks this story of the triune God's work with sinners so that more of Christ's freedom can wreak its havoc and create anew. It takes courage to preach this publicly, as Luther once observed about the Psalmist's need to pray: "O Lord, Thou wilt open my lips, and my mouth will announce Thy praise."[1] Gerhard Forde begins his work, as scripture does, with the distinction between "God preached" and "not preached" and carries this through to its end. All of theology is therefore tuned to the proclamation of Christ crucified for the sake of sinners as its end and goal. Forde understands that all theology is to show Christ, to *give* Christ to sinners through the hearing of the Word or, as he often puts it, "to *do* the text to hearers." His enduring impact will no doubt be on this central matter of the very person of Jesus Christ, given in the present to the ungodly such as to kill and make alive.

Forward to Luther

This means that Forde goes against the grain of most systematic theology by refusing to speculate at any length about God outside Christ. The result of this confession is a blunt honesty that is both refreshing and alarming. When Forde rears back to "tell it like it is," he exposes a fake theology that would peer into God's naked majesty and nervously explain away any threat by substituting its own word for God's. Speculative theologians need to rehear that it is a fearful thing to fall into the hands of such a *living* God who refuses to be found other than in the word, who stands silently back behind sheer abstractions like "omnipotence," and yet is frighteningly near — not even giving sinners room to spit, as Job once put it. Forde lets this unpreached God stand and judge. What else could one really do? Forde is one of the few theologians who has ever abided by the old Socratic saying: "Things above us are no business of ours" *(quae supra nos, nihil ad nos).* This particular worship of the unpreached God that leaves God alone, refuses to be God's earthly defender, and has a healthy fear is rarely encountered among barnstorming theologians. So Forde's writing is always "edgy" and provocative, throwing considerably new light on whatever topic he pursues. Yet, Forde does more. He follows Luther's own insistence not only to let the unpreached God alone, but to run at once to the preached God. That is why Christ is always in his mouth.

What follows in Forde is a "broken" systematics, snapped at just the right place, so that theology does not become its own end. Instead, it pro-

---

1. LW 12:393.

duces the one thing necessary for people who are actually bent low by God's wrath at sin: forgiveness of sin by the only one who can really forgive it. The only way to deal with an unpreached God is to get a preached one. Or, in Forde's inimitable style — the only solution to the Absolute is absolution! The purpose of theologizing is not to speak about, but to give. Sinners need to have both their sin and its forgiveness declared to them. There, in proclamation, we have plenty to do with God. Proclamation of the Word comes to sinners as law and gospel and so this distinction becomes the source of what theology can and must say about God *for us.* What are we to preach in a world awash in information and the schemes of idea(l) mongers? As Forde puts it in *Theology Is for Proclamation,* "What is to be proclaimed is what God has decided, in fact, to do." And what is that? To justify his chosen sinners through the preached word on account of Jesus Christ alone, apart from works of the law.

It certainly can be said that all of Forde's writing has its center and focus in justification by faith alone. We have included in this collection several essays devoted precisely to the theme that troubles all — especially Lutherans — concerning the relationship between forensic justification and sanctification. The next generation of pastors and theologians should follow Forde's lead here, recognizing the necessary truth of holding to a forensic justification by the sheer, imputative declaration of the Word. Nevertheless, this is not understood as leaving sinners just as they were, only *thought of* differently by God. Rather than discuss the nature of sinners according to an ontological scheme in categories of being, and so construe the law as something "tamed" for good Christians, Forde recognizes that *all* depends upon Christ, his Holy Spirit, and so the new creation as a resurrection from the dead. Of course this means we must speak of "Christians" with the mark of the eschatological divide — simultaneously sinner and saint while the old world continues. Progress is always that of God's kingdom, the coming of the Lord to us in a kind of sacramental reversal from that of normal, sacrificial religion. Sanctification is misunderstood when seen as the progress of a continually existing subject, a pilgrim striving toward an ethical goal. So, Forde has always prided himself as *weak* on sanctification, while *strong* on the bondage of the will. This has provided a new generation of theologians with an opportunity to overcome the consistent Lutheran problem (to say nothing of other Christian confessions) of having to wed a clear and powerful Christology to a weak and decadent anthropology. What gave all to Christ on the one hand attempted to take it away with the other by rescuing the free will as a potent force that combines with grace in some mixed-up synergism called "regeneration" or "Christian life" and sanctification. Thus, what started well with the likes of Martin Luther was all taken back in an attempt to save the myth of the free will and its concomitant "continually existing subject" before the law of God.

But the gospel is more radical yet. Forde has helped us find a way past such a limping synthesis, back behind Melanchthon in his later years and the fears of losing precious human powers that alone seemed to make life worth living and faith worth having. He simply stays with a true Christology whatever its end — and a new beginning — for humans. For this reason he has consistently called theologians to go back to Luther himself, who has been a recent rediscovery even among those called by that name. In Luther we typically find a steady application to humanity of what God has decided to do in Jesus Christ. This is especially seen in the unmasking of the bound will. It comes as no surprise to people who have lived just a bit that it is God who *elects*, however frustrating that becomes for free-willers. But if that is not offense enough, then using the *preaching office* to get the job done adds offense to offense — "it pleased God through the folly of what we preach to save those who believe" (1 Cor. 1:21). And to top it off, Forde constantly points out the final straw of the content of that electing proclamation that breaks the camel's back. True preaching absolves actual sinners by an *unconditional* promise: "Your sins are forgiven on account of Jesus Christ." What red-blooded person, trying to do the right thing before almighty God, would not be offended by that? Americans are awash in an enthusiasm that refuses God's work of justification on account of Christ's cross alone through what the Lutheran confessions call "means."

One of Forde's greatest theological contributions is his development of a doctrine of the ministry straightway from the doctrine of election. After all, God's act of choosing, and so the faith of sinners, turns on Christ's unthwartable promise to them. But rather than clinging to the promise, the self-righteous can only see the specter of the unpreached God acting in complete freedom outside the law. Offense at Christ and his preachers has never much troubled Forde. In fact he would expect no less from those who have come under the working of the law. Future work on this doctrine of election could bear much fruit.

Theology as the Art of Distinguishing Law from Gospel

Unpacking what it means in actual human lives for the law to be at work is the reason why Forde's theology will continue to be essential reading. Early on, Forde identified the chief matter of a theology that did more than just describe God. He recognized that truth depended upon the place of the law in one's theology. This was elaborated in the history of an early controversy concerning atonement among Lutherans and published as his first book, *The Law-Gospel Debate.*

The distinction of law and gospel is always a target for demolition by theologians who would solve the problem of God by explaining the divine "system." They begin by describing God's being and nature, move to God's attributes, then proceed to why and how God creates. Having somehow determined all that, they propose a description of the human fall from such original order, and then imagine what it would take to get things back in that order again. Currently the vogue is ontologically to chart God's inner being as a triune community of relations, then to explain how humans fell out of "participation" in God's relational being, followed by the exhortation to re-participate in Christ in order to get *back in* through the church, such that the church can have a "public effect" in the world. Once you know the system, the mind of God, it is simply a matter of turning idea into act. Yet, such a system cannot abide the real distinction of law and gospel that actually announces an end to the law since righteousness is presumed not to be Christ, but the law, the system, or the return to original order itself. Forde recognized that one can try to collapse righteousness into law or duty, that one can attempt to shy away from it into a Romantic idyll of a pre-law relation to God, or one can attempt to go through law and beyond to establish a higher form of law in relation to God. But these attempts always fail. Such theology does not know who Christ is and what Christ does, and they imagine that theology itself becomes a means of escaping the sting of sin and death itself. Forde caught the sense of what Luther repeatedly taught, but which has proved so elusive, that theology is the art of distinguishing law and gospel. One can only do that when Christ and his cross are the stuff of theology, and so the discipline of theology stands between yesterday's proclamation and tomorrow's. Theology has no place to stand outside of this passing on, not even allowing the theologian's own person to escape the working of the law and its condemnation of our lack of trust. Too much of theology and subsequent talk about appropriate order within the church has simply been the theologian's personal defense against Christ.

It has been said about Lutherans that they are identified by having Christ always in their mouths. In addition to Christ's person, one of Forde's most respected theological contributions concerns the doctrine of atonement like that in his locus on the work of Christ in *Christian Dogmatics*. Atonement theories have historically shut down preaching rather than fostered it by attempting to solve the problem of God "on paper." That means that their effect for faith is more often doubt than certainty. How can it be that God would have to fight the devil in order to reclaim creatures? Is that not Manichaean? Is it not too violent for God, or beneath God's dignity? Is it not all too apocalyptic or mythological? And how does the balancing of accounts help when God's wrath seems to be appeased on the one hand by a sacrifice of his own unguilty Son on the other? Or if in fact the cross is God's great example of love how does this love finally find expression in weak human natures? But when the system of thought and its attempt to protect sinners by the law is no longer the lens through which Christ's cross is seen, something rather clear comes through. Christ's death is a historical crime, not a sign, or myth, or piece of the system of salvation. At once not only are the falsifications of church dogmatics regarding Christ's cross laid bare, but so is a long history in the church of interpreting scripture according to the method of *alleosis* by which Christ's divine and human natures are carefully distinguished so as not to offend human reason with such things as the death of God, the crime of deicide, and the experience of being "caught in the act" of doing away with the savior and creator of the world who has come down to meet us. The death of Christ is just that, a death, and moreover the pinnacle of a long-lasting rebellion against trust in God's own word as the only worthy worship of the true God. When Christ and his cross are preached "for you," they do not announce the key to the system, but pronounce your guilt, your end. In him your *eschaton* has come.

Forde is thus not only drawing from the great Reformation tradition, but is drawing out the fruit of modern historical, critical analysis that is even now being buried again under "postmodern" myths. Christ is an eschatological prophet. He came and announced the end for sinners. The time was up. He was about to do something new. For this, Jesus of Nazareth was killed. One of the great links between Luther's own theology and the modern situation is a return to the origin of Christian proclamation itself, the eschatology that drives away from a mere speculation to a present proclamation of your end. Law and gospel, Christ and his cross, and so preaching all assume a radical eschatology that is operating through the word — a real end and new beginning. For sinners that means a death and resurrection. At the center of all that theologians say must be an unbridgeable chasm when it comes to system, continually existing being, nature, or ontology. It is there that Forde has made his sharpest criticisms of the continual use of substance categories that go all the way back to original doctrines of the Trinity and Christ's two natures. Instead he has pushed theologians to recognize the relational descriptions that establish and constitute reality, especially the new creation that does not subsist in itself, but rather outside itself in Christ.

In Forde, this is far from being "existentialist," as if we were preaching a new heroic standpoint or a moment of decision. Forde's eschatologically driven theology is no different than Luther's here, and is something many Lutherans (to say nothing of all who have been affected by Luther's teaching) have badly mistaken. From the beginning of the proclamation of the gospel there has been a constant desire to return to the comfortable fleshpots of Egypt or the integrity of the Torah or the authority of Rome or the attempt to map the mind of God or the yearnings of the spiritual virtuoso. Lutherans have badly erred by falling into a series of struggles that have continued to this day on the elaborate distinctions of forensic declaration of forgiveness and effective appropriation of holiness by sinners. Forde's contribution in theology here can be great if we take up his call for the preaching of "a more radical gospel," even pointing out as he did in a series of memorable lectures that the Lutheran Confessions themselves are at times too timid in publicly clarifying the central matter: justification is a matter of death and life. Forde's lectures were published as *Justification: A Matter of Death and Life* and these provide a window into the next generation's responsibility to refuse a Kantian version of forensic justification, an "as if" theology. But at the same time Forde refuses the temptation to return to an ontological description of the effect of justification on a sinner, and the group of sinners gathered by the word, the church itself. Death and its sting are constantly denied, especially in the theological quest for building systems and the personal quest for a righteousness that can be called our own rather than one that remains ever Christ's as a sheer gift. Forde frequently speaks of the eschatological limit that cannot be transgressed without attempting to transform the gospel into human righteousness before God according to the law. In Christ the law really reaches its goal *(telos)* and comes to an end *(finis)*. Several of the essays and speeches included in this collection address how this limit to the law utterly changes our understanding of authority in the church. The gospel establishes the proper limits and use of the law in this old world, and gives a peculiar, new authority attributed especially to the Holy Spirit who creates anew, out of nothing. Without a radical preaching of the gospel that leaves off speaking *about* forgiveness and actually *gives* it to real sinners, there is only confusion of law and gospel. Where such confusion reigns, authority takes on the coercive and accusing aspects of law, especially in the church. Gospel authority, on the other hand, results in real freedom: "Where the Spirit of the Lord is, there is freedom" (2 Cor. 3:17).

One of the important future contributions in all of Forde's work is the subtle understanding of the actual working of law and gospel in real lives. He is able to address an ongoing debate in Lutheranism, and beyond, regarding the "overlap" between law and gospel. Such overlap is not a confusion. It is the means by which law pushes toward the gospel where the voice of the law ends, and at the same time the gospel establishes the truth and limits of the working of the law. With regard to humans this means law and gospel as Spirit and flesh, not in the sense of two ideals or the relation of self to the material things around it, but as two persons opposed to each other with a grave between them. One cannot simply assert a continually existing subject for the sake of satisfying a system of thought that avoids bringing death and resurrection into the center of theology and its goal in preaching. So when it comes to describing humans, theological anthropology must take up the troublesome and necessary *simul* — wholly sinner and wholly justified at once.

Scripture, Authority, Ecumenism

Forde's work in hermeneutics springs from this same source and will be an abiding interest for the future. He especially identifies the sacramentality of the preached word itself. God's gospel, unlike the restraining and persevering law, creates anew — even out of nothing. It does what it says, says what it does. Scripture as the source of this word is the battleground for the problem of dealing with an eschatological word that raises from the dead. And a pitched battle it is. Since the letter kills and the Spirit gives life the problem of interpretation of scripture is key for all matters of church and theology. You cannot secure the truth of scripture by asserting that you have more Spirit than the next person. But neither can the church in the form of a teaching authority diachronically preserved through time by apostolic succession in the laying on of hands succeed in preserving scripture's word. That simply repeats the problem in a "massive subjectivity" embodied in the office of the papacy. Forde makes good use of Luther's discovery that Rome and the spiritualizers have a common root that repeated the original sin of enthusiasm, God within-ism. Enthusiasm always seeks to ground the word in itself, rather than let the word do its work of killing and making alive. So Forde frequently elaborates two of Luther's insights about scripture's authority. First, that there is an internal and external clarity to scripture's word as preached publicly to sinners: "My sheep know my voice." Second, that scripture actively interprets itself. Instead of the exegete working on understanding and preserving a written text for modern use, the text as preached works on the interpreter. The spaces opened there for discussions of the current issues of authority, the relation of text and interpreter, and the yearning for true freedom are many.

Hermeneutics especially opens up the impact Forde has had and hopefully will have on ecumenical relations. If it is true that the churches have come through some of the hostility and isolation of previous centuries to a greater understanding and desire to communicate and cooperate "ecumenically," then it must also be said that the ecumenical movement must now learn to face the truth when confessions have opposed teachings. For someone like Forde such candor is not simply trying intractably to preserve Lutheran tradition. Forde is addressing children of the Reformation especially to change their mode of operating along with some of their cherished traditions. He does not want Lutherans, for example, to remain the same. In fact, he has recognized their faulty synthesis of Christ and free will. He wants them and all Christians to come to the radical gospel of justification by faith alone, apart from works of the law. The church and its ordering cannot be the basis for "visible unity," but justification by faith alone must be. It alone is catholic and preserves the ecumenicity of the church. That is why Forde occasionally likes to joke that he has no ecclesiology. This radical approach alone will open new relations because it does not allow subservient matters to become the real stuff of church ecumenism. Differences in liturgy, order, cultural accoutrements, etc. cannot only be tolerated but even enjoyed, but if and only if the true agreement on preaching the gospel of Jesus Christ and him crucified is what makes the church the church. Aside from this we would come to a truly "catholic impasse" — a fight that has gone on since the first preaching of gospel outside the Garden of Eden. Thus, you do not find in Forde the direction of current attempts to reach vague agreements about justification by faith alone only to have all collapse because of disagreements over the office of episcopacy. He insists on coming to the only agreement possible, the preaching of the pure gospel and right administration of the sacraments, thus agreeing that justification by faith alone is the truly ecumenical principle for the church and its theology.

Eschatology: The Last Word First

The first three essays recognize that eschatology is not merely one topic among many, the one that deals with the doctrine of the "last things." Rather, eschatology has a comprehensive focus. Forde accentuates and centralizes the eschatological metaphor of "death and resurrection" and in this way teases out the "effective" dimension of justification latent within God's imputative word, thus countering the charge that the doctrine of justification *sola fide* is a fiction having no bearing for lived experience. Forensic and effective perspectives on justification are not opposites because they are formulas for a word that says what it does and does what it says — calling forth new life within and among people.

"Radical Lutheranism," published first in *Lutheran Quarterly* in 1987, is a programmatic piece that passionately argues, with the prospect of the new Evangelical Lutheran Church in America (1988) on the horizon, that for missional effectiveness Lutherans must appropriate the more radical eschatological gospel that was rediscovered at the origins of the Protestant movement. Forde notes that Lutheranism, both world and North American, has been plagued with identity crises. Should we focus on individual salvation or social justice? More to the point, we are obsessed with the relevance of our message. We assume that there should be therapeutic or prophetic consequences for our work or there is no "pay off." Forde notes that our questioning is far more important than we often acknowledge: the gospel is at stake! Hence, he argues that in contrast to conforming with the standards of this age for the church as either offering ways to help people as individuals cope with the mechanistic, impersonal, and bureaucratic social structures of modern life or to help people as oppressed groups change social structures to get a fair hearing or shot at a "larger piece of the pie," the church must return to a gospel that is neither conservative nor liberal but instead radical. We must acknowledge that the Pauline view of the gospel will always be at odds with or homeless in this age.

Even the "Evangelical Catholic" conviction that the church is a "movement within the church catholic" is inadequate in relation to Pauline radicalism — it tends to seek a compromise between an eschatological gospel and the view of the church as a visible body. We need, Forde emphatically states, to recover Luther's "theology of the cross" (*theologia crucis*), the death and resurrection of Jesus *done to us* by the proclamation of its fact. Both the focus on individual salvation and social transformation assume an anthropology derived from the conviction that humans possess "free will" *coram deo*, at odds with Luther's. In this regard, Forde notes that despite all the alleged discontinuities between the medieval and modern worlds, both medieval scholasticism and the modern views latent in Renaissance Humanism shared an anthropology governed by the affirmation of "free will." Forde argues that the old being is *bound* to reject God's mercy as a matter of self-defense against God. The "free choice" perspective assumes a subject who stands over against the gospel as an object that he or she can either accept or reject. In contrast, Luther understood the being or person of the human as such to be fundamentally receptive or passive. Unfortunately, post-Reformation Lutherans attempted to combine Luther's radical gospel with Aristotelian anthropologies that could not tolerate it. Humanism could accept the *sola fide*, but not the bondage of the will (understood as our bondage to a quest for moral improvement as our salvation). The only answer for Lutheranism is to return to Luther's radical gospel which liberates us *from* our incurved selves and *for* God's glory and the world as new creation — gift.

In "Apocalyptic No and Eschatological Yes," given at a Summer Karl Barth Conference at Luther Seminary, Forde ambitiously but perceptively aims to look at the basic systematic structure of the church through the ages and how it relates to hermeneutics, the interpretation of scripture. Affirming the position of the early Barth, Forde asserts that Christianity must be "thoroughgoing eschatology" or it has no relation to Christ! Forde notes that eschatology was not to prevail in the church. In the most primitive church many were apocalyptic. When the apocalypse did not occur — when there was no immediate redemption closing history, then early

Christians turned their attention to an anticipated redemption "from above." Some became Gnostics — "disappointed *apocalyptikers.*" However, even "orthodox" Christians who rejected Gnosticism did so on Gnosticism's own grounds — at the expense of eschatology. Hence, Irenaeus offered a true "gnosis" in opposition to the false one of the Gnostics. In this deeply "ontological" perspective, hermeneutics is not configured by the performative word — a word in action to set people free from incurvation — but that of signification, symbolizing an ontic or psychological reality either within or above the interpreter, independent of the language that conveys it, providing information about how we can conform to or mimic the ontological scheme and achieve its goal. Hence, doctrine is thought to be conveyed allegorically in the scriptures and incites the virtue of faith. Morality is conveyed tropologically and incites the virtue of love. Mystical experience is conveyed anagogically and incites the virtue of hope. Luther rediscovered the gospel as eschatological by means of a new hermeneutics of an active, promising word. Again, Forde notes how anthropology failed to conform to this Lutheran insight. Humanist and early modern views of human nature reasserted the Aristotelian ontological priority of possibility over actuality and opened the door for the hermeneutics of signification, albeit configured differently from the ancients. For orthodoxy, the allegorical approach ruled in its quest for pure doctrine. For Liberalism, the tropological approach presided with the concomitant quest for pure morality. Only with twentieth-century thinkers' despair over inhumanity as expressed in world wars and massive acts of cruelty and violence has an eschatological word — anagogy — been allowed to be heard. Nevertheless, the tropological move is not easily dismissed. Humanity's faith in itself is shaky, but not totally lost. Tropology, the view that only our ethics could render justification effective, continues to guide the church. What would it take for us to trust God's ability to establish the new being in faith?

The third essay, "Lex Semper Accusat," an early work from 1970 published in *dialog,* also conveys the theme of eschatology as applied to law. Given the Reformation stance that the law always accuses *(lex semper accusat),* can there be any positive construal to the law? If the law is a source for human pretension, then what value could it have for the new life? This essay provides a detailed analysis of the role of law in modern thinkers and movements: Kant, Hegel, Schleiermacher, Marx, and Democratic Liberalism. Forde's insight is that when there is no limit to law —

when it is absolute (as it was for Kant), it becomes intolerable. People will seek an alternative to law — they will attempt to be "antinomian." Yet, such antinomianism is futile, because human life *in this age* must be ordered. No matter how much we aim to be rid of the law, law always returns under a different and often more repressive guise. Both the proposed antinomianisms latent within liberalistic individualism, which kills the individual's constitutively social nature, and Marxist collectivism, which kills the individual's uniqueness, fail to rid humanity of law. Only faith in Jesus Christ, unbound from law, sin, death, and the devil, opens a new sphere of agency freed from compulsion towards self-affirmation and self-justification governed by law. Faith alone allows us to see law in its positive light as providing stability and order in the world for the flourishing of life.

Legal and Evangelical Authority

The second set of essays deals with the question of authority in ministry by establishing a distinction between legal and evangelical authority. Given the pervasive individualism of North American culture that lends itself to highly subjective approaches to interpreting scripture, many preachers struggle to find an authoritative public voice as a basis to do their ministry. It is temptingly romantic to idealize a "historic episcopate" that might help them secure a perceived authority derived, allegedly, from the apostles. In contrast to this return to law, Forde seeks to reestablish authority in the church as based upon and subject to the gospel itself as given in scripture. In contrast to the modern tendency to situate the human subject as the epistemological and/or ontological center of reality, Forde notes that we are always decentered by the God who claims us in the scriptural and oral word.

The fourth essay, "Authority in the Church: The Lutheran Reformation," presented at an ELCA synod assembly, notes that the Reformers needed to forge a path between the papal view of authority — "too much" authority, and that of the Enthusiasts — "too little" authority. The Reformation position relativizes the papal and the Enthusiast's views of authority. In reality, those two views are less opposed than would first appear. As noted earlier, Forde acknowledges that papal authority can be viewed as a "massive subjectivism" that counters the subjectivism of individuals. The

Reformers, of course, appealed to scripture as the sole authority in matters of faith and life. Forde immediately raises and discusses the well-known problem with scriptural authority: scripture may be *sola*, but interpretations are *multi*. In order to counter this problem, Forde discerns that gospel authority is different from that of legal authority. Gospel authority is unique because as a living, world-establishing word, it is creative, it sets free. Its "power-over" individuals is freeing: if this authority holds me, it is not because I have to, but want to. Gospel authority cannot be forced or threatened. Legal authority can and, given our sinfulness, often should be. It holds that if you transgress the law, you are on the way to perdition. Gospel authority, by contrast, opens new horizons for the world when it does its task of setting limits to law. The gospel is the end, as goal *(telos)* and limit *(finis)*, to the law. The human temptation is to use the law to help bring in the kingdom of God. However, apart form the gospel, (1) the law oversteps its limits and (2) we are bound to try to end the law's authority. However, apart from the gospel, the law has no end. The socially constructive goals of the law can only be established, counterintuitively, by faith. Faith does all *(fac totus)*, as Luther says. Faith allows us to live "outside ourselves" for our neighbors' well-being and thus spontaneously do or even improve upon what the law threateningly commands. God will bring in his kingdom at his own time and in his own way. In establishing its proper authority in relation to law, faith thus puts limits on authoritarianism without fostering relativism.

In the following essay, "*Scriptura sacra sui ipsius interpres:* Reflections on the Question of Scripture and Tradition" given as a background paper for the Lutheran/Roman Catholic dialogue, Forde further specifies the relation between scripture and gospel by means of the hermeneutics of the active, creative word. Such a hermeneutic opposes attempts to reestablish an authoritarian office in the church as a means to curtail subjectivism in the interpretation of scripture, even for ecumenical purposes. The old opposition between Protestants and Catholics — caricatured as "Papalism versus Biblicism" — has long been discredited since papal authority is dependent upon the recognition of individuals and the Bible, and has been formulated by human, church tradition. Forde points out that were we to acknowledge the Reformation outlook on *sola scriptura*, then we would have to move beyond what the scriptures might mean to what the word *does* in and through them. We would discover that it is scripture that interprets the exegete and not vice versa! Properly understood, exegetes are not subjects standing over the scriptures as their object. Rather, beyond any blending of horizons of interpretation between interpreter and scripture, the interpreters find themselves to be hearers of the word, indeed *exegeted* by the word. As exegeted by the word, one in turn can tell — preach — it to others. Scripture, in the Reformation understanding, claims the hearer. With this in mind, one can reappropriate historic, churchly traditions of exegesis. Tradition is then not a source or judge of authority but is what Forde calls a "hearing aid." The company of hearers summons us to hear scripture more closely.

"The Irrelevance of the Modern World for Luther" was given at Roanoke College in Virginia. In it Forde carries on the polemical subversion of modern forms of hermeneutics, indebted to the ongoing spirit of the Enthusiasts. His whole point is: do not try to make Luther relevant! Luther's contemporary power will be unleashed when his voice is allowed to critique modern assumptions. Faithful theology recognizes that when God takes charge, the ethics and theology of the old being lose power and control. One of the most interesting parts of this essay is when Forde unmasks secularism as highly religious — indeed, we might say, superstitious, since it no longer distinguishes between God's judgment and self-esteem. Modern perspectives aim to protect themselves from coming to an end in justification by faith alone, especially protecting its affirmation that we are fundamentally victims, not sinners, and the modern self-centered attempt to "tranquilize itself with the trivial." Forde concludes that in light of today's superstitions Luther would not change his message that "afflicts the comforted and comforts the afflicted." Neither should we.

Atonement and Justification: Christ Unbound

In the essays in this section Forde cuts through any attempt to reduce the gospel to morality, theory or feeling. We walk by faith alone, and not by sight or deeds. God's promise of commitment to us is not only necessary but also sufficient for us. In his famous essay, "Caught in the Act: Reflections on the Work of Christ," published in *Word and World* in 1984, Forde critiques traditional theories of the atonement. Anselm's understanding of mercy is enmeshed with concerns about legal transactions between the divine and the human. From Forde's perspective such theories are insufficient to provide certainty for the anxious conscience. The questions that ought to govern our concerns with the atonement are highly unspeculative, since God hides outside his particular words. Forde's claim is that "absolution is the answer to the absolute." The question "Will God have mercy?" can only be understood by resorting to the question: "*Does* God have mercy?" In this regard, Forde notes that Jesus was raised from the dead in order that his ministry of forgiveness might be vindicated and reconciliation for sinners can be received in his name.

Forde agrees with Abelard that the death of Jesus is a murder in which we are implicated. The problem with Anselm's theory of the atonement is that it allows us to exonerate ourselves of this murder by blaming the necessity for the cross onto God. Since Anselm is so tied to legal imagery, the question is raised: If Jesus' death was a payment to God, then how is the reconciliation he establishes one of mercy? However, Abelard's theory is no less moralistic, since it sees Christ purely as example *(exemplum)* and not sacrament *(sacramentum)*, gift. The early church's "Christus Victor" theory is also problematic in that it raises the issue: Was Jesus' death necessary to defeat the demons? Indeed, why is Christ's death *necessary* at all? Forde's radical response is that — it was not! Why could God not just forgive us? He did! Unfortunately, we would not have it. Unlike the obscuring of sin present in each of the three dominant atonement theories, Forde charges that we wasted Jesus in self-defense. We think that we cannot survive the "attack," one might say, of Jesus' mercy to our world bound in sin and law. Jesus shatters our sense of order by radically believing God. We are thus caught *in* the act of rejecting Jesus, but also, *by* this act — God will not be satisfied until he has mercy on us, until we become people of faith.

In "Loser Takes All: The Victory of Christ," a 1975 *Lutheran Standard* article, Forde claims that Jesus cannot serve as an idol of our projections for self-empowerment. Jesus' victory, in spite of our rejection of him as a "loser," was that, unlike the first Adam who sought deity, he sought to be fully human in a life of service. His resurrection means that God approves of and reestablishes this kind of life.

"In Our Place" was presented at a Luther Seminary conference on feminist criticisms of atonement theories. Forde specifically takes up Rebecca Parker and Joanne Carlson Brown's rejection of traditional, Anselmic views of the atonement. He shares their concerns about Anselm. However, he refuses their tropological, moralistic reading of the tradition in which Christ is only and always an example, never a gift. Forde appreciates their criticism of the legalism embedded in the tradition, but their solution offers only a more vicious legalism — an uncompromisingly pure, heroistic, utopian proposal of how to get to a place free of sexism. They cannot conceive of Christ as sheer, unmerited, lavishly given gift, but only an ethical model — and thus bypass any real hope for salvation for the world.

"Forensic Justification and the Christian Life: Triumph or Tragedy?" is a preliminary study concerning the work of Christ for Volume 2 of the *Christian Dogmatics* (edited by Carl E. Braaten and Robert W. Jenson). Far from the critiques that allege forensic justification only lends itself to social quietism, Forde allows the new life inherent in the doctrine of forensic justification to be unleashed. With its radical negation of self-transformation, it acknowledges the reality of God's kingdom coming among us with its own transformative power. Quite un-quietistic, it recognizes that sanctification is the *source*, not the goal of good works. A life captured by and captivated to God is the self-centered, incurved sinner's demise and the beginning of a new life expressing itself daily in acts of love towards one's neighbor.

When justification is no longer taken as the starting point for the Christian's struggle toward righteousness, the questions always arise about Christian ethics. Forde responded in his lecture "Luther's 'Ethics'" at Capital University. Freed *from* the need of justifying ourselves before God, we are free *for* service. Counter to all anthropologies based on the development of human potential, which quickly become the obligation to develop such potential ("Be all that you can be!"), Forde responds with a kind of "narrative identity" approach to ethics. Jesus' story becomes my story in the gospel. Christian ethics teaches us not to get in God's way as he does his work in us and through us for the world. It recognizes that God's kingdom comes without our prayer, but we pray that it would also come among us. Radically worldly, secular — though not in the secularistic sense, Christian ethics has nothing to do with saving the world or transforming the self. As such, we are free to offer service through worldly vocations to others.

Unecclesiological Ecumenism

In the final essays of this volume Forde reflects on issues concerning the ecumenical relationship among churches from his experience over decades as a member of the Lutheran–Roman Catholic dialogue. While Forde often teases that he "doesn't have an ecclesiology," these essays indeed will demonstrate that Forde has a robust ecclesiology, not driven by highly abstract, romantic views of the church that elevate the supposed structural unity of the Middle Ages as our current ideal. Instead, the word reigns supreme and church unity is held by faith and not by sight. "The Meaning of *Satis Est*," originally an address at the second St. Olaf Conference (1990), argues against the dominant trend of ecumenism in the ELCA that the *satis est* clause of the Augsburg Confession (1530) could be understood as a minimum requirement for church unity to which other standards could be added, such as the historic episcopate. Instead, "it is enough" is a "limiting concept" of what can be imposed upon churches and still be faithful to the freedom of the gospel. In contrast to those who seek visible church unity, Forde argues that the unity of the church is *hidden* as a necessary implication of the gospel itself. If we are justified by works, then our ecclesiology will suggest that we must either be separate from the world (as monasticism and the Radical Reformation sought) or remake the world in light of its eschatological hope (as Kantian- and Marxist-influenced positions teach). However, if we are justified by faith, then the visible marks of the church can only be the word and sacraments that bear and sustain the church. The *satis est* clause thus provides an "eschatological limit" to institutional forms of the church.

In "Lutheran Ecumenism" Forde notes that ecumenism can be motivated by three reasons: (1) political, (2) ecclesial, or (3) theological correctness. The first reason is the simple-minded proposal that there is no fundamental difference between church confessions that has not been relativized by history and that structural unity between churches is now desirable for the sake of a unified witness against secularism (as if throngs would now join such an institution who are not joining now). The second is a response to the first, an attempt towards ecumenism in order to establish an authoritative voice in the face of theological fuzziness that leads to the first brand of ecumenism. "Home to Rome" would seemingly offer an authoritative magisterium that would counter such corrosive theological diversity. The third, the only viable route for Forde, argues that ecumenism can be justified only for the sake of testing the integrity of one's confessional position — does it stand the test of fidelity to the gospel? The criterion for such a test is whether or not a transformationist approach to justification is as true to the gospel as that of simultaneity, i.e., that we are totally saints and totally sinners at the same time. Since there are good reasons to maintain the latter, Forde affirms that it is not the scandal of division that is to be feared, but that of union. In "The Catholic Impasse," published in *Promoting Unity: Themes in Lutheran-Catholic Dialogue Today* (1989), Forde again raises the question of integrity in ecumenics. Why would a contemporary, postliberal Lutheran be catholic? It is simply due to the fact that the radical gospel preserves the catholic faith as it is embodied in the three ecumenical creeds.

We have included several of Forde's sermons that demonstrate the liberating power of the unbound Christ in the preached word. Since theology is for preaching, here we can begin to see how Forde preaches so as to *do* the gospel to his hearers instead of talking about bible texts, God, and our feelings about things. Forde's sermons were largely preached in Luther Seminary's chapel over the long course of his teaching.

Finally, what we have received in Forde's teaching, writing, and preaching all along is a theologian of the cross. In his most recent book, *On Being a Theologian of the Cross,* he laid out the implications of having a God who, contrary to human desire, is a loser-takes-all God. Preaching this Christ, the one crucified, means that in the radical gospel God chooses sinners, bound and determined to be righteous by the law, only by the public announcement of their forgiveness on account of Christ alone. It puts them to death (in the only real meaning of that term) and raises them up to new life since "it depends not on human will or exertion, but on God who shows mercy . . ." (Rom. 9:16). With appreciation for what Forde has accomplished and with an eye to what this can mean for the future we offer this collection of essays. May it further the artistry of distinguishing law and gospel so that public proclamation makes sinners free to the glory of Christ and his kingdom.

MARK C. MATTES
STEVEN D. PAULSON

ESCHATOLOGY:
THE LAST WORD FIRST

Radical Lutheranism

Lutheran Identity in America

For some time now, Lutherans both here and abroad have been suffering from what contemporary jargon calls an identity crisis. Lutherans do not seem to know anymore what they ought to be or to do. On the international scene this is demonstrated by persistent studies sponsored by the Lutheran World Federation/Lutheran World Ministries going back some twenty years or so. John Reumann chronicles and sums up this study under the rubric, "The Identity of the Church and Its Service to the Whole Human Being." The big question precipitating the crisis is indicated by the title. It becomes most evident, no doubt, in connection with the mission of the church, particularly in the "third world." Is the church to be concerned now with proclamation or development? Individual salvation or social justice? Peace with God or peace among humans?[1] Lutherans seem to have a difficult time deciding which way to go.

The crisis in identity is in many ways intensified on the national scene.[2] For the most part Lutherans in America are just lately emerging

1. See the introduction to John Reuman, ed., *The Church Emerging: A U.S. Lutheran Case Study* (Philadelphia: Fortress, 1977), pp. 1-31. The entire book is an interesting testimony to the agonies of Lutheran identity today.

2. The prevalence of that word in the debates and documents of the newly forming Evangelical Lutheran Church in America is noteworthy. "Crisis" and "identity" appear quite often in current Lutheran self-scrutiny, both at home and abroad. Robert H. Fischer, profes-

3

from geographic, ethnic, and synodical isolation onto the broader American scene with ambitions towards "inclusivity." We used to be predominantly Germans, Swedes, Danes, Norwegians, Finns, and a smattering of other northern European and Nordic folk, and it was probably more our geographic isolation and ethnicity that kept us together and determined our identity than our Lutheranism. Now that we are apparently about to launch out more into the mainstreams of American Christianity, the identity question is posed with heightened urgency. Who or what in this opulent religious cafeteria shall we be? Shall we be conservative, liberal, confessional, orthodox, charismatic, neo-pentecostal, fundamentalist, or "evangelical" (perhaps "fundagelical," as someone recently put it)? Shall we be sectarian or ecumenical; Protestant or Catholic; high, low, or in the middle? Lutherans are pulled in all these directions today. They seem to be looking for someone to sell out to.

Is "Lutheran" anything to be in America today? Chances are Americans don't even know how to spell it. It usually comes out "Luthern" or something like that. In the "homeland" established Lutheranism was predominantly a folk religion, a quasi-political and ethnic reality, closely identified with national and social life. Take all that away and what is left? What is Lutheranism at rock bottom? Some of my colleagues like to say — and I have echoed the thought myself — that Lutheranism is a confessional movement within the church catholic, or that its primary reason for being is that it has a dogmatic proposal to make to the church catholic,[3] or, as Tillich used to say, it advocates the "Protestant Principle" vis-à-vis a catholic substance.[4] But what then is the core, the substance of Lutheranism? Can a "movement" or a "proposal" or a "principle" give identity to the long haul, not to say serve the human soul for daily bread? Other Christian denominations are recognizable at least by distinctive forms of polity or

---

sor at the Lutheran School of Theology at Chicago, observes that "For many reasons North American Lutheranism is confronted by an identity crisis. In its larger dimensions this is a crisis in understanding both our churchly mission in the world and our Lutheran identity within the Christian ecumenical scene" (*The Church Emerging*, p. 6). See also Martin E. Marty, "Scenarios for a Lutheran Future: A Case Study of Identity," *Lutheran Forum* 9 (May 1975): 6-10.

3. Eric Gritsch and Robert Jenson, *Lutheranism: The Theological Movement and Its Confessional Writings* (Philadelphia: Fortress, 1976), pp. 2ff.

4. See the essays in Paul Tillich, *The Protestant Era*, trans. James Luther Adams (Chicago: University of Chicago Press, 1948), especially pp. 161ff.

perhaps even what are today called types of spirituality. Lutherans dabble pragmatically in whatever forms and types seem to work best in a given context, but canonize none of them.

Who then are we? The new church proposes to call itself "The Evangelical Lutheran Church in America." But what would that mean? "Evangelical," "Lutheran," "in America"? The debates and suggestions floated in the Commission for a New Lutheran Church are themselves indicative of the identity crisis. Several people thought we should at last drop the adjective "Lutheran" and call ourselves "Evangelical Catholics." Others thought we should probably drop both "Lutheran" and "Catholic" and just call ourselves "The Evangelical Community in Christ" or some other generic title. Some thought we should drop the adjective "Evangelical," since it is misleading today and already redundant when put together with "Lutheran." How can a Lutheran not be evangelical? But in the end we decided we are still Lutherans after all and Evangelical to boot! But what that means still seems to be a matter for debate. Is retention of the name anything more than romantic nostalgia? Even the protracted and hesitant debate over a headquarters site indicates something of our uncertainty about who we think we are, or hope to become. We feared being identified with parochial interests and looked for a "world-class city." But what business do we have to do there? The arguments seemed to assume that it would be good for us to be *affected* by such an environment; the question of whether we have anything to *effect* there was largely unanswered.

The most persistent and serious identity crisis is manifest at the grass-roots level. These Lutherans seem somewhat at a loss as to what to make of the American religious scene. For the most part they do have a sense of the importance of the *evangel* and seem more ready to support the outreach mission of the church than anything else. Perhaps basically conservative, they are often puzzled and confused by clergy and leadership that seem to be leading elsewhere — just where is not very clear. The incessant drive for "inclusivity" can give the impression that they have been abandoned, perhaps, for a more desirable clientele. Emerging from their ethnic past, they can be impressed by and drawn to those who can dress a cause or a human longing in appealingly religious trappings. They remember there was something vital they were supposed to be for, and thus they are tempted by those whose piety seems impressive and/or offers more solace. They are attracted by "American" religion: "fundagelicals," charismatics, the Hal Lindseys, Jerry Falwells, Robert Schullers, etc., and sometimes even by high-liturgical Anglo-Catholicism. Is "Lutheran" any recognizable thing to be any more? Garrison Keillor says he can always get a laugh when he mentions Lutherans. Why? Is it something to be apologetic about?

In an article on Lutheran identity written some ten years ago, Martin Marty saw Lutheranism standing between two forces, ". . . both of them attractive and capable of overwhelming Lutheranism, permitting it to remain as a shell or husk or form, but not as a confessional witness or a promise."[5] Reformed neo-evangelicalism is one force, Marty wrote, and the most likely winner, because America is "genetically programmed to tilt toward" it, and Lutheran conservatives and even some moderates are attracted by it. The other force, in Marty's view, is a "more natural kin," but less likely to prevail: it is "a kind of evangelical Catholicity."[6] Today it seems obvious that both of these forces are powerfully at work dividing the Lutheran house.[7] Marty's analysis still leaves us with the question, however: Is one or the other overwhelming Lutheranism?

Without wishing unduly to complicate matters, I want to mention at least one more force today. One might call it decadent pietism. Lutherans who came to this country were for the most part pietists of one stamp or another. Under the pressure of American Arminianism, Personalism, psychologism, individualism, human potential movements, and what not, pietism simply becomes decadent. The old pietism thought it vital first of all "to get right with God" through the experience of grace in conversion. But now, since God is, in general, love and no longer wrathful with anyone, God more or less drops out of the picture as a serious factor with which to be contended. In decadent pietism, since God is "affirming" in general, the task is to "get right with oneself." The old pietism contended that conversion was to be manifest in a morally upright life of service. Decadent piet-

---

5. Marty, "Scenarios for a Lutheran Future," pp. 8-9.

6. Marty, "Scenarios for a Lutheran Future," p. 9.

7. Marty remarks: "I think that the typical conservative Lutheran congregation today has not the faintest idea of how to sort out Francis Schaeffer or Anita Bryant, Billy Graham or Johnny Cash, Robert Schuller or Hal Lindsey from their own tradition. And some Lutheran moderates fall under the same sway" ("Scenarios for a Lutheran Future," p. 9). No doubt Marty is right. But one should also add that the typical "Evangelical Catholic" congregation or theologian today likewise has not the faintest idea of how to sort out the work of a Gregory Dix, Odo Casel, J. A. T. Robinson, a Schillebeeckx or an Aidan Kavanagh, from their tradition.

ism seems to hold that the way of the Christian is to become "affirming" of others in their chosen life styles. Along with this there is very often a rather sanctimonious "third use of the law" piety centered mostly around current social causes and problems. No longer concerned with one's own sins, and certainly not the sins of those one is supposed to affirm, one shifts attention to the sins of those other entities (more or less anonymous) that inhibit the realization of our affirmed and affirming human potential. Generally, these are summed up under the rubric of "the establishment" or perhaps personified by those who happen to be in power.

Is it fair to call this a pietism? We need not quibble about the nomenclature. In any case one has only to visit contemporary churches and note the religious fervor and piety with which the view is promoted (especially among contemporary clergy, I fear) to get a sense of its power as a contending force in the battle for identity. Among Lutherans, the gospel is equated mostly with this general drive toward being permissive, affirmed, and affirming. Ministers must become therapists, church gatherings must be therapeutic and supportive if they are to meet people's needs, and ministry must be "prophetic" and have a social payoff if it is to be at all relevant.

Theological Identity: Radical Lutheranism

One could continue discussing the problem of identity endlessly, since there are so many dimensions and aspects to interpret and haggle about. My purpose here, however, is not to belabor the problem but rather to propose a way towards a solution, to suggest a course for the future that is helpful, promising, and faithful to the tradition. My thesis is that Lutherans, to be true to their identity, yes, even to reclaim their identity, or rather be reclaimed by it, should become even more radical proponents of the tradition that gave them birth and has brought them thus far. The crisis in identity indicates the necessity for staking out some turf on the ecclesiastical map. What shall we be? Let us be radicals: not conservatives or liberals, fundagelicals or charismatics (or whatever other brand of something-less-than gospel entices), but radicals: radical preachers and practitioners of the gospel by justification by faith without the deeds of the law. We should pursue it to the radical depths already plumbed by St. Paul, especially in Romans and Galatians, when he saw that justification by faith without the deeds of the law really involves and announces the death of the old being and the calling forth of the new in hope. We stand at a crossroads. Either we must become more radical about the gospel, or we would be better off to forget it altogether.

We should realize first of all that what is at stake on the current scene is certainly not Lutheranism as such. Lutheranism has no particular claim or right to existence. Rather, what is at stake is the radical gospel, radical grace, the eschatological nature of the gospel of Jesus Christ crucified and risen as put in its most uncompromising and unconditional form by St. Paul. What is at stake is a mode of doing theology and a practice in church and society derived from that radical statement of the gospel. We need to take stock of the fact that while such radical Paulinism is in itself open to both church and world (because it announces a Christ who is the end of the law, the end of all earthly particularities and hegemonies), it is, no doubt for that very reason, always homeless in this age, always suspect, always under attack, always pressured to compromise and sell its birthright for a mess of worldly pottage.

Lutheranism, we have said in the past, is not so much a denomination as a confessional movement with perhaps a proposal of dogma to make to the church catholic, a critical principle to apply over against a catholic substance. I wonder more and more of late whether such at once over-modest and pretentious estimates of self-identity will serve the radical nature of the gospel as Paul, for instance, saw it. Would Paul have been satisfied with such a description of his own mission? What is the catholic substance, after all? What if it turns out to be a fantastic universal synthesis between this age and the next that quietly ignores or disarms New Testament eschatology and absorbs it in its universal ecclesiology? What if all critical principles and proposals of dogma are benignly ordered somewhere in the hierarchy of truths and filed away in a Denzinger? Can there really be such a thing as a *catholic* church? Should not someone be asking whether it is not likely that the radical eschatology proclaimed especially by Paul will have to be pursued to the end of the age? Is what Lutherans have stood for a passing fancy?

I don't know that I am prepared to give full answers to all such questions yet, but I do want to pursue the proposition that Lutheranism *especially* in America might find its identity not by compromising with American religion but by becoming more radical about the gospel it has received. That is to say, Lutherans should become radicals, preachers of a gospel so radical that it puts the old to death and calls forth the new, and practitioners of the life that entails "for the time being."

We must realize there is not just external reason for our identity crisis but deep theological and, for want of a better word, existential reason. It lies simply in Lutheranism's fateful attachment to the Pauline gospel in a world whose entire reason for being is opposed to it. All who adopt such a stance will find themselves constantly on the defensive not only before the world but especially before the religious enterprises, not to say the churches, of the world. Witness already Paul's own anguished and repeated defenses of his own apostolate against "those reputed to be something."

If we are to probe to the root, the *radix*, of our identity crisis, however, we must dig beneath even the world's general disapproval. Theological anthropology, the understanding of human existence itself before God, is perhaps the place where the crisis becomes most apparent. The fact is that the radical Pauline gospel of justification by faith without the deeds of the law calls for a fundamentally different anthropology and with it a different theological "system" (if there be such!) from that to which the world is *necessarily* committed. The radical gospel of justification by faith alone simply does not fit, cannot be accepted by, and will not work with an anthropology that sees the human being as a continuously existing subject possessing "free choice of will" over against God and/or other religious goals. The radical gospel is the *end* of that being and the beginning of a new being in faith and hope.

This is readily apparent in virtually all of Paul's writings (especially in Romans and Galatians) when he pursues the logic of justification by faith alone to its end. The law does not end sin, does not make new beings; it only makes matters worse. Where the old continuity is maintained, sin does not end. No matter how much religious pressure is applied, sin only grows. But, Paul has the audacity to say where sin abounded, grace abounded all the more. But this is disaster for the old and its thinking. For then, it seems, the floodgates of iniquity are opened! Shall we not sin the more then, that grace may abound? Here we arrive at the crucial point. Here the pious old Adam can only recoil in horror from the thought of unconditional grace and try to protect the continuity of the old self by making compromises: some fateful mixture of grace and law, a little bit of human cooperation, perhaps the addition of a third use of the law, some heavy breathing about sanctification, and so on.

But the radical gospel will have none of that. Shall we sin the more that grace may abound? By no means! Why? *For you have died,* and how can you who have died to sin still live in it? The reason why abounding grace does not lead to sin lies in the fact that in its radicality it puts an end to the old, not in some species of compromise with the old. Furthermore, we miss the radicality of that if we do not see that this death is announced as *accomplished* fact: you *have* died. The death is not something yet to be done, one last act of spiritual suicide for "free choice." If Jesus died for all, then all have died (2 Cor. 5:14). The being of the hearer is simply stamped with the *theologia crucis,* the death and resurrection of Jesus is done to us by the proclamation of the accomplished fact. There is no justification except by faith alone. The radical forgiveness itself puts the old to death and calls forth the new. It is simply not possible to work with an anthropology that assumes a continuity that survives the cross, and turns it into an object for free choice to dally with.

The continuing crisis for anyone who is grasped by that radical gospel comes both from the fact that the world and its church cannot do other than resist and attack that gospel (as a matter of self-defense), and from the fact that they cannot escape the constant temptation to make compromises that disguise or blunt the sharp edges of its radicality. Lutheranism in particular, and perhaps especially now in this country where it is losing its more "worldly" folk-trappings, finds itself in this crucible. Lutheranism was born because Martin Luther was grasped by the radical gospel. Doctrinally he prosecuted his case predominantly as an attack on the anthropology derived from and dependent on the belief in free choice of the will. An even cursory study of the genesis of his theology demonstrates this, from the very first disputations *(Against Scholastic Theology,* the *Heidelberg Disputation),* on through the radical attack on emerging humanistic anthropology in the *The Bondage of the Will,* to the final massive *Commentary on Genesis.* In basic anthropological presupposition there is no difference between scholasticism and modern humanism or, for that matter, various other brands of contemporary Christianity, be they catholic, evangelical, charismatic, or even Mormon.[8] The differences among them on this score are more or less in-house disputes about how what is left of the

---

8. Cf. "Lectures on Galatians (1535)," in *Luther's Works,* ed. Jaroslav Pelikan and Helmut Lehmann (St. Louis: Concordia; Philadelphia: Fortress), v. 26, pp. 295-96. "Whoever falls from the doctrine of justification is ignorant of God and is an idolator. Therefore it is all the same whether he then returns to the Law or to the worship of idols; it is all the same whether he is called a monk or a Turk or a Jew or an Anabaptist."

continuously existing free choice can be cajoled, enticed, controlled, frightened, persuaded, impressed, etc., into making "the right choice." But in a pluralized society, the will is unable to make such a choice and can only lapse into a skepticism that has to settle for relativism. Whatever is right for you is the right choice.

In his debate with Erasmus, Luther saw that the attempt to combine the radical Pauline gospel with even the slightest hint of free choice could only lead to thoroughgoing skepticism, a permanent "identity crisis."[9] Hans-Joachim Iwand, a theologian little known in America because most of his work was published posthumously and remains untranslated, demonstrates this most clearly and consistently.[10] The positing of free choice means that the subject stands over against the gospel as an object, a theory that is to be accepted on grounds dictated by the subject. But what could such grounds be? Can the subject will its own death? Willy-nilly, the subject, claiming to be free, constructs a defense mechanism against the gospel, and permanent skepticism is the outcome. One can avoid it, perhaps, only by submitting to the authority of an institution like that of the Roman Church. Freedom is given with one hand only to be taken back by the other! From this point of view the Enlightenment is simply a kind of institutionalization of skepticism over against ecclesiastical authoritarianism.

The tragedy of post-Reformation Lutheranism and the theological root of its identity crisis is to be found in the persistent attempt to combine the radical gospel of justification by faith alone with an anthropology that cannot tolerate it. Thus, as Iwand maintains, Lutheranism has for the most part been a house divided against itself. "The doctrine of justification was retained, but it was combined with an anthropology which had its entire pathos in a faith in the freedom of the will." Thus, the radicality of the gospel was blunted and frittered away. The anthropology was borrowed largely from humanism. ". . . Humanism from Melanchthon to Ritschl indeed permits justification to occur even *sola fide,* but nevertheless breaks off the spearhead by which it would itself be mortally wounded, the bondage of the will."[11] The attempt to combine two diametrically opposed

9. Martin Luther, *The Bondage of the Will,* trans. J. I. Packer and O. R. Johnston (Westwood, N.J.: Fleming H. Revell, 1957), p. 140.

10. See, for example, the collection of essays titled *Um den rechten Glauben,* Theologische Bücherei, Neudrucke and Berichte aus dem 20. Jahrhundert. Bd. 9. Systematische Theologie (Munich: Chr. Kaiser Verlag, 1959).

11. *Um den rechten Glauben,* p. 17.

theological positions can only issue in a fundamental skepticism in thought and hesitancy in practice.[12]

This is the source of what we might call the inner and outer aspects of Lutheranism's crisis. The attempt to combine two incompatible views means that internally it has always had to battle its fundamental skepticism, its uncertainty about the basis for its faith. So in its practice it has resorted mostly to a dogmatic absolutism largely dependent on a view of scriptural inerrancy, which usually brought with it disguised moral absolutisms of various sorts as well. A will that supposedly begins in a state of freedom ends in captivity. The message becomes a perverted mirror image of itself. "Yes, you are free, but you jolly well had better choose to believe in justification by faith alone or you will go to hell. The Bible says so! And then you had better show your thanks by your sanctification."

The outer side of the crisis comes from the fact that justification by faith alone without the deeds of the law can only appear dangerous, if not somewhat ridiculous, to the outside world premised on free choice of the will. Thus, Lutheranism easily becomes the target of religious disapproval, not to say ridicule. The litany of complaint is a familiar one: "How can there be serious evangelism if there is no free choice?" "Lutherans don't believe in good works." I have a Baptist friend who likes to say that the trouble with Lutherans is that they never get any better! "Lutherans preach cheap grace; Lutherans are quietists, Lutherans don't have any social ethics; Lutherans are too passive; etc." Many Lutherans themselves seem to take masochistic delight in rehearsing this litany. No doubt it is a way of getting back at justification by faith turned into dogmatic absolutism.

The division of the house against itself is thus quite evident. Lutheran theological ranks, especially in America, seem filled by practitioners who on the one hand are spooked by the ghosts of past absolutisms, dogmatic and moral, and on the other are somewhat embarrassed by Lutheranism's fateful attachment to the gospel of justification by faith alone and, of course, frightened to death of "exaggerated" assertions about the bondage of the will and such unpleasantries. So where then does one end? Somewhere in the middle, no doubt, in a theological no-man's land where one will be shot at from all sides. "Yes, justification is nice, but it's not the only choice in the biblical cafeteria." A little criticism and relativism to counter the absolutism, a dash of "free grace" to relax the moralism

---

12. *Um den rechten Glauben,* p. 9.

(but not to be overdone), a little resorting to the Lutheran Confessions when in a tight spot (but not to be exaggerated), and a general tailoring of the message to "meet one's needs." The result is a loss of recognizable identity, a tendency to fade into the woodwork of generic religion, and an almost complete failure of nerve.

Proclaiming the Radical Gospel

What is to be done? Whither Lutheranism? The analysis leads to a crossroads. The radical gospel of justification by faith alone does not allow for a middle-of-the-road position. Either one must proclaim it as unconditionally as possible, or forget it. We must somehow muster up the nerve to preach the gospel in such fashion as to put the old to death and call forth the new. In one sense, of course, the litany of complaint against Lutheranism is all too true. Preaching the gospel of justification by faith alone *to* old beings in such fashion as to leave them old can only be a disaster. The proclamation either makes the old beings worse, or it puts an end to them to make them new. If Lutheranism is to recover a sense of its identity and mission today, it must begin to consider what it means to preach the gospel in radical fashion.

A short paper such as this is not the place to attempt laying out such a program. But in the space remaining I will venture some observations about the dimensions of the task. First of all, we do not adequately gauge the depth of the problem unless we see that it is ultimately a problem for the *proclamation* (Word and Sacrament) of the church. Of course, theological reflection is vital. But one does not preach justification by faith alone or the bondage of the will and such doctrines. They are presuppositions for preaching. It is the *proclamation* that makes new beings, not theology, or even ethics. If we begin with the presupposition of bondage, it is obvious that the difficulty we face, as Iwand likes to insist, is not merely a logical or even a historical mistake.[13] If it were so, it could simply be corrected theologically. The fact, as we have maintained all along, that justification was combined with the wrong anthropology could be fixed simply by getting a new and improved dogmatic anthropology. But if the will is in fact bound, we must deal with what, for want of a better term, is an exis-

13. *Um den rechten Glauben,* pp. 17 and 18.

tential matter. To persist in the wrong anthropology is not just an exegetical or dogmatic mistake but a *temptation* about which the old being *per se* can do nothing, precisely because it wills to do nothing. And it wills to do nothing because it has no hope and no vision of the new. There is no freedom here; everyone theologizes as they must.[14] Whatever talk there might be about a new anthropology based on death and resurrection, for instance, would only be turned into metaphor for moral improvement. The old remains bound.

What does this mean for theology? Is this a new and more vicious form of absolutism? The ramifications for theology and its task are indeed many, and we cannot tackle them here. The point, however, is not that a new absolutism is proposed, but that theology comes to realize precisely its limit and must give way to the sheer proclamation of grace. Theology does not make new beings. It is precisely the business of a theology that knows about bondage to see this, and thus to drive toward a proclamation in Word and Sacrament which by the power of the Spirit *ubi et quando visum est deo* will do it. When theology learns its task it will be relieved of its endless theoretical skepticism and can proceed with regained confidence. Such theology is neither absolutist nor relativist, conservative nor liberal. Theology drives to proclamation. Its thinking is dedicated to making that proclamation hearable in a given context as a radical gospel that sets free from bondage and makes all things new. Whither Lutheranism? Here we might find a way into the future worthy of the tradition that gave us birth.

Secondly, it follows from all we have said that the proclamation, to be radical, must be uncompromising, *sola gratia, sola fide.* The most common failing, the most persistent temptation, is a failure of nerve. A pastor said to me the other day after a lecture on absolution, "I think we know we are supposed to do the unconditional absolution, but I suspect we just don't dare!" Who has not experienced the fear of perhaps having gone too far this time in preaching the gospel, and perhaps has been afraid of having wrecked the whole program of the church, so carefully built up! After all, for the time being we do stand in the old age; we see through a glass darkly. We walk, and talk, and prophesy by faith, by hope. But there is no middle ground in this matter. Certainly that was the burden of Luther's argument against Erasmus. If there is to be any point to the continued existence of

14. *Um den rechten Glauben,* p. 19.

Lutheranism (not to mention Protestantism in general), we must simply be ready to prosecute the case for this radicality.

Virtually all the failures and shortcomings of Lutheranism can be seen in the hesitancy to proclaim the gospel in uncompromising, unconditional fashion, to proclaim as though we were about the business of summoning the dead to life, calling new beings into existence. Most generally, it seems, the gospel is preached as though it were a repair job on old beings, a "new patch on an old garment." It is preached *to* old beings instead of *for* new beings. When that is the case, the litany of complaint turns out to be mostly true. Its understanding and proclamation of the gospel undercuts and enervates the moral projects of old beings and seems only to invite license. When the gospel is not "anti–old Adam/Eve" it just becomes antinomian. The only way one can rescue it from absolute disaster then is to make compromises with the projects of old beings. But that is the end of the gospel. Either the gospel must be preached in radical fashion, or it is best left alone altogether.[15]

A radical Lutheranism would be one that regains the courage and the nerve to preach the gospel unconditionally; simply let the bird of the Spirit fly! There is too much timidity, too much worry that the gospel is going to harm someone, too much of a tendency to buffer the message to bring it under control. It is essential to see that everything hangs in the balance here. Faith comes by hearing. Will the old persist? Will we understand ourselves to be continuously existing subjects called upon to exercise our evanescent modicum of free choice to carve out some sort of eternal destiny for ourselves? That depends. It depends on whether someone has the courage to announce to us, "You have died and your life is hid with Christ in God!" "Awake you who sleep, and arise from the dead!" It could be that we will be only continuously existing subjects doomed to our own choices. Is the law eternal? It could be and will be if Christ is not preached so as to end it for us. We tremble on the brink of freedom. Is this all, this old age, this confusing mixture of *regnum mundi* and *regnum diaboli?* It could be. That is the terror of it. And it will be for us unless someone sounds the trumpet of the *regnum dei* with an absolutely uncompromising clarity. How shall they hear without a preacher? We have a hard time realizing that everything hangs here on the unconditional announcement, the absolutely new

---

15. Luther maintained that semi-Pelagianism was much worse than outright Pelagianism! *Bondage of the Will,* p. 292.

start of God in the resurrection of Jesus. The vision, the hope, yes, even the ecstasy or the "rapture" as even Luther could say,[16] hang on the radical unconditionality of the proclamation.

Finally, it is only out of this radical unconditionality that an appropriate understanding of the life of the Christian for the time being can arise. We simply do not understand the pathos of the Reformer's utterances about faith doing the good spontaneously and naturally unless we see this. Precisely because the declaration is unconditional we are turned around to go into the world of the neighbor to carry out our calling as Christians. The works of the Christian are to be done in the world, but not as conditions for salvation. The persistent and nagging debate about the two kingdoms among Lutherans arises mostly out of reluctance to be radical enough. Precisely because the gospel gives the kingdom of God unconditionally to faith, this world opens up and is given back as the place to serve the other. Will it be so given? That depends, of course. It is not a static affair. To the degree that one is grasped and set free by the unconditional gospel, to that degree one can be turned from the sort of life created by the self (and its supposed free but actually bound will) to the world of the neighbor. To the degree that the theological use of the law comes to an end in Christ, to that degree a political use of the law for others becomes a possibility. If somehow this could be grasped, perhaps we could cease the silly debates about whether the church's mission is proclamation *or* development, personal salvation *or* social justice, etc., and get on with the business of taking care of this world and the neighbor as lovingly, wisely, and pragmatically as our gifts enable.

Radical Lutheranism? Is there, and can there be such? That depends, of course. It depends, for our part, at least, on whether or not we are "encouraged" enough to preach that radical and unconditional gospel. Beyond that, of course, it depends on the Spirit. But after all, in spite of our reluctance and timidity, it isn't some Herculean task we are being asked to do. It has all been done. All we have to do is say it; just let the bird fly!

16. Luther, *Bondage of the Will*, p. 311.

The Apocalyptic No and the Eschatological Yes:
Reflections, Suspicions, Fears, and Hopes

When I was invited to speak at this conference, I was reluctant because I fear I have said everything I have to say about Karl Barth. But informed about the subject of the conference, "The Necessary 'No!' and the Indispensable 'Yes!': Theological Controversy, Christology and the Mission of the Church Today," the subject of the conference called to mind the dominical warning from the Sermon on the Mount, "Let what you say be simply 'Yes' or 'No'; anything more than this comes of evil." Perhaps we can take that to mean that in these matters we should always say "yes" or "no" but not "maybe." Buoyed by the apparent latitude and even a kind of dislike for the "maybe," I decided to develop the theme "The apocalyptic 'no' and the eschatological 'yes.'"

The original description of the purpose of this effort reads: "This lecture will reflect on both apocalyptic and eschatological themes in contemporary theologies and respond to them from the perspective of christological dogma." Feeling that to be overly ambitious, I have given this exercise the subtitle: "Reflections, suspicions, fears, and hopes." In short, I will attempt something rather presumptuous: a reflective look at the shape or basic systematic structure of the church's theology through the ages and how that might relate to some of our problems today. It will be a kind of attempt — albeit audacious and outrageous — to gather together out of my past a number of theologoumena and bits of history that have bothered me and aroused certain suspicions, fears, and hopes. I will attempt to bring some of these reflections to bear on current questions. In my thinking, these reflections and suspicions increasingly circle around questions of apocalyptic and eschatology.

So, where have we arrived at today with the likes of our "ecumenical consensus building," our "Jesus seminars," or our general return to moralism of one sort or another — our outrageous fancies and nonsense? It may seem inappropriate to throw such disparate operations together but, looked at from the perspectives of apocalyptic and eschatology, are they really all that much different? So the problematic and even perhaps what might be called the thesis for this lecture is suggested by the words from Barth's *The Epistle to the Romans* that launched this theological century — quoted in the prospectus, "If Christianity be not altogether thoroughgoing eschatology, there remains in it no relationship whatever with Christ." Those are strong words. In them, there is a "no" and a "yes," but there certainly is no "maybe." How would we fare today if we were to be measured by that dictum? Where have we arrived? Does what we do theologically bear any relationship to Christ? Does it bear the stamp of "thoroughgoing eschatology"? Or, have we decided to dismiss Barth, given up, and gone back to finding our salvation in our ontologies? After all, like all "apocalyptikers," the Barth of the Romans Commentary was a little bit crazy. It was in his maturity that he settled down and became more sensible. So we have learned to comfort ourselves. When he became a university professor, he could not make such outrageous statements. We can write this off as the foolishness and rashness of an overheated Protestant youth.

Extinguishing the Apocalypse

But the words echo from those of Franz Overbeck, who, if he had not caught the apocalyptic bug, at least knew it when he saw it and whose work bothered Barth as he set out on his theological journey. Barth's review essay on Overbeck bears rereading in these theological dog days. Barth gave the essay the title *"Unerledigte Anfragen an die heutige Theologie,"* translated as "Unsettled Questions for Theology Today." I wonder if it should be translated even more pugnaciously as "The Unfinished Business of" or "Unanswered Charges Leveled against" the theology of today. By giving the essay such a title Barth wants to raise again for his day — and ours — the same question that Overbeck hurled at his. Have these really been *"erledigt"* even now? We do not have the time here to rehearse them all lest this become an essay on Overbeck.

For our purposes, we can simply say that Overbeck was a clear-eyed reader of the New Testament who was able to penetrate to the apocalyptic root of it all. Like Ernst Käsemann, he was able to see that apocalyptic was the "mother of Christian theology." Overbeck looked at the New Testament and then at the Christianity and theology of his day and came to the conclusion that they really had little, if anything, to do with one another. Now, in itself, that is not such a novel operation. Pious folk are always doing that. But usually their attack is a moralistic one, made on the basis of the "Religion of the Sermon on the Mount," seeking a Jesus "without frills" or the "Q Jesus." Frightening! Unrelenting judgment! Instead, Overbeck's attack came more from the apocalyptic character of the New Testament. The New Testament is not about "revelation in history" but about "supra-history" (*Urgeschichte,* Overbeck called it), i.e., about that in which history is enveloped, about the beginning and the end, the *Urzeit* and the *Endzeit,* as the Germans would later say. The apocalypse expected and awaited is the utterance of the final "No!" to history and this entire evil and adulterous age. The announcement was that it shall be burned to a crisp, as can be found, for instance, in 2 Peter 3:10ff.:

> But the day of the Lord will come like a thief, and then the heavens will pass away with a loud noise, and the elements will be dissolved with fire, and the earth and everything that is done on it will be disclosed. Since all these things are to be dissolved in this way, what sort of persons ought you to be in leading lives of holiness and godliness, waiting for and hastening the coming of the day of God, because of which the heavens will be set ablaze and dissolved, and the elements will melt with fire? But, in accordance with his promise, we wait for new heavens and a new earth, where righteousness is at home.

Christianity, on the other hand, at least as Overbeck in his day saw it, was not at all about that. Christianity was a form — no doubt the highest — of culture. Christianity was all about this world and its possibilities. Christians were more likely to be interested in postponing than "waiting for and hastening the coming of the day of God"! Apocalyptic was to be read — if at all — as a kind of secret code to be translated by expert decoders into relatively harmless moral and cultural platitudes.

Theology that supported this enterprise, Overbeck averred, was "the Satan of Religion," tempting Jesus with the gift of this whole world if he will only worship the devil. Theology, then, would be the attempt to impose Christianity on the world under the explicitly hallowed garb of modern culture by concealing and even denying its basically ascetic (and we might add apocalyptic) character. Theology, in that light, is the business of misleading people into Christianity by making it all "so nice" — akin to a sign on a colleague's door that reads: "God is nice. We should be nice. Isn't that nice?" The apocalyptic "no" was no longer heard, simply ignored, so that the "yes" became theological marshmallows.

Have the *unerledigte Anfragen,* the "unanswered charges," coming from an Overbeck via Barth been somehow *erledigt,* at least to the degree that they do not come back to haunt us in contemporary theology? I, for one, have a hard time ridding myself of the suspicion that they have not. That is why I speak in my subtitle of suspicions and fears. Is there not — even in the increasing tendency to relegate Barth, especially of the Romans Commentary, to an honored but relatively insignificant place in history — a steadfast avoidance of the apocalyptic "no"? Is there perhaps in, say, our ecumenical theology, an obscuring of real differences at just this point? Is the supposed "catholic" *oikumene* with which we are converging not just another form of "culture"? Are we borrowing from an ontological bank where we have no capital to invest our bishops with a sort of power that eschatology can never afford? Is it, for instance, altogether a great boon that we are now proposing to announce in a formal and binding fashion that the "mutual condemnations" of the Reformation era no longer strike "today's ecumenical partner"? What if — just what if — those very condemnations of the Council of Trent, for instance, taken as a whole and not just one by one, were really aimed at the apocalyptic and eschatological shapes implicit in Reformation theology itself? If the condemnations no longer strike, could it perhaps mean that the apocalyptic fire has gone out? Shall we huddle together in our clubhouse now that the light has gone out and call it "full communion"? Ah, love, let us be true to one another. . . . Imagine the irony: instead of burning everything to a crisp, the apocalyptic fire went out! But did the fire just go out or did someone put it out? Perhaps we could add another image to Overbeck's derogation of theologians: they are the firemen of the apocalypse, experts at putting out apocalyptic fires — so they will cause only minor damage!

I am suspicious about these and many related questions. Have they now been settled? So in what follows I will do some reflecting on the problem and place of apocalyptic and eschatology in the history of the church's theology. This can be done here only in broad and sweeping terms. It is risky and perhaps audacious to attempt, but I have been at this enterprise long enough now to venture some risks.

Ontologizing Jesus

To get to the root of our problems with apocalyptic and eschatology, we have to go back almost to the beginning. To clarify matters, we need to make a distinction between apocalyptic and eschatology. Apocalyptic is always hard to specify since there are so many strands of it. However, for our purposes here, it is the story of the beginning, the catastrophic misadventure, and coming cataclysmic end of the present age. Salvation is largely a future possibility given from out of the ashes of the fire from which those who are righteous must wait — no doubt with a certain anxiety. Its power and theological utility and truth is in the impending "No!," the swift, sudden, and sure judgment against a creation that has turned against its Lord, the insistence that this cannot go on forever. Rather, there shall be a cut-off time, a final "too late." And certainly, in the apocalyptic view, not everyone is going to make it. The "NO" will have its day. So, for that reason, apocalyptic continues to have its rightful place.

Eschatology, on the other hand, is more the story not so much of how we shall fare in the future cataclysmic end, but how the future will come to us in Jesus, how the end and the new beginning breaks in upon us in Jesus' life and deeds among us, especially his death and resurrection. Here, the end comes to meet us. The eschatological "yes" invades our present. To be sure, it is clothed in the "no," in the hiddenness of the cross and even the utter unconditionality of its graciousness. It is the story of how God's sovereign future invades our present, ending the old and the beginning of the new. The apocalyptic clash of the ages remains, but is now christologically anchored and done to us in the living present.

I have claimed that we need to go back to the beginning to discern what happened to apocalyptic. How then might we think about what happened back there? The problem with apocalyptic thinking and speaking was precisely that it had no way to deal with the salvific deed of Christ in the present. The apocalyptic scenario was formed without Christ, and "apocalyptikers" often had a difficult time fitting Christ into the picture. A Christ who shatters the apocalyptic "no" with the eschatological "yes" breaks up the apocalyptic scheme. To the true-blue "apocalyptiker" it was, no doubt, something of a disappointment. What apocalyptic expected seemingly was not realized in Jesus. There are some overtones and undertones of that in the relation between John the Baptist and Jesus when John, incarcerated for his fiery preaching, sends disciples to ask Jesus, "Are you he who is to come or are we to look for another?" John might well have asked, "Is this all? Where is the ax laid to the root of the trees? Where is the winnowing fork and the unquenchable fire into which everything that does not measure up will be tossed?" Jesus' answer is an implicit eschatological one: "Go and tell John what you see and hear. The blind see, the deaf hear, the lame walk, the poor have good news proclaimed to them. And blessed are those who take no offense at me." But that is probably somewhat disappointing, maybe even offensive, to the true-blue "apocalyptiker." Jesus tends to break up the apocalyptic scenario by his eschatological claims. So apocalyptic expectation tends to shift to yet another future possibility when it will all still come true: to the return of Christ, the *parousia,* and the notorious problem of its "delay." For an even more apocalyptic vision, it is the delay that is the problem. It seems always to be "too late!" But in eschatology it is the pre-occurrence that is the problem. It is always too soon, too much! But even as the *parousia* is anticipated one could expect it only with a certain sense of dread and fear. Christ takes on more the character of the fearsome apocalyptic ruler and judge, the Son of Man who comes on the clouds with great glory to settle all accounts. It is something of the attitude one sees expressed on those bumper stickers that announce: "Jesus is coming soon, and is he ever pissed!"

But the fascinating question is, Whatever happened to our "apocalyptikers"? I have always been persuaded by Robert Grant's highly significant thesis that many of them became Gnostics. Gnostics are disappointed "apocalyptikers." They got tired of waiting for the apocalyptic scenario to work itself out. Instead of looking for the redeemer in the future, they looked for a Gnostic redeemer from above. They transcendentalized it all. When the apocalypse does not occur, Jesus gets ontologized. In one way or another that seems always to be the case. The Christ who is always present is substituted for the Christ who does not present himself. So it was with the Gnostics. Christ is the messenger from an absolutely new and hitherto unheard of "alien God" aeons beyond the cosmic disaster in which we find ourselves trapped in torpid ignorance. But, as is well known, this move drives to a metaphysical dualism. Apocalyptic's temporal dualism of the ages is replaced by the eternal dualism of the "below" versus the "above," the sensible against the intelligible, the realm of change, decay, and death opposed to that of unchanging, immortal, and eternal spirit. With it, as we all know, came the rejection of this world and its "creator" God, Yahweh, together with his "covenant." The human Jesus tends to be only the temporary disguise of the Gnostic redeemer. Indeed, in some Gnostic systems, he does not really suffer crucifixion at all but exchanges the cross with Simon of Cyrene and stands by in the crowd observing, amused with the curious proceedings! In sum, the apocalyptic "no" is transformed into a metaphysical "no." Perhaps we could say that what the old apocalyptic failed to destroy physically the Gnostic "apocalyptikers" destroyed metaphysically — a linguistic destruction is substituted for a real one. Except, of course, that in their asceticism some sought a sort of destruction of themselves! Where there is no eschatological "yes" the apocalyptic "no" always seems to assert some sort of destruction.

But now the interesting and puzzling thing here is how we are to assess the general reaction to all of this from what we have come to call the more "orthodox" theology that developed in the church. For reasons that now seem to us to be quite obvious but were not to them, those who became the teachers of the church rejected Gnosticism. But, what bothered me is the question of how and on what grounds this was done. My suspicion is that it was done by attempting to meet the Gnostics theologically on their own ground, by a move to an ontology in which they hoped to engage the challenge of Gnostic dualism. Or, perhaps, it was a kind of synthesis between biblical teaching and Hellenism, in which the more egregious elements of Gnosticism and Hellenism were countered by the biblical word. The "false *gnosis*" was confronted by the "true *gnosis*" (Irenaeus). So Yahweh was reinstated as the one and only God. The Old Testament was reinstated as a Christian book. Creation and incarnation countered the disparagement of this world. "Free choice" was established as a defense against Gnostic and Manichaean fatalism. Out of the Gnostic crisis emerged a kind Christian Gnosis.

Now, of course, it has to be said that this kind of move is entirely understandable, even necessary, given the circumstances. The problem, however, is that eschatology is the casualty. I do not want to presume that this happened with every theologian at the time. But it does seem to be an appropriate generalization. The presence of Christ is guaranteed by the ontological system since he is the union both of temporal and eternal being rather than by the inbreaking of the eschatological promise as word into the present. We cannot help but wonder: Is ontological presence always the hallmark of the demise of the apocalyptic and eschatological viewpoints? Certainly, the fight against metaphysical dualism reinforces the view that the eschatological duality of the old and the new simply was eclipsed along with it. Anything "new" became suspect. What was left of apocalyptic and eschatology was relegated to the last chapters in dogmatics and also in life itself. It now had to do with "The Last Things," but not with anything of pressing concern in present experience, except perhaps that one should "be prepared," the tyranny of the future, shall we say? Thus, the import of eschatology is eclipsed since you can wait until you or your loved ones are facing the end.

That eschatology became a casualty very early in the church is a matter of considerable consequence. Virtually everything is affected — soteriology for starters. The eschatological "yes" ending the old and ringing in the new through the word of the cross and the resurrection does not sound. All you are likely to get is an ontological "maybe" — maybe you will be saved if you acquire proper ontological credentials and are properly "transformed." The church and the ministry take on ontological trappings; they become ranked in appropriate hierarchies. Instead of the Gnostic aeons and aeons we have, à la pseudo-Dionysius, the Celestial and the Earthly Hierarchies. The church on earth is a reflection of the one in heaven, the "militant" versus the "triumphant" church. However, most fateful of all is the problem of the interpretation of scripture. Gnostics, we can affirm, were honest enough to see that the scriptures, particularly the Old Testament and its God, could not be assimilated to their ontological systems. So they just rejected the idea that it was about the same God who sent the redeemer. Marcion, as we all know, carried the matter even further. More than just rejection of the Old Testament, he constructed his own New Testament canon, rejecting even those portions of the New Testament writings that did not fit. In sum, the Gnostic answer to the interpretation of scripture was flat-out rejection of that which did not fit.

But now, what did the more orthodox-minded who had taken the road of meeting Gnosticism on its own ground do? Scripture, we should be aware, has always posed a very serious problem for us when we are tempted towards an ontological direction. What are we to do with the God of the Old Testament and all the moral misadventures of his people? What evolved was the practice of interpreting the scriptures — especially the portions that are most offensive, "spiritually" as many would have called it, though "symbolically" would perhaps be more accurate. In this regard, Jan Lindhardt's book, *Martin Luther: Knowledge and Mediation in the Renaissance,* is vitally important. The scriptures were "bent," we might say, to fit a more ontological point of view.

The great distinction between the literal/historical sense and the spiritual or symbolic sense was used to support this enterprise. Interpretation was a matter of penetrating to what the text "really" symbolized. The text, to use Lindhardt's apt image, was something like a secret code requiring experts to decode it in order to find its original and true message. This parallels the Gnostic system itself where it was held that the Gnostic redeemer imparted secrets to be understood only by the initiated! What evolved already in Origen and right into the Middle Ages was the much celebrated "fourfold" method of scriptural interpretation. The basic assumption was that words are signs or symbols that signify things. Since ultimate truth is already fixed by the ontology, words do not really do anything or alter anything. They can only signify what was (in time, the eternal and unchangeable past) or (in eternity, ontologically) what always is and so, on that basis we hope, will be at the end. Unchanging reality is our anchor!

But words that only signify or symbolize deliver neither an apocalyptic no nor an eschatological yes. They do not actually do much of anything except inform us about what to do in order to conform to the demands of the ontological scheme. So the fourfold method issues largely in instruction. The literal/historical sense, the account of what happened way back then, has in itself "meaning" at best as a preliminary or elementary sense for the simple-minded. That the text, for instance, says God rescued his people from Egypt and led them through the Red Sea and the wilderness for forty years is of no great import in and of itself. Indeed, the Pauline dictum that the "letter (the literal/historical sense) kills while the spirit gives life" was taken in a Platonizing sense to mean that the literal was insufficient. The text, then, does not deliver an apocalyptic "No!" It is merely judged inadequate. Interpretation overtakes soteriology. One must get beyond the literal to the spiritual, that is, in order to be rendered significant the literal text must be decoded. The fourfold method sought to deliver such significance on any or all of three levels: (1) allegory (a doctrinal level), (2) tropology (the moral), and (3) anagogy (the mystical or eschato-logical). So, on the allegorical plane, one might draw conclusions about the nature of God, i.e., that he is a redeemer who looks on his people with steadfast love and mercy. Tropologically, one could say that the Exodus event symbolizes the necessity for the moral transformation of us all. "Leaving the flesh-pots of Egypt" is a phrase that still hangs on in lan-guage. Tropology — treating the text as though it were really a symbol of a deeper and more eternal meaning — accentuates the necessity for moral renewal and transformation. Anagogically, the Exodus could be decoded as the mystical journey of the soul from the many to the one through purga-tion (leaving Egypt, the journey through the wilderness, etc.), illumination (vision of the promised land), and union (although like Moses, as many mystics held, we cannot attain the final union here, but can only see it from afar on Mt. Nebo). But the mystical journey of the soul is what it is really all about at its deepest level. That is the ultimate message once it has been decoded.

So the fourfold method really delivers only instruction as to what we are to do, instruction to fortify the theological virtues of faith (allegory), love (tropology), and hope (final enjoyment of the mystical vision). The method sidesteps a view of language in which the word does something to us. Rather, it attempts to render the text meaningful so that we will imple-ment it. It instructs us about what we are to believe, to do, and to hope. Where words are merely symbolic, where they only signify "meaning" in an ontological scheme, everything revolves on the free choice of an acting subject. Hermeneutics and methods of interpretation are not theologically neutral or unrelated exercises. Every hermeneutic, every method of inter-pretation, is an implicit soteriology. Here the apocalyptic "no" and the es-chatological "yes" are effectively blocked out.

Renewal of Eschatology

Now the Reformation was something of an eschatological interlude in our story. This is certainly true when one looks closely at Luther's struggles with the interpretation of scripture. Since this is all relatively well known, I will not dwell on the fine points but rather situate it with broad brush-strokes as I continue our story. What emerged from Luther's struggle with scripture was quite evidently an eschatological use of the word and the preaching of it. The word "eschatology," of course, was not then in use, but he particularly intuited the eschatological shape of the New Testament message. Luther himself, contemporary research increasingly likes to say, was, like many in his day, something of an "apocalyptiker" and often spoke of his role as a Reformer in apocalyptic terms and images. It could be said that Luther's actual thought and social counsel was more eschatological than apocalyptic — as I have here tried to delineate this difference.

The key, once again, is the interpretation of scripture. Is scripture to be read and preached as an eschatological word that *does* the end of the old and the new beginning to us now, or is it to be read as a book of symbols, pointing to some deeper ontological meaning accessible only to expert decoders? For Luther, it was certainly the former. He rejected the fourfold method as a way to get from letter to spirit. He is reputed to have insisted on the literal or grammatical historical meaning as the only legitimate sense of scripture. Actually, that is something of an oversimplification since he continued to use allegory for interpreting scripture most of his life. Jan Lindhardt is more correct, it would appear, when he says that what Luther really rejected was the practice of symbolic interpretation, which treats scripture, as we have seen, as though it were a symbolic code open to decoding in at least the four different dimensions of the method. In that way, scripture would become, as Luther said, "a wax nose" that could issue in several different "meanings," one supposedly as valid as another. Luther's insistence on the literal meaning counters this by saying that if you are looking for "meaning," there is only one and that is to be found in the literal, or as he preferred to call it, the "grammatical historical." To find the "meaning," one must employ all the historical and grammatical tools available.

But beyond the question of meaning, there is the question of the use *(usus),* the question not just of what the words mean, but what they do, how they work on us, and indeed how we in turn might consider using them. So Luther took the passage about the "letter killing and the spirit giving life" differently from the earlier — and, we can infer, later tradition. That the "letter kills" was not due to its inadequacy but rather to the fact that as "preached word," it functions first as law. It accuses and kills. The history of God with his people leads to one place, the cross, and it spells one thing for old beings, death. The apocalyptic "NO" begins to sound. That the Spirit gives life is not taken as the result of an interpretative process but rather what is to occur through the preaching of the gospel. Spirit,

Luther says in his argument with Emser over letter and spirit, may be spoken of, as St. Augustine held, as gospel without law. "Without law" here can be taken as the unconditional word whose aim is to bring the dead to life. The eschatological "YES!" is to ring out from the pulpit.

The Reformation, seen in this light, was an inbreaking of the eschatological word into the church's proclamation. But alas, as subsequent history shows, it was only an interlude. Not that the Reformation did not go on and spawn churches in their own right. But the question for our purposes is: Did they become bearers and preachers of the eschatological word? Perhaps, here and there, now and again. But there is something here that does not love the eschatological word. It is too much for the old age to take. An unconditional gospel-promise will always be suspected of fostering all sorts of theological and ethical mayhem: quietism, formlessness, antinomianism, cheap grace, social irresponsibility, and moral laxity. The ills of the modern world sooner or later will be blamed on the gospel — or some distorted form of it. "Now that the gospel has come," Luther quipped, "men have learned the fine art of blaming all the evils of the world on it! As if these evils were not in the world before the gospel! Just as men blame education for the fact that as education spreads their own ignorance is exposed!"[1]

At any rate, taken as a whole, from the eschatological perspective, the later followers of the Reformation tended to cave in to incessant complaints of the gospel's "impracticality." This is perhaps most evident again in the understanding of the interpretation of scripture. Luther's searching attempts to see the *usus* of the word as killing letter and life-giving spirit were largely buried in manuscripts that were not published or read very widely. All that remained was the insistence that scripture should be interpreted according to its literal sense and that when one got in a tight spot one could invoke a bowdlerized version of Luther's dictum that "scripture interprets itself." The word lost its active character as eschatological word doing both the end and the new beginning and reverted to a mere signifier.

But what did such a bare literal word signify? Exegetes, of course, continue their work on the literal word. But criticism and word studies do not a theology make. To make a long story short, I would contend that the old fourfold method did not just go away but actually continued in a seriatim fashion what the Middle Ages did simultaneously. That is, allegory,

---

1. LW 33:55, translation altered.

tropology, and anagogy continued as methods of interpretation *one after another* in the various periods and movement of modern church history. Orthodoxy repeated the allegorical search for the doctrinal sense. The move away from this culminated finally in liberalism, which practiced tropological exegesis — searching for the moral meaning. If we can say that anagogy was akin to the eschatological sense, then it would be not entirely inaccurate to say that for a time, in the early and middle parts of this century, anagogy had a brief moment in the sun. We almost made it! Barth's statement quoted at the beginning of this paper to the effect that if theology is not thoroughgoing eschatology it has no relation to Christ, together with the *unerledigte Anfragen* inspired by Overbeck, are indications of that. The dialectical theological movement, the recovery of the apocalyptic and eschatological messages of the scriptures — all of this could be termed anagogical in type.

But, alas, it was only brief: the eschatological interpretation of scripture seems to have enjoyed but a short time in the sun. For the most part, the theological world seems to have slipped back into various species of tropological exegesis. As always, ethical questions swarm to the attack like angry hornets. The eschatological "yes" grants too much too soon. It is too dangerous for this world. Its grace is "too cheap." This is the same charge that was leveled at the time of the Reformation. Unconditional, "forensic" justification is ineffective. It must be rendered effective by our ethics. Back then there was the "third use of the law." Today we have other attempts to repair the damage: peace and justice concerns, neo-Marxist theologies of Hope, Liberation Theologies, rights movements, ecological concerns, and self-affirmation support groups. We even have our friends in the Jesus Seminar insisting that Jesus did not preach an apocalyptic or eschatological message at all, but was rather a wandering near-eastern sage. This ancient tropology is now to be polished up and presented to us as "a New Vision."

Resistance to Eschatology

What is one to do with all of this? Of course the eschatological word is dangerous. Furthermore, if it is taken merely as a word that signifies and does not do what it says — doesn't kill and make alive — then either the old being reads it as an excuse for license or the death of which it speaks becomes (à la Marcus Borg) just a metaphor for "spiritual transformation." The tropological Jesus is being pitted against the Christ of Dogma!

How, then, should we respond to all this? If you listen to Luther in the *Lectures on Galatians* (1535), you will find that he has no solution other than to go on preaching the Word in spite of everything. Commenting on Galatians 3:19 ("Why then the law? It was added because of our transgressions," etc.), Luther remarks about the resentment evoked among those angered by Paul's limitation of law to a penultimate status:

> For when the rabble hear from the Gospel that righteousness comes by the sheer grace of God and by faith alone, without the Law or works, they draw the same conclusion the Jews drew then: "Then let us not do any works!" And they really live up to this. What, then, are we to do? *This evil troubles us severely, but we cannot stop it.* When Christ preached, He had to hear that He was a blasphemer and a rebel, that is, that his teaching was seducing men and making them seditious against Caesar. The same thing happened to Paul and to all the apostles. No wonder the world accuses us in a similar way today. All right, let it slander and persecute us! Still we must not keep silence, on account of their troubled consciences; but we must speak right out, in order to rescue them from the snares of the devil. Nor should we pay attention to how our doctrine is abused by the vicious and wicked rabble, who cannot be cured whether they have the law or not.[2]

One could, of course, write reams about a passage like that. The temptation, always, when confronted by a mess like the current one, is to bring the law to bear in more stringent form — resorting, perhaps, to structure, order, authority, or high office. All of that, no doubt, can find its rightful place *if* one makes a proper distinction between this age and the next. But Luther refused to resort to the law to shore up this sagging enterprise even in his day. Those who abuse and ridicule the eschatological proclamation are not likely to be saved by the law in any case. There is nothing to do but to stick to the proclamation in all boldness so that troubled consciences may be rescued from the fire. This is itself an indication of Luther's "apocalyptic" view of his calling. He did not expect that the gospel proclamation was going to save everybody. He saw his mission as that of saving the

---

2. LW 26:305 (emphasis added).

"elect" before the apocalyptic fire came. Thus, he was not about to deceive his hearers by compromising the message. Luther felt that slander and persecution were unavoidable. Indeed, he says at another place that the gospel cannot be preached without such complaint and outcry. If people are not complaining about your mistreatment of the law and all that, you probably are not preaching the gospel! The biggest mistake we are likely to make is to think that we are going to remedy things by imposing more law. The eschatological word bites. Indeed, it kills the old Adam and Eve. It is a two-edged sword. The "yes," perhaps we should say, in its own way hides the uncompromising apocalyptic "no" to all human religious aspiration within itself just as — as Barth knew well — the apocalyptic "no" hides the "yes."

Reassessing the Condemnations

But now, as we move toward the conclusion, there are of course other *"unerledigte Anfragen an die heutige Theologie"* that arise from the perspective of the eschatological Word. Virtually all aspects of theology are affected. But as was indicated at the outset, one of the more immediate problems is the ecumenical one. If we can say that the overcoming of Gnostic dualism by the Christian ontological scheme rendered New Testament eschatology a casualty and that the Reformation carried an implicit rebirth of that eschatological faith, what does it mean to say that the two are now "convergent" or that the differences between them are only a matter of "emphasis"? Can that really be the case? Is it not more likely that the eschatological viewpoint is once again gradually being smuggled out of sight?

Or, what does the "solemn and binding" agreement that the condemnations of the Reformation era no longer strike today's ecumenical partner imply? Why "no longer"? Did they strike somebody before? If so, who ducked? Or, is it rather the case, as suggested, that the apocalyptic and eschatological fires are going out — especially given the move in general toward moral tropology in theology. It seems terribly attractive for us to speak of declaring the condemnations inoperative today. Who, after all, would affirm cursing at one another? But, is it really all that complimentary to be told that you are no longer even worth shooting at? What if all those condemnations, especially the endless lists one finds in the Council of Trent, taken as a whole and not just one by one as was done in the Joint

Ecumenical Commission, really turn out to be a massive attack precisely on the eschatological shape of theology?

Look, for instance, at the first of the condemnations on justification. It says: "If anyone says that, without divine grace through Jesus Christ, man can be justified before God by his own works whether they were done by his natural powers or by the light of the teaching of the [Mosaic] Law; let him be anathema." It looks innocent enough because it is directed not so much at the Reformers, but even more at nominalist distortions within the Roman Catholic fold. Anyone who claims to be saved by one's own works under the law without the aid of grace is anathema. Lutherans, without ado, are likely to say "Amen!" But what is the assumption behind it? Read in the context of the Council and its anathemas as a whole, the assumption is that one can be saved by works performed *with* the aid of grace, where grace is understood as an infused quality in the soul. Consequently, later in the eleventh condemnation, it is held that anyone who claims that justification comes by the imputation of Christ's righteousness alone, or the remission of sins alone, or that the grace which justifies is the sheer favor of God (and *not* a quality in the soul) is anathema.

It is difficult to escape the supposition that this argument is precisely about the matters of which we have here spoken. The question about grace — whether it is a quality in the soul or the sheer divine promise *is* a question of ontology versus eschatology. Is "grace" a new eschatological reality that comes *extra nos* and breaks in upon us bringing new being to faith, the death of the old and the life of the new, or is it rather to be understood in ontological terms as an infused power that transforms old being? Can the eschatological perspective really be so accommodated as to be no longer struck by these condemnations? If so, who ducked? Shall the eschatological view once again be swallowed up by an ontological view that really amounts to little more than another tropology — perhaps now a tropological cake with grace as a kind of frosting?

I am not exactly sure how to end this exercise. Perhaps it is because one *unerledigte Anfrage* just uncovers another, and another, and another. So I will just conclude where I started, with Barth's dictum: "If Christianity be not altogether thoroughgoing eschatology, there remains in it no relationship whatever with Christ." Such a statement leaves *us* with our *unerledigte Anfrage:* How are we doing?

Lex semper accusat? Nineteenth-Century Roots of Our Current Dilemma

> Do we then overthrow the law by this faith? By no means!
> On the contrary, we uphold the law.
>
> *Romans 3:31*

J. Edgar Hoover liked to quote Lincoln's saying that reverence for law should be the political religion of the nation.[1] But we seem today to have arrived at a point where such words meet with something far less than enthusiastic or unanimous approval. Indeed, the very fact that they are thrown at us by the head of a major law-enforcement agency is likely only to increase antipathy in many circles. Reverence for law is just not "in."

There are, of course, many reasons for this general malaise in the attitude toward law — reasons that arise out of the complex political, social, and cultural situation in which we find ourselves today. My purpose here cannot be an attempt to untangle that mess, much as that is needed. Rather I would like to reflect a bit on the *theological* understanding of law and to ask whether theological development may have contributed, perhaps unwittingly, to the current difficulties and if so, how these might be sorted out. Such a restricted theological approach cannot pretend, to be sure, to provide a comprehensive answer to the problem of law today, but it might at least help Christians to find their bearings in a confusing time.

---

1. See his article on that subject in *Event* 1.9, no. 1 (January 1969): 3-6.

To do this I think we must look back a bit to the century immediately preceding our own, for it is here that we will find the roots of many of our current difficulties. Perhaps also before we begin it should be made clear that in considering the theological understanding of law we are dealing with the problem of law in a more or less general sense, not with particular laws or legal systems as such. There may be particular laws or even legal systems that one would not want, as a Christian, to support. But our question here is the more general one of the theological understanding of the function of law as such. The question is: What ought the Christian attitude to law and the rule of law to be?

The Reformation View

When the question is put in this way it becomes immediately apparent that Christians have had a difficult time giving a positive answer. The reason, of course, is that law has always suffered from its unfavorable contrast with the gospel. The law makes irksome and even impossible demands that "the flesh" in its weakness cannot fulfill. The gospel, on the other hand, grants forgiveness and comfort. In this scheme of things the law was granted a primarily *negative* function. The law exposes man's weakness and short-coming *so that* he will turn to the gospel for help. As Melanchthon put it, *lex semper accusat,* the law always accuses. In contrast to the gospel the law is looked upon as a tyrant from which one hopes to be delivered by the gospel.

Now the question is, if this is the case, how is one to come to an understanding of the positive function of law? It would be interesting to speculate, no doubt, about the part this primarily negative view of law might have played in the development of the modern antipathy to law. But such speculation would lead us, I think, too far afield. The reformers, it should be noted, did have devices by which they sought to establish a more positive attitude to law. This came in their distinction between the *uses* of the law. The accusing function of law related to its *theological* use, i.e., its use for man's relationship to God. Here the law always accuses. That is to say that man can never use the law to earn his way to God, to establish his own righteousness in the final judgment. The situation was quite different in relation to human society, however. Here one encounters the law in its civil use. Here the law is understood as a force, backed by the power of the state as God's representative in civil matters to restrain evil and to preserve human society. In this it could be argued that there was at least the beginnings of a more positive evaluation of the place of law. Christians must have respect for law as the means through which God intends to preserve and extend human society.[2]

The Nineteenth-Century Problem

By the time of the nineteenth century, however, the Reformation view of law had been largely forgotten or discredited. The major reason for this, no doubt, was that man, full of the confidence inspired by the Enlightenment, came to resent the idea that he needed a gospel backed by ecclesiastical authority to help him.

What the Enlightenment and, with some reservation also, the nineteenth century rebelled against was what they called the "positivity" of the Christian religion, the fact that it was supposed to be revealed in positive historical facts unrelated to reason. A truth revealed in historical facts and imposed by ecclesiastical authority could only appear arbitrary, a heteronomy, a law imposed from without. And it was, of course, the gospel that suffered from this attack. The law, on the other hand, was quite reasonable, being the presupposition of the universal natural religion of mankind. It was, you might say, a new kind of gospel discovered now really for the first time in man's "coming of age," his "enlightenment," his newfound independence from feudal and ecclesiastical heteronomies.

With revelation and the gospel thus discredited, the religion of reason, i.e., morality and law, gradually took over the theological scene. Thus it was that Immanuel Kant came to write his treatise on *Religion Within the Limits of Reason Alone,* a work that was epoch-making in the theological understanding of law and in many ways decisive for the nineteenth-

2. Some of the reformers, of course, liked to speak also of a third use of the law, the law used as a guide to conduct for the redeemed Christian. Since, however, this is a rather specialized use, pertaining to the Christian life alone and not to the attitude toward the laws of society in general, it can perhaps be left out of account here. I say *perhaps* because some would no doubt dispute this. But to enter here into the complex debate about the third use of the law would be impossible. For further guidance the reader is directed to Elert. W., *Law and Gospel* and Althaus, P., *The Divine Command* (Facet Books, Social Ethics Series), nos. 16 and 9 respectively (Philadelphia: Fortress Press).

century problematic. The very title is significant. Reason, once the repressed poor relative of revelation, has now expanded its province to take in all that is essential in religion.

But this could only mean that religion would be reduced to the dimensions of law and its rewards. There were, of course, difficulties in doing this. For our purpose the most formidable one was the problem of freedom. If religion is to be reduced to the dimensions of law, how could man be said to be free? Having just escaped from the heteronomy of ecclesiastical law was man now to be bound by a new and perhaps even more exacting taskmaster, the moral law of reason?

To solve this problem (as well as other related ones that we leave unmentioned here) Kant fell back on the idea of the moral law *within*. Man hears *within* himself the voice of the moral law demanding that he do the good for the sake of the good. And since the moral law comes from within, it is at the same time the guarantee of freedom. That is to say, man is not subject to any legislation from without because he is a law unto himself; he is autonomous. This freedom is finally impervious to any threat that might be posed from without, be it that of ecclesiastical or political heteronomy, or scientific or psychological determinism. Man hears within the call, "du kannst denn du sollst" (you *can* because you ought). Nothing short of degeneration into bestiality can silence that call, and man's highest religious duty is to recognize it as the call of God. "Religion is (subjectively considered) the recognition of all our duties as divine commands."[3]

This surely is the high-water mark, in modern times, of the positive appreciation of law. The moral law is the guarantee of the most precious gift: freedom — the ultimate deliverance from all heteronomies. Action in accordance with that law can alone be called truly good. The inner law evoked, for Kant, virtually a religious veneration. Two things, he said, filled his mind with ever new and increasing awe: the starry heavens above and the moral law within him. The pinnacle upon which law has been placed presages in an interesting fashion the words that Hoover borrowed from Lincoln: ". . . The highest goal of moral perfection of finite creatures — a goal which man can never completely attain — is love of the law."[4]

The similarity between Kant's statement and Lincoln's is not, I

3. Immanuel Kant, *Religion Within the Limits of Reason Alone*, trans. T. M. Green and H. H. Hudson (New York: Harper, 1960), p. 142.

4. Kant, *Religion Within the Limits of Reason Alone*, p. 136.

think, just coincidental, for an understanding of law like Kant's is basic to modern liberal democracy.[5] Man is liberated from feudal heteronomies and external legal persuasion to the extent that he becomes a responsible citizen, a law unto himself. Respect for law is the foundation of social existence.[6] But is this the positive view of law we are looking for? Whatever its advantages, the fact is that most nineteenth-century theologians recoiled in horror from this stringent moralism. Indeed, one could say that from one point of view, the very problem posed for the nineteenth century was that of escaping from the rigors of Kant's view of the law. And this certainly indicates an important point about the search for a positive understanding of law. When law is made so absolute that it dominates everything in this fashion, it becomes intolerable. Men turn away from it in horror. From a theological point of view I suppose I can say that the trouble is that there is no end or limit to law. There is nothing outside it or beyond it, no "promised land" beyond its reach. And that is to say that there is no gospel, no eschaton to alleviate the unbroken reign of law. Kant did not escape the *lex semper accusat,* he succeeded only in making it more absolute.

---

5. The term liberal democracy is used here and throughout the paper not in a partisan sense, either theological or political (i.e., not as a contrast to conservatism), but simply to designate modern Western democracy *per se.*

6. There is, of course, something of a tension here between the law within and external statutory law. When Kant extols love of law as the highest moral perfection, he means the law within. But love of the law within does not take place at the expense of respect for statutory or external law. It means rather that one enters a higher state of moral existence in which external law is no longer needed. To oversimplify a somewhat complex picture, Kant sees man's moral progress in three basic stages. The first stage is one of "lawless external (brutish) freedom and independence from coercive laws." This is a state of savagery, "a state of injustice and of war, each against each." Man must leave this for the second stage, that of a political commonwealth where the war of each against each is restrained by coercive laws. But on this stage there is still conflict between the true inner law, the principles of virtue and the inner immorality provoked by coercive law — the immorality of doing good only in order to receive personal advantage. Thus the truly moral person must bestir himself to join an ethical commonwealth (Kant's idea of the church) where one lives freely according to the inner law and does good for the sake of the good alone. But looking down from this height, the virtuous man respects statutory law, the laws of the political commonwealth. Love of the law within and the freedom it grants is the source of one's respect for statutory law. See Kant, *Religion Within the Limits of Reason Alone,* p. 88.

The Negation of Law

There were many attempts by nineteenth-century theologians to escape the moralism of Kant. If one can generalize without too much oversimplification, I think one can say that these attempts were of three sorts. More traditionally minded theologians did not attack the view of law frontally, but sought to use it as proof of man's need for grace and supernatural help. This attempt, in some ways laudable, could not really succeed however, since the idea of revelation had been so seriously eroded. Its only recourse was to fall back on an idea of scriptural inerrancy that meant a return to the heteronomy men were trying to escape. Thus its attempt to mitigate Kantian moralism was frustrated by the tendency to make the gospel itself into a new law.

Others, like Schleiermacher, sought escape by falling back upon an immediacy prior to law and conceptualization, in the dimension of feeling. Kant, it was held, *had* done violence to the moral life by picturing it as a constant and never-ending struggle between the principles of virtue and natural inclinations. What they sought was a harmony between inclination and will in which the problem of law could be more or less bypassed. What is needed, they thought, was the cultivation of the proper feelings that would restore the lost harmony.

Such feelings and sentiments could be aroused, for Schleiermacher, through the Christian gospel, through the communication of the perfection reached in Jesus. We need not dwell here on the intricacies of this theology. Suffice it to say that here law is virtually eclipsed. Like all conceptualization, law is always at one remove from the immediacy of feeling. The question of law for Schleiermacher can arise for the Christian only as "an accident of memory."

To be sure, he admits, "something like legislation will always exist in Christian life in . . . certain spheres," but this is only "to guide the actions of those who lack insight." And this is where civil law and such things enter the picture. But law itself can be conceded no value whatsoever in the sphere of sanctification for, says Schleiermacher, "love always is, and does, more than law can be or do." Thus Schleiermacher counsels the dropping of the imperative mood altogether in Christian ethics, preferring instead simply a description of how men live in the kingdom of God.[7] This type of

---

7. F. Schleiermacher, *The Christian Faith*, ed. H. R. Macintosh and J. S. Stewart (Edinburgh: T. & T. Clark, 1956), pp. 522-24.

thought gave birth to a long line of purely descriptive ethics in the nineteenth century that sought more or less simply to bypass the problem of law — at least for the Christian.

Undoubtedly there are many things that could be said in favor of attempts like Schleiermacher's. For certainly everyone — and not just Christians — would find quite desirable a state of harmony in which law is no longer necessary. That, surely, must be what the kingdom of God is about. The question is, however, if such a state is attainable in Schleiermacher's fashion, i.e., by returning to a state of immediacy prior to law. Does such an attempted return really take the concrete realities of the human situation under law seriously enough?

However one may answer that question today, G. W. F. Hegel in the nineteenth century answered it in the negative. This brings us to the third and for modern times, I think, the most important reaction to Kant. Though he shared with Schleiermacher the desire for a harmony beyond the reach of Kant's grim moral struggle, Hegel did not think one could find it by a retreat into feeling prior to law and conceptualization. To sink back into undifferentiated and indefinite feeling was to sink, he said, into that "night where all cows are black." "The spirit," as he put it, "appears so poor that, like a wanderer in the desert who languishes for a simple drink of water, it seems to crave for its refreshment merely the bare *feeling* of the divine in general."[8] One cannot escape the Kantian law by retreat; one can overcome it only by going *through* it to something *beyond* it. And this, in Hegel's mind, demands the hard labor of thought and not merely the cultivation of appropriate feelings. One must conquer the problem of law through understanding, not emotion.

But how is this to be done? The beginnings of Hegel's attempt to move beyond Kant can be seen especially in one of his early writings, "The Spirit of Christianity and Its Fate." His complaint is that Kant did not really reach the goal he set for himself, that of freeing man from the "positivity" (heteronomy) of religion. For simply to move the moral law from without to within is not really to set man free. It merely means that whereas once God was seen as being external to man demanding obedience without question, now God is within. Whereas once there was opposition between Jehovah and his creatures, in Kant there is opposition be-

---

8. G.W.F. Hegel, *Preface to the Phenomenology of Mind*, quoted from the edition by W. Kaufmann, *Hegel: Texts and Commentary* (Garden City, N.Y.: Doubleday, 1965), p. 16.

tween the moral law within and man's natural inclinations, which are coerced rather than freely persuaded to acquiesce. For even if the voice of law comes from within, man is still a slave, if only to himself.[9]

In this early writing, Hegel asserts that one can get beyond law only when something higher than law takes the place of law and thus annuls or negates law in its legal form. This "something higher" is the love that Jesus taught and exemplified. Love is a concrete thing, an "is," which is the fulfillment and thus the negation of law in which law loses its form as law. Love is therefore the unification of inclination and moral will missing in Kant.[10]

The important thing to notice, it seems to me, is the way in which even in this early essay, Hegel tries to get beyond the problem of law by employing the idea of negation *(Aufhebung)*. The form of law, its character as an abstract universal command, is negated or *aufgehoben* when the concrete love that it demands is realized. In comparison to Schleiermacher this means that one does not sink back into an indefinite state of feeling prior to law but that one moves through the negation of law to a higher state. Kant's mistake, then, was not his discovery and formulation of the moral imperative, but his inability to get beyond it.

One must have law, one must conceptualize if one is to escape the "night where all cows are black." But such conceptualization must in turn be negated by a higher concrete realization. Such negation does not mean, of course, direct obliteration or cancellation. It means rather a suspending in which what is essential is taken up on the higher state. Thus Hegel speaks of the *form* of law (its universality, its character as abstract demand) being annulled while its *content* is realized in the concrete instance of its fulfillment.

But what is this higher concrete realization, this higher state reached through the negation of law, and how does such negation actually take place? Quite obviously, if man is to be released from the coercive domination of law both from without and within, he will have to be taken up in a higher community in which he does his duty freely and spontaneously, in which he freely relinquishes his individual inclinations for the sake of the whole. The higher community will then supersede the Kantian inner law. In *The Spirit of Christianity and Its Fate*, this higher community is the community of love inaugurated in Jesus which is the fulfillment and thus

---

9. G. W. F. Hegel, *On Christianity*, trans. T. M. Knox (New York: Harper, 1961), p. 211.
10. Hegel, *On Christianity*, pp. 209-16.

the negation of law. Attractive as this idea may be, Hegel is not at this early stage very clear about how this community comes to be or just what the negation involves. He toys rather vaguely with the idea that the Spirit that was in Jesus is to become the common spirit of the group. But this, I shall argue later, is precisely where a fruitful beginning comes to naught. The idea of negation is a fruitful one, but Hegel does not, I think, know how to exploit its full theological potential.

Hegel's own assessment of the failures of the community of love is decisive for the road he was to take in developing his mature system. The trouble was that the original community of love founded by Jesus was not and could not be universal enough. It was a small and restricted group existing in opposition to the world. But the true religion must be universal; the true God is the God of the whole. If Christians were set in opposition to the world, they were, in effect, without God. Thus, they were without a proper object for their worship. And to make up for this lack they made the earthly Jesus, now understood to be risen from the dead, the object of their worship. Instead of *becoming* love themselves, they worshiped the *symbol* of love. This was the sad fate of Christianity. Thwarted from true universality because of its separation from the world (and thus from God) it became a positivistic and heteronomous sect in opposition to the world.

This devastating critique of Christianity already indicates the direction in which Hegel will have to move in order to find his higher community in which law can be negated and there will be a more universal and concrete unification between inclination and moral will. It must be a community more universal than the church, involving all the people and all of life. But since it was at the same time to be concrete, it could not be just "the world" or "humanity in general," for that, too, was an abstraction — the favorite abstraction of enlightenment. The only answer then was that it must be the nation, the concrete state. It is in the state and its ethos that man is caught up in something higher than himself to which he freely gives his allegiance. In Hegel's view, the restraints that one's country lays upon one will not be experienced as imposed from without, they will not have the alien character of Kant's moral law.[11] On submitting to the state

11. "The state is the actuality of the ethical idea. It is ethical mind qua the substantial will manifest and revealed to itself, knowing and thinking itself, accomplishing what it knows and insofar as it knows it. The state exists immediately in custom, mediately in individual self-consciousness, knowledge, and activity, while self-consciousness in virtue of its sentiment toward the state finds in the state, as its essence and the end and product of its ac-

one is not submitting to external control, but only to what is really an extension of oneself.

This is an idea which, of course, sounds excessively dangerous to modern ears. It is usually cited as the reason why Hegel's thought could lead to political absolutism of the most arbitrary sort. Whatever the justification for such charges — and we cannot argue them here — one must not overlook the fact that Hegel felt himself protected from them because his understanding of the state was the culmination of his philosophy of history, the long struggle of human freedom, the process by which the spirit comes to realize its true self in perfect freedom. And it is in this process, finally, that we see what has happened to the idea of negation.

The spirit progresses toward realization of itself, toward freedom, through the process of negation. This is, of course, a difficult thing to grasp. If we can oversimplify it and put it in terms of law, perhaps we can say it looks something like this. As society progresses its needs are conceptualized in the form of law. But law as a universal and abstract concept is alien to life itself; it is itself a negation of life. However, the alien form of law is itself negated when what the law demands is concretely realized. There is a higher synthesis through the negation of the alien form of law, through a continual process of conceptualization and negation something like this: the Spirit reaches in man the ultimate harmony between what ought to be and what is, and this ultimate harmony is absolute freedom.

The state is therefore the current expression of this progress toward freedom. The law as a form alien to concrete life is negated in the perfect harmony between national ethos and individual inclination. In other words, one might say, Hegel had dissolved the problem of law and gospel into a philosophy of history, culminating in the bourgeois state.

Law and Revolution

Whatever one might say for the intellectual brilliance of Hegel's attempt, the suggestion that history culminates in the bourgeois political state, that here man finds his true home, virtually cries out for critical protest. This is true especially in those instances where it becomes evident that the liberal-

---

tivity, its substantive freedom." G.W.F. Hegel, *The Philosophy of Right,* quoted in W. H. Walsh, *The Ethics of Hegel* (London: Macmillan, 1954), p. 45.

ism of the bourgeois political state is hard pressed to solve its problems. Hegel's own followers were, as is well known, of two minds. Those who were quite satisfied with things as they were (the right-wing Hegelians) used Hegel to justify the status quo. At best they were in favor of extending the system and instituting liberalizing reforms to patch up the cracks. On the other hand, those who felt victimized by the bourgeois state, or who were sensitive to the manner in which it did victimize people (the young, or left-wing Hegelians) drove the system on toward one more ultimate negation: critical attack and revolution against the bourgeois state itself. This kind of negation reached its fruition in Karl Marx.

We need not argue here which of these groups were true followers of Hegel or whether the revolutionary program of Marx is a materialist inversion of Hegel's dialectic. The important thing for us to see is the way in which the revolutionary impetus has grown quite directly out of the attempt to solve the problem of law, the attempt to escape the *lex semper accusat.*

It is the result of the search for "the promised land" beyond law, the haven of true human freedom beyond heteronomy. Hegel sought to get beyond the endless moralism of Kant by means of a higher synthesis in the bourgeois state. For someone like Marx, however, the bourgeois state does not liberate man, it only enslaves and alienates the major part of its citizenry. The so-called "rights of man," the laws of the state, are not universal human rights, they are merely bourgeois privileges, laws that protect and perpetuate the greed of the moneyed classes over against the less fortunate. What is needed, therefore, is one further act of negation, a revolution that will eventually abolish the state itself and lead to the land of true and universal human freedom. The significance of this progression, in the light of current problems, can hardly be exaggerated. The animus against law culminates in revolution.

But what is the promised land beyond the bourgeois state, beyond the "long arm of the law"? What does it look like and is it in fact attainable? These are questions, of course, that do not admit of easy answers. For Marx it was the classless society, the communist society. It is instructive to note, however, that not all of his fellows among the young Hegelians agreed with him in this.[12] Max Stirner, for instance, declared that Marx, too, had not gotten rid of the last vestige of heteronomy because he had

12. See the informative book by David McLellan, *The Young Hegelians and Karl Marx* (London: Macmillan, 1969).

simply subjected the individual to the demand of the whole of society in general.

Stirner believed in a society of absolute egoists in which each individual, free from all universal concepts and demands, makes of his life what he can. Marx rightly retorts that this was nothing other than the apotheosis of the bourgeois Protestant individual, a return to the primeval battle of "each against each" from which man sprang. Bruno Bauer, on the other hand, seemed to look not for the end of the state, but for its strengthening, a new kind of absolutely secularized state in which bourgeois freedom and egoism would be surrendered. He longed for a ruler strong enough to take over and create this "paradise." Others, like Donoso Cortes, opted in favor of a Christian dictatorship. And there were other suggestions as well.

This argument among the young Hegelians is significant, I think, because it anticipates in such an interesting way the confusion of today's revolutionary. The violent reaction to the bourgeois liberal concept of law may have its justification, especially where such law has become oppressive. But where does one go beyond law? Hegel dreamed of a "higher synthesis" in the state. Marx found this oppressive and sought a higher freedom in the classless, eventually stateless, society. It is a sobering fact that this allowed his disciples to pay lip service to the ideal of freedom while actually implementing totalitarianism.

The Return to Liberalism

The latter half of the nineteenth century found itself unwilling or perhaps even incapable of dealing further with these problems. Perhaps it was because the times were such that they were not yet forced to face them, perhaps it was due to sheer exhaustion of spirit. At any rate, the theology of the time as well as the philosophy and the politics quite generally forgot the questions of the young Hegelians and returned to the liberalism of Kant.

Theology busied itself mainly with historico-critical questions and "degenerated," to use Karl Löwith's somewhat harsh words, "into history of dogma and church history, comparative religion and psychology of religion."[13] It is hardly surprising, therefore, that the most influential theology

---

13. Karl Löwith, *From Hegel to Nietzsche,* trans. D. Green (Garden City, N.Y.: Doubleday, 1967), p. 118.

of the late nineteenth and early twentieth century was a Ritschlianism built largely on the foundations of Kantian liberalism and remembered mostly for its historical research.

This means, I think it fair to say, that in the mainstreams of thought there were no really new attempts to grapple with the problem of law.[14] To be sure, the harshness of the Kantian moralism was ameliorated somewhat by assimilating the moral imperative to the commandment to love — a love inspired by being taken into the historical community made possible by Jesus' redemptive act. But Christianity is viewed, nevertheless, in Kantian fashion as the perfect moral and spiritual religion in which one is raised above the restrictions and inhibitions of natural inclination and natural causality. Freedom is achieved when one acts spontaneously out of love, independent of natural necessity or reward. As with all Kantian-based liberalisms, such a view would seek to solve the ills of society by persuading men to leave nature behind and to join the kingdom of moral and spiritual freedom, the kingdom of love, the kingdom of God. It will advocate reform rather than revolution, reform that will seek to extend the benefits of individual freedom to the largest possible group.

Such a view makes it rather easy, of course, to associate the cause of the gospel with advancing social reform. The words of Adolf von Harnack are perhaps typical.

> The gospel aims at founding a community among men as wide as human life itself and as deep as human need. As has been truly said, its object is to transform the socialism which rests on the basis of conflicting interests into the socialism of a spiritual unity.[15]

One cannot fault the nobility of such aims. The question, however, is whether the comfortable association of the gospel with the liberal faith can remain viable. Is it really possible to transform a socialism of conflicting needs into a socialism of spiritual unity? Our own time hardly encourages optimism of that sort.

---

14. This is not to say, however, that there were no important developments in lesser-known circles that were to bear fruit later. For an account of such developments see R. Schultz, *Gesetz and Evangelium in der Lutherischen Theologie des 19. Jahrhunderts* ("Arbeiten zur Geschichte and Theologie des Luthertums," vol. 4 [Berlin: Lutherisches Verlagshaus, 1958]), and my book, *The Law-Gospel Debate* (Minneapolis: Augsburg, 1969).

15. Adolf von Harnack, *What Is Christianity?* (New York: Harper, 1957), p. 100.

The End of Liberalism?

It begins to appear now as though the return to liberalism, with its existentialist aftermath between the wars, might have been only an interlude. At any rate it is apparent that liberal democracy is finding it increasingly difficult if not impossible to cope with the problems of contemporary society. The attack upon law from all sides, the erosion of public morality, can only mean that the liberal faith is dying or is already dead. And liberalism is nothing without its faith, without the belief that the telos toward which man strives is the true "ethical commonwealth" where there is a perfect wedding between natural inclination and law, where man spontaneously and freely does the good for the sake of the good. Without that faith the liberal state degenerates into a system of competing needs, where law is the enemy of natural inclination, and the battle of each against each is always a threat if not a reality.

In such instances the liberal state is forced against its will to become totalitarian. The majority enforces its will by sheer weight of numbers. In the wake of such developments, the sinister character of some "law and order" campaigns is evident. But if liberalism is dead, this spells the end of its noble attempt to foster a positive attitude toward law as well. Though it was in many ways theologically naïve, its passing is hardly a cause for rejoicing. The fascism of the reactionary right and the nihilism, the grim self-righteous confusion of the revolutionary left, are certainly vastly inferior, to say the least.

Toward a Positive View of Law

We must attempt, nevertheless, to pick up the pieces. The rebellion against the liberal view of law that has been incubating for so long has in recent days burst upon us with a fury that has shocked and surprised. If we had been more attentive to the history of the nineteenth century, perhaps what is happening would not seem so strange. The rejection of liberalism means that we are once again confronted with all the questions raised by the young Hegelians and the confusion resulting therefrom. In attempting to develop a positive view of law in a postliberal age, perhaps we need to go back to that time and try to discover, from a theological point of view at least, what went wrong.

The difficulty lies, it seems to me, in the development of the idea of negation. Hegel quite rightly saw that it would take a negation of law, at least in its form as law, to get beyond the moralism of Kant. But Hegel is not exactly clear, I think, about how such negation is possible or who actually accomplishes it. He seems to think that man does the negating, or at the very most the Absolute Spirit immanent in human society working through the human spirit. Once one rejects Hegel's doctrine of spirit, however, as did the young Hegelians, the result is unambiguous: man is the negator of law. Thus the idea of negation, shorn of whatever Christian trappings it may have had in Hegel, produces the revolutionary, the man who takes upon himself the right to negate the law and bring in the golden age of freedom.

From a Christian point of view this is impossible. For the Christian view is surely that only God can negate the law and that such negation can only be eschatological; it can come in its completeness only with the passing of "this age." That does not mean, however, that one must wait in submission to law until the end of the world. For it is in *the gospel* that such negation has occurred in our time in Jesus Christ. But such negation is not mere negation of law in a purely objective historical sense; it is rather more the negation of the man who lives under the law and for whom law is necessary. It is, in theological terms, the death of the "old Adam" and the raising of the new. In other words, this age and its law remains until the new man appears who no longer needs it.

But this new man appears not as a matter of course, not as the result of the legal process, not as the fruit of the dialectical progress of Spirit, and not as the product of a revolutionary program, but as the result of the death and resurrection of Jesus Christ who works that ultimate negation and new life in men. From the Christian point of view, the end of the law, the freedom from heteronomy, for which all men seek — the search to which the nineteenth century bears such eloquent and tortured witness — is available. It is the gift of the gospel.

This theological understanding of the idea of negation provides a vantage point from which one must raise questions about the Hegelian idea and its revolutionary offspring. If man is the negator of the law, he can easily usurp for himself the place of God. Perhaps that is why some revolutionaries find it so easy to preside over questions of life and death. Perhaps, too, that is the reason for the grim, humorless, self-righteous piety of most revolutionaries. It is a tough and serious business to play at being God! And perhaps as well that is the reason for the confusion of the revolutionary.

Having supposedly negated the law, he doesn't really know what to do with the world. Either he will have to end by imposing much more stringent and totalitarian laws than ever before in order to realize his revolutionary goals or, recognizing the incongruity of that, settle for permanent negation, permanent revolution. This is not to say that there may not be legitimate forms of revolution, revolutions in which a Christian ought to participate. Nor is it an argument for the status quo in society. It is merely to point out that there is at the root of the modern idea of revolution something incompatible with the Christian gospel. This, I think, is something that needs to be said today. For if one sees that it is God and not man who holds the ultimate power of negation and that he has done this in such a way in Jesus Christ as to negate not merely law but the old Adam, things begin to look quite different.

From this vantage point, too, perhaps we can begin to develop a more positive attitude toward the use of the law. The nineteenth century, as we have seen, spent a good deal of its energy trying to escape the idea of endless law. It was quite rightly recognized that it was the very endlessness of law that made it impossible to bear. They were wrong, however, in thinking that law could be ended by theological or philosophical artifice or even by revolution. Here, I suppose one could say, the *lex semper accusat* still holds. There is no escape from law in that way. But there is an end to law far more real than that, the end that comes with the breaking in of the new in Christ, the end of the old Adam and the creation of the new. It is when man realizes that there is really and truly an end, a goal, a telos, that he can begin for the first time to listen to the law, to let it speak to him and hear what it has to say. When one sees that the end, the goal of it all, has happened and is on its way through God's initiative one can begin to see law in a positive light. For then one sees that law is not forever; it is for this age, for this world.

The point is that faith opens up an entirely new sphere of possibility and action, *this* world bounded by the end. Here the law can be viewed in a positive way. That is why, I think, the reformers could speak about a "civil use" of the law according to which actions here and now could be judged as good. If the law is eternal, if there is no distinction between this age and the next, there is no way to speak of the goodness of our actions in and for this age; everything is judged by the moral absolute.

There is little chance, too, then, of really arriving at a positive attitude to law. For it is the supernatural pretension of law, its unbreakable absoluteness that makes it unbearable and drives man in his endless quest to be rid of it. When it has an end, however, a real end, one can see its positive use. In view of the end in Christ we can see that the law is intended for *this* world and that a new kind of goodness is possible, a goodness in and for this world, a "civil righteousness." Faith in the end of the law establishes the law in its proper use.

To say this is not, it must be insisted, to defend the status quo or to fall into the old trap of unqualified obedience to the state. That kind of thinking arises only when one has not grasped what faith in the end of the law means — both on the part of its proponents and its critics. For faith in the end of the law leads to the view that its purpose is to take care of this world, not to prepare for the next. That means that we do not possess absolute, unchangeable laws. If the law no longer takes care of this world, it can and must be changed. As even Luther put it, we must write our own decalogue to fit the times. Furthermore, whenever anyone, be he reactionary or revolutionary, sets up law or a system by which he thinks to bring in the messianic age, that is precisely the misuse of law against which Christians must protest. That is why, I would think, not even revolution is entirely out of the question for the Christian if that appears the only way to bring about necessary changes. But it must be a revolution for the proper use of the law, for taking care of this world, in the name of purely natural and civil righteousness and not in the name of supernatural pretension. That is to say, it must be a positive revolution and not a revolution of negation.

It is too much (or perhaps too little?) to say, I think, that respect for law must be the political religion of the nation. That seems to imply that law is an absolute before which we must all unquestionably bow. It would be better to say that care for the proper use of the law must be our constant and never-ending concern in this world. For we are not called merely to be law-abiding, but to take care of this world, and law must be tailored to assist in that task.

LEGAL AND EVANGELICAL AUTHORITY

Authority in the Church:
The Lutheran Reformation

At the time of the Reformation the churches faced two major problems with institutional authority. On the one hand, they faced the problem of *too much* authority, i.e., excessive, grandiose, and often tyrannical claims to jurisdiction and authority on the part of institutions, both church and state, symbolized by pope and emperor. On the other, they faced the erosion of public authority — *too little* authority — by (1) Enthusiasm, manifest in those individuals who claimed to be possessed by the Spirit, i.e., those whom Luther disparaged as folks who thought they had "swallowed the Holy Ghost, feathers and all" and even, we can say, (2) nascent Rationalism, found in the biblical criticism of some Humanists and anti-Trinitarians, including the questioning of scripture one finds in Erasmus' argument with Luther over the clarity of scripture.

Now, how do the Lutherans meet this double challenge: too much authority — an authority that had overstepped its bounds — on the one hand and too little on the other — tendencies that erode all institutional authority? The first move, of course, is to reassert the sole authority of scripture. They took as their own the principle of *sola scriptura*. That was not originally a Reformation slogan — it was already abroad in the church — but they adopted and declared it as the very first principle from which to challenge all other claims. From its inception it was employed as a polemic against the use of "tradition" to support teachings that had no basis in scripture. The *sola* was set against the "and" in "scripture *and* tradition" where the "and" was understood as a plus sign. Tradition had come to be understood not simply as the *paradosis,* the act of the handing on *of* scripture, what scripture has to say, but as an addition *to* scripture. Over against this, the Reformation insisted that scripture is the sole source and norm, the primary and final authority, for doctrine, faith, and life in the church. That is the rock, the foundation, on which all authority must stand.

But the problem of authority is not settled simply by slogans. *Sola scriptura* is not the end of the matter, but rather something of a beginning. For throughout the history of the church, the problem has been not so much *whether* scripture is the source of authority, but *how* to interpret it and, of course, *whose* interpretation is to be accepted as the right one. Where does the buck stop in the interpretation game? That is the reason why there was always an appeal to some "final authority." In Rome the buck stops with the magisterium and finally the pope, the one who as the properly ordained vicar of Christ has the charism, the special spiritual gift, to exercise such authority. This, of course, could lead to uniformity on disputed questions. But, even more importantly, it leads to a transgression of limits, a violation of the eschatological line in making absolutist claims. On the other end of the spectrum, such absolutism might be manifest in the charismatic individual — one who claims to be endowed with the special gifts of the Spirit and who asserts the right to an authoritative interpretation. This, of course, could lead simply to chaos — perhaps not unlike what we experience today. Incidentally, Luther thought both of these claims were tantamount to the same thing, and thus equally preposterous. The papal claim to possess the Spirit was hardly different from individual claims to such possession. As T. F. Torrance once remarked, Rome proposes a "massive" subjectivism to counter the subjectivism of individuals. Either would lead eventually to some sort of tyranny.

Between the two extremes, there is a third possibility. One might place the scholar between pope and enthusiast. Instead of claims to possess the Holy Spirit by special ordination or occasional experience, one could perhaps offer the spirit of scholarship, and a graduate degree, as attempts objectively to arrive at authoritative interpretation by scholarly investigation. But is the scholar to become the final authority? Of course, scholarship is necessary and essential. Yet, in the end, usually because it wants to be "objective," it tends to back off from "authoritative" answers to our questions and presents us rather with a smorgasbord of "learned opinions" from which we might pick an interpretation amenable to our tastes. Scripture may be *sola* but interpretations are *multi.* So we are back at square one. The problem of authority cannot simply be solved by appealing to the *sola scriptura* principle. It is a start, but the question of authoritative interpretation remains largely unanswered.

The Dialectic of Authority in the Reformation: Law and Gospel

Renewed understanding of what the gospel is and does together with its distinction from law and its uses brought a fundamental revision of the nature of authority in the Lutheran churches. To make a long story short, it can be said that they met the challenges in the problem of authority by dividing the issue into two modes of the exercise of authority. Naturally enough these could be called the gospel mode and the law mode. There are, no doubt, more sophisticated and even accurate ways of putting the matter, but this will do for now. We are making a long story short here. The task of interpretation of scripture that led to the distinction between law and gospel enabled the Reformers, on the one hand, to meet the problem of excessive institutional authority, particularly that of the church, by insisting that the ultimate exercise of authority in the church is in the preaching of the gospel. On the other hand, they attempted to confront the problem of the erosion of authority by individualistic and spiritualist claims by insisting on the external clarity of the word as law. This results in a kind of dialectic of authority based on the proper distinction between and uses of law and gospel. In what follows we shall attempt a closer look at this.

Gospel Authority

Even though sanctified Lutheran custom might dictate that I speak of law before gospel, it is helpful to start here with the gospel. This is due to the fact that this mode of exercising authority is often overlooked and its significance ignored. It is usually not understood as a mode of exercising authority at all. But gospel is the key to the question, and only when we realize that will we properly get to the heart of the matter. In the view of the Lutheran Reformation, the ultimate exercise of authority is the preaching of the gospel as the end of the law, the release from bondage to sin, death, and the devil through what God has done in Jesus Christ. The old being is put to death and the new summoned to life through the gospel in the power of the Spirit. True authority, in this light, is what sets you free — in the ultimate sense, from sin, death, and the devil. Authority, as you will remember, comes from the Latin *auctoritas* and means creation or creative power. An author in that sense is a creator. The preaching of the gospel is authoritative because it exercises that sort of power. It creates. It brings into being a new creation over against the old. The word of God, as Luther insisted, is not a dead letter, but a living voice. It does not just lie about waiting for approval from those reputed to be "authorities," or awaiting authoritative interpretation. Rather, it works. It does something. And, as we shall see, it even interprets itself. This gospel authority, as Paul put it, is set over against the old authority of law: "For neither circumcision nor uncircumcision counts for anything, but a new creation" (Gal. 6:15).

Gospel authority is compelling because of its sheer attractiveness, not because it imposes itself by the power to dominate and force. It grasps and holds me in the Spirit because it sets me free. The real problem of authority from this perspective is not how to bind but how to set people free. The basic assumption is not that the real problem for people is that they are living too loosely, but that they are bound — to the tyrants of sin, death, and the devil. The true exercise of authority in the ultimate sense is through the Holy Spirit. "Where the Spirit of the Lord is, there is freedom" (2 Cor. 3:17). If the church wants to talk about exercising authority in the proper sense, it had better learn first and foremost how to preach the gospel and distinguish it from legal authority. If I hold on to this authority — or better, am held by it — it is because I want to, not because I have to. Furthermore, this means that there is no way this authority can be imposed upon me by a power move, force, or even argument. To be grasped by it is to be reborn or converted to it. That rebirth or conversion is a death to the old and a resurrection to the new.

Now, if one is going to exercise such authority, one has to preach it as sheer good news. To do that, one has to learn how to distinguish law from gospel. This means that there are some rules that come into play here about properly distinguishing law and gospel and that administering these rules will also be involved in the question of ecclesiastical authority. But that will occur on a different level, the level of legal authority, which we will speak of later.

The 1995 visit of Pope John Paul II and the various accounts of it were an interesting study of the issues that are at stake here. The *U.S. News and World Report* essay of October 9, 1995 began like this:

"Woe to me if I do not proclaim the gospel!" St. Paul wrote to the Corinthians some 2,000 years ago, explaining why he persisted in preaching the sometimes difficult teachings of the Christian faith. Pope John Paul II cites the biblical passage often these days. The 75-year-old pontiff arrives this week for his fourth papal visit to the U.S. and will stand firm in proclaiming what he believes are immutable truths in an age of moral relativism. "It has never been easy to accept the gospel teaching in its entirety," the leader of the world's 960 million Roman Catholics told U.S. Bishops in Los Angeles in 1987, "And it never will be." Just what constitutes the gospel "in its entirety" is, of course, a matter of some dispute, especially among many American Catholics who disagree with the Vatican's strict stand on sex and gender issues. (p. 72)

Later, in discussing the problem of moral decadence, the article says that "John Paul thinks one way to combat such decadence, especially in America, is through strict reiteration of church doctrine — and tough enforcement of it. 'There was a sudden flaccidity, a weakening of discipline' in the church after the Second Vatican Council in the mid-1960's says Michael Novak, a Catholic scholar in Washington, D.C. 'But John Paul has restored unity and discipline,' says Novak, by his 'clear teaching' and by showing American clergy 'You don't have to be a weenie to curry favor; you just have to stand for the gospel'" (p. 74). What is of concern here is not the pope's judgment about American decadence or even the attempts to reassert discipline. He can be applauded for much of what he says and for his courage in doing so. But the problem in the exercise of authority is the tendency to confuse law and gospel. There seems to be an attempt to purchase favor for the law by calling it the "teachings of the gospel," or "the gospel teaching in its entirety," or perhaps speaking of "fundamental ethical values." Of course, the pope is not alone in this. Just read some of the proposals of ELCA task forces and notice how often we are informed about "what the gospel teaches" on the matter at hand. And in general, law is rarely, if ever mentioned. At best there will be talk of "values" and "commitment." The attempt seems to be to sugarcoat the bitter pill of law by calling it the teachings of the gospel. But that is the gateway to rampant confusion. Two things happen at once. The law loses its punch and the gospel no longer sets people free.

Gospel authority as that which sets one free cannot by its very nature be compelled. For all his blustering, Luther always insisted that the gospel could never be forced on anyone. It is itself a matter of freedom. Either I am set free by it in the exercise of its authority through the power of the Spirit or I am not. There is no way you can argue that I must or ought to accept it. It works strictly by the power of its own goodness. In the last analysis, when the Reformers were asked where the authority in their teaching lay, they tended simply to quote Jesus in the Gospel of John: "My sheep hear my voice." "I know my own, my own know me." And that is that! Furthermore, Luther especially affirmed that being set free by the gospel of Jesus Christ enabled one accurately to judge all doctrine and practice and to be certain about it for oneself. One could sort out truth from heresy if one knew the difference between law and gospel. What he meant by that was that one who has been grasped by the gospel and freed by it will be able to tell when he or she is being sold back into bondage. One who knows the gospel and its distinction from law develops a very sensitive "crap detector." But even so, the ability to judge doctrine is for oneself. It is a private *discretio,* not public. The public judgment leads us, once again, to that different level that is coming into view, that of law or legal authority.

When trying to get this across to students, I sometimes use the image of a "charter of freedom." The documents of the church, the scriptures and the confessions, function in this perspective like a charter of freedom, or perhaps, a letter declaring a slave free. The charter or letter has power and authority just because it sets me free. It does something. And I hang on to it for dear life not because I have to but because I want to. It sets me free. It is my very life. I become sensitive to all attempts to sell me back into bondage. But once again, we are very soon led to a different level of authority. This charter of freedom also has protective power in a hostile world because of its legal character. So, in a hostile world that wants to enslave me, I hang on to it, preserve it, study it, make sure it is understood, interpret it to fit new contexts, and guard its language from corruption. But it also means that I become aware that freedom can be lost, not the least of which is by my own negligence or laziness. Just because I have been set free, I cannot simply "go on a moral vacation," so to speak. If I do, I find myself right back in bondage — perhaps all the worse now because I do not even know it. So the charter of freedom calls me to guard that freedom. As Paul could put it, "For freedom Christ has set you free. Stand fast therefore and do not submit again to a yoke of bondage." A charter of freedom has not only gospel authority, but also participates in and establishes a kind of protective legal authority.

Law (Legal) Authority

The discussion of gospel authority tends quite naturally to lead to a discussion of the nature and place of legal or what we will call here law authority. When the gospel grasps one, one begins to see that law authority works differently from gospel authority. Law authority works by coercion, pressure, fright, threat, force. This is an insight, it is to be noted carefully, to which one comes *ex post facto* by being freed by the gospel. It is not an insight that one comes to in all its fullness naturally. The coercion that law authority exerts is first and above all of a spiritual sort: it attacks and plays upon the "conscience." In its most basic form it simply threatens that if you transgress the law, you are on the way to eternal perdition. Institutionally it can mean excommunication. Such spiritual coercion can give the church extraordinary power. But coercion can also be of a more mundane sort. If you transgress and get caught you could end up in prison. Or, if you don't do well, you will get laid off, or won't get promoted, or won't get your scholarship, and so on, endlessly. In the old days this was socially codified by the question, "What will the neighbors think?," surely one of the most oppressive forms of coercion. It was H. L. Mencken who quipped, "Conscience is the little voice inside you that tells you someone may be looking!" Today it is questionable whether we even know or care about what the neighbors think. Nevertheless, law has countless ways of imposing its authority. In that sense it is very powerful and, in spite of all modern devices, inescapable.

From the perspective of the gospel, the fundamental problem of the law is that it is not creative. According to the Lutheran doctrine of the law's uses, it has a perfectly good but nevertheless limited use. It restrains evil and exposes sin, but does not create. It can kill, but cannot give life. At best it preserves but does not save. The difficulty with this kind of authority on the institutional level — and this especially includes the church — is the tendency to misuse it, to overstep its proper limits. Institutions in this age, in this left-hand rule, are indeed called to the proper use of the law to take care of the creation and its creatures. But the overwhelming temptation is always to overstep the limits, to attempt to use legal authority to bring in its own version of the kingdom of God, whether it be named the "Third and Eternal Reich," or the "classless society," or "ethnic cleansing," or even "making the world safe for democracy." Or, in the church, it could be to use such authority to enforce its institutional hegemony by the threat of excommunication, inquisition, heresy proceedings, or the founding of holiness sects and various other devices. The temptation is always to dream that law authority is creative. But it is not. Whenever it oversteps its bounds, as it inevitably seems to do, tyranny is the result and someone is sacrificed. It was not without reason that Paul called it the dispensation of death.

The Relation of the Two Types of Authority

The crucial question for the exercise of authority in the church is that of the relation between gospel authority and law authority. As we said at the outset, the problem for the Reformation churches was too much authoritarianism, an institution that had overstepped the bounds, on the one hand, and too little regard for the institutional exercise of authority, on the other. How can these two problems be met in terms of what we have said about the two kinds of authority? The preaching of the gospel of freedom in Jesus Christ is the highest exercise of authority in the church. Saying that frightens a lot of folks. The fear, of course, is that the gospel is just going to wipe out the law — that the gospel will then become just a mushy permissiveness, one of the besetting sins of the age and the reason for the erosion of authority in the church. What does the gospel do for the authority of law?

The answer lies in the fact that there is a very subtle dialectic of authority in the relation between gospel and law. The understanding of authority and its exercise resonates between two poles. On the one hand, the gospel is the end of the law: "For Christ is the end of the law so that there may be righteousness for everyone who believes" (Rom. 10:4). Lutherans have always taken that to mean both *telos* and *finis,* both that Christ is the goal and the goal line, the realization and fulfillment of that to which law can only point. In Christ it is over. But note well, *only* in Christ is it ended. Law ends to the degree that we are in Christ, not on account of some general permissiveness. On the other hand, faith in the gospel *establishes* the law. Hence, "Do we then overthrow the law by this faith? By no means! On the contrary, we uphold the law" (Rom. 3:31).

The preaching of the gospel both ends and thus limits the authority of law and at the same time establishes or gives law its rights. How does this work? Where the law knows no bounds or limits, which is to say, where the gospel is not preached, at least two things happen. First, law oversteps its limits. In the absence of the gospel, the law is the only proffered salvation and so it takes over the role of the authority that is going to bring in the Kingdom. The result is tyranny. Authority is exercised by coercion. Christ as head of the church is displaced by human rulers, popes, bishops, charismatics, and self-appointed prophets. But second, where law oversteps its limits sooner or later we must take steps to end its tyranny. We do not uphold but seek instead to remove or somehow dilute the law. Rebellion against the authority of law is the inevitable result. That is the reason why law has virtually disappeared from our vocabulary. So we talk about "the teachings of the gospel" instead of speaking forthrightly about the commandments of God. We have thought to escape the burden of law as did the antinomians — just by erasing it from our texts and our speech. But that, of course, is folly. The ironic thing about antinomianism is that it is an impossible heresy, a drama played in an empty theater, as Luther once put it. For the fact is that apart from the gospel law *has* no end. It just changes its form and gets worse.

One can see a prominent example of this in our problems with the Sixth Commandment these days. There really was much more freedom for openness and sound relationships between men and women when that commandment was established and held in some honor. Men and women could relate to each other without as much suspicion or fear. Now that we seem to have taken steps to disregard or get rid of it, however, things have gotten much worse. Now you cannot be sure what the other person has in mind. Whole sets of new laws begin to appear, such as laws against harassment, which can mean anything from saying the wrong thing in class to touching someone. Persons are not supposed to have a private conference with members of the opposite gender with the door closed. People are half afraid to smile at one another and even say hello. There was a celebrated incident in my town in which there was some complaint on the part of women that workmen were ogling them unduly. We now have a law about ogling: You are not allowed to ogle for more than nine seconds at a time. People, particularly women, do not feel safe. Before you know it we have as many laws as in the Sabbath laws of old that Jesus excoriated in the gospels. Law does not go away when we try to end it; it just sneaks back again, usually in far worse form. Only where law is ended in Christ, i.e., only where gospel is preached radically as the end of law, will it truly be established.

This dialectic of ending and establishing the law holds the answer to the two problems the Reformation had with authority. First of all, faith in the gospel of Jesus Christ as the end of the law puts limits on the authoritarianism that oversteps its bounds or — what is the same thing — transgresses the eschatological limit. Earthly institutions always try to appropriate for themselves the role of the eschatological Kingdom. The Reformation was a massive protest against such a grandiose ecclesiology. The placing of limits on such authoritarianism can be seen clearly in the various moves they made to correct abuses. The idea that the pope was the head of the church by divine right was rejected by insisting that Christ was the head of his body the church. That meant that the gospel was the ultimate authority, not human law dressed up in divine disguises. The distinction between divine right and human right itself indicates the limiting of ecclesiastical claims to this age, refusing them to be extended to the next. Even though the distinction between divine and human right has been largely discarded in ecumenical discussion today, it still has something to tell us about the problem of authority in the church. Humans could be granted the right and authority to oversee the *earthly* affairs of the church only by human right, but not by some supposed divine right. Bishops and pastors act by divine right only when they properly preach and act on behalf of the gospel. By divine right they are to preach the gospel, judge and condemn doctrine that is contrary to the gospel, and exclude from community those whose conduct is detrimental to the church's witness to the gospel. In other words, by divine right they are to be custodians of the gospel. But "divine right" is exercised only through and in connection with the gospel. Everything else is by human right (see the Augsburg Confession [*CA*] 28, paragraph 29). Always they were concerned to make a careful distinction between what belongs to this age and what concerns the next. The regulation of marriage belongs to this age, as does secular political concerns. The rejection of the greater Ban, and retention only of the lesser, is an indication of the same move. Luther could even insist that the church as such had no right to establish or define doctrine authoritatively since only Holy Scripture could do that. The refusal in *CA* 28 to allow bishops to use ecclesiastical power to force political ends and vice versa demonstrates the same thing, evidencing a pattern manifest in all these areas having to do with authority. A clean distinction must be made and limits must be set in order to prevent the exercise of authority from overstepping its bounds and thereby destroying itself. If the role of authority in the church is to be sorted out properly, then the critique must start at home for the church.

The church must begin by carefully discerning just what kind of authority it is supposed to exercise.

Scripture as Clear and Self-Interpreting

Now we will consider the second problem the Reformation had with authority, i.e., the problem of too little authority, the erosion of ecclesiastical authority in the face of individual claims — charismatic, scholarly, rationalistic, or otherwise — to interpret scripture according to one's own lights, or even to have access to divine truth apart from scripture. Even though this is a more modern problem, it can be said that the Reformation already faced it in various forms. It is not only a more modern problem but also a more difficult problem. Here the difficulty is not just authoritarianism (even though many charismatics, scholars, and rationalists are quite authoritarian about their own doctrines!) but rather relativism — a "chaos of thought and passion all confused," precipitated by the claim that everyone has the right to think and believe as he or she sees fit and that the church has no right to impose its doctrinal decisions on anyone. How is this chaos to be confronted according to the Reformers? Or better, how is authority to be exercised by the church in the midst of such chaos?

As has been pointed out, the fundamental starting point is the authority of scripture and the *sola scriptura* principle. Holy Scripture is the first principle, the sole source and norm for all exercises of authority in the church. However, we have also seen that slogans like *sola scriptura* are not in themselves sufficient to solve the authority problem because the question is always about who will have the final say in the battle over interpretation. The problem of interpretation seems of itself inevitably to lead to some sort of ecclesiastical absolutism. The Reformation met this kind of move by insisting that the gospel of Jesus Christ is the end of the law, and so set limits to legal authority. The freedom of the gospel, however, threatened a general collapse into relativism.

The Reformers, particularly Luther, met the challenge posed by competing interpretations by two further moves. The first was to make a distinction between the internal (subjective) and the external (public) clarity of scripture, and the second was the insistence that Holy Scripture interprets itself *(scriptura sacra sui ipsius interpres)*. We shall look at these more closely.

First, the distinction between internal and external clarity of scripture is rather subtle and needs much more attention than can be given here. But, the problem we have in interpreting scripture is that we do not understand it from the inside out, i.e., we do not see or more likely do not accept it in its internal clarity. But the fault in that does not lie in scripture, since scripture is in itself "externally" or "publicly" perfectly clear. Granted, there may be historical and grammatical problems here and there but for the purposes of this argument those can be passed over. The fault in the matter of interpretation lies rather in us, not because scripture is unclear, but because we do not like what we read. Mark Twain once remarked, "It's not what I don't understand in the Bible that bothers me, it's what I do understand." In other words, it is because scripture is so clear externally that internally we cannot take it. Thus, Luther could say that without the Holy Spirit we do not understand a word of it. As Lief Grane aptly put it, "It is not because Scripture is unclear that we need the Holy Spirit, but because it is so clear!"

Luther himself illustrated this point when he argued with Erasmus about the hardening of Pharaoh's heart. Luther's argument, ostensibly, is that the passage in which God says, "I will harden the heart of Pharaoh" is externally perfectly transparent. However, since Erasmus does not "internally" agree with it, i.e., does not understand its internal logic, finds it necessary to avoid what it says and so must have recourse to "interpretation." He must interpret it figuratively to mean that somehow Pharaoh hardens his own heart. The price, however, for such "interpretation" is the loss of the entire "internal logic" of the biblical narrative. For then the Exodus event really depends on Pharaoh's disposing and not on God's!

The appeal to the Holy Spirit, however, also gives rise to the insistence that the Holy Spirit enables one to understand and interpret the scriptures clearly and indicates Luther's agreement with the entire Reformation reaction to Roman authoritarianism. Indeed, Luther insisted that every Christian, by the power of the Spirit, could interpret scripture aright for himself or herself and judge all doctrine and heresy. However — and here comes the move to the role of the church — such interpretation is entirely private, subjective, and "internal." But if I am going to claim authority or exercise it publicly, then I cannot do it on the basis of a claim to possess the Spirit. I cannot conduct a public argument with you by claiming that I have the Spirit, or more of it, or even a better faith, than you have. Instead, public argument can proceed only on the basis of the *external* word and the assumption of its clarity. Thus, when Luther participated in public debate, what we might call public exercises of authority, for instance with Zwinglians over the Last Supper, he did so strictly by repeatedly sticking to the external word of scripture and its clarity. So he simply stuck to the words, "This is my body," and would not budge, as he said, unless an article of faith or necessary reason can be induced to make him move.

Public exercises of authority in the church, in this light, can proceed only on the basis of the external clarity of scripture and appropriate argument about it. There is, no doubt, a relation between the internal and external clarity in all of this. Only one who through the Holy Spirit has been grasped by scripture's internal clarity and logic is likely to let the external clarity be. Luther, at any rate, could hardly restrain himself from the suspicion that those who refused to allow the external clarity to come to expression were somewhat lacking in the Spirit department. Hence, one recalls his words to Bucer in the argument about the Supper, "You have a different Spirit," and his repeated complaint that Erasmus' words were "Spiritless." In any case, the important point here is that the Holy Spirit is not "swallowed" but speaks authoritatively through the external word. So Luther always insisted that the Spirit comes through external means, the Word and the Sacraments.

The second move the Reformers, particularly Luther, made was to answer the persistent question about interpretation by asserting that Holy Scripture does not need interpreters but that it interprets itself *(scriptura sacra sui ipsius interpres)*. This principle can and has been interpreted in a rather simplistic sense, to wit, that the obscure passages are to be interpreted by the clearer ones. But that is rather the argument that goes with quite another principle, that of the perspicuity of scripture. Is this not more a principle of the Reformed? Actually, the principle that "scripture interprets itself" is much more an attempt to deal with the central problem of authority that has been nagging us all along — the question of the subjective caprice of the interpreter. Once again, we have an issue that demands much more attention and will have to make a long and complex story short.

The assertion that "scripture interprets itself" arises out of the reader's encounter with scripture. It proposes a radical reversal in the relation of the text and the exegete/reader/hearer. In the usual model, the exegete stands as a subject over against the text as an object to be interpreted. But this means that the exegete, as subject, always remains in control and one always winds up in the swamp of subjectivism. Usually, such subjectivism can subsequently be overcome only by submission to the collective subjectivity of the whole, either by some kind of consensus or by recourse to a teaching office that supposedly has the gift or the power to close the argument.

In the model proposed by the claim that "scripture interprets itself" the roles of exegete and text are exactly reversed. The Word of God speaking through the scriptures is the acting subject and in such acting the exegete soon finds himself or herself as the object to be interpreted. The encounter with scripture puts the exegete in a subordinate position. The Word finds him or her as a sinner, not merely as an "objective" student. Scripture is not, in the final analysis, to be understood as raw ore to be refined by the interpreter but rather as the means through which the Spirit works on and creates a true hearer. Attention moves beyond what the word means to what it does. The movement in the direction of the living word is, of course, unmistakable here. The exegete is put in the position of a hearer who upon being addressed and exegeted by the Word becomes in turn a speaker, a preacher of the Word. The Word, in this encounter, works its way with the hearer and in so doing interprets itself. It argues and prosecutes its own case. It ends the subjectivism of the exegete by establishing its own authority over its hearers. All of which is to say that scripture establishes itself as authoritative because it is gospel, justifying word, that sets its hearers free from sin, death, and the power of the devil. The insistence that scripture interprets itself is simply the hermeneutical correlate of justification by faith alone. The church is the community called into being by the hearing of the Word whose reason for being is to speak that Word in all the world.

But now, even though much more would need to be said, it is apparent that we have come full circle. We started by insisting that the preaching of the gospel was the highest exercise of authority in the church, and that is where we arrive again at the end. But that is, I hope, all fitting! So I will close by making some concluding observations. First, last, and always, the preaching of the gospel of Jesus Christ crucified for our sins and raised for our justification is the highest exercise of authority in the church. But second, if this authority is to be exercised today, it shall have to be preached much more radically as the end, both *telos* and *finis*, of the law which actually establishes it for the time being. From the Reformation perspective, the problem in the church is not finally to be traced to a lack of nerve in asserting the law, but rather in the failure to preach the gospel in all its radicality. There is absolutely no way that the proper authority and uses of the law are going to be established in the church's message without that radical gospel. This call for a more radical gospel is the *raison d'être* for my teaching. Since the Reformation, beginning even with the Saxon Visitations (the "graveyard" of the Reformation?) where Melanchthon tried to shore up the sagging enterprise by preaching the law more strenuously, just about all the remedies have been tried. We have about used up all our coupons. We have only one left. We should try it — a more radical gospel. If the tree does not bring forth good fruit, spread it on a little thicker! And wait! Have a little patience! Yes, the pope is right in quoting St. Paul. "Woe is me if I preach not the gospel!" But it better be the gospel and not just another confusing mixture with law. The church has no right and no call to flex its authoritative muscle if it is not going preach this gospel. Furthermore, if the analysis suggested here is right, it will not work — and is not, as a matter of fact, working. To see that, all you need to do is read the statistics. If we are not prepared to preach a radical gospel we can just as well enter into competition with the Kiwanis Club. No doubt we do need to find ways to exercise more discipline. But why should people accept the discipline if we have nothing to offer that they cannot get elsewhere? If they want to escape the discipline, they can just go down the street to some other religious sideshow or support group. If we do not preach the *gospel* in such a radical fashion that it ends the law, then there will be no establishment of the law either and the role of authority in the church will disappear altogether.

Scriptura sacra sui ipsius interpres: Reflections on the Question of Scripture and Tradition

It will not be possible, at least from a Lutheran stance, fruitfully to engage the question of scripture and tradition without some attention to what is today called hermeneutics. The disagreements over relating scripture to the subsequent interpretative activity of the church arise because of some quite different perceptions of the relationship between the text and the exegete (either as an individual or a collective). What shall be attempted here is to offer for discussion what these different perceptions are. It will not be possible in this short essay to do that in anything other than rather facile and broad generalizations. Nevertheless, my aim is that this presentation will move our discussion in a fruitful direction.

Perhaps there is no clearer indication of these different perceptions than in the traditional antithetical assertions about where final authority resides in the interpretation of scripture: with the church and its magisterium or rather with scripture itself, especially as comprehended in Luther's audacious claim that the sacred scriptures interpret themselves *(scriptura sacra sui ipsius interpres).*[1] In this hangs the hermeneutical di-

---

1. *"Praeterea cum credamus Ecclesiam sanctam catholicam habere eundem spiritum fidei, quem in sui principio semel accepit, cur non liceat hodie aut solum aut primum sacris literis studere, sicut licuit primitivae Ecclesiae? Neque enim illi Augustinum aut Thomam legerunt. Aut dic, si potes, quo iudice finietur quaestio, si patrum dicta sibi pugnaverint. Oportet enim scriptura iudice hic sententiam ferre, quod fieri non potest, nisi scripturae dederimus principem locum in omnibus quae tribuuntur patribus, hoc est, ut sit ipsa per sese certissima, facillima, apertissima, sui ipsius interpres, omnium omnia probans, iudicans et*

vide we need to get at. In the one case, tradition, taken as something additional to scripture — whether as extra-canonical material or as interpretation or extension of the canonical text — plays a prominent role, whereas in the other it comes under radical critique.

The differing attitudes toward tradition are engendered by basically different hermeneutical "models," different perceptions of the relationship between exegete/interpreter and text. In the first and perhaps most universally assumed model, the exegete, as "subject," stands over against the text understood as the "object" that is to be interpreted. The interpretation yields doctrine and practical mandates. Faith equals acceptance of such doctrine and practice. The problem immediately engendered by such a model is the subjectivity or potential arbitrariness of the exegete. How can one be assured that the interpretation or application or extension of the text is "correct," i.e., not distorted by the *spiritus proprius* of the individual exegete?[2] How is the subjectivism of the exegete to be transcended? By the historical method?

At this point tradition, in one form or another, enters the picture. The tradition stands as norm of or guide to interpretation. But then what does one do if the tradition does not always agree with itself? The hermeneutic, it would seem, inevitably drives to an authoritative office to oversee the interpretive process, apply the tradition, and be the place "where the buck stops." As Joseph Lortz put it, ". . . No religious objectivity is possible where it is not certified again and again, from case to case, by a living interpreter, i.e., through an infallible, living teaching office."[3] The subjectivism

---

illuminans, sicut scriptum est psal. c.xviii [119:130]. 'Declaratio seu, ut hebraeus proprie habet, Apertum seu ostium verborum tuorum illuminat et intellectum dat parvulis.' Hic clare spiritus tribuit illuminationem et intellectum dari docet per sola verba dei, tanquam per ostium et apertum seu principium (quod dicunt) primum, a quo incipi oporteat, ingressurum ad lucem et intellectum." See *Assertio omnium articulorum M. Lutheri per Bullam Leonis x. novissimam damnatorum* (1520), WA 7, 97, 16-29. This quote from Luther is a *locus classicus* for the *sui ipsius interpres*, but the same can be found in other places: WA 14, 566, 26-29; WA 10 III, 238 10 f, etc.

2. Luther uses the term *spiritus proprius* (which is apparently interchangeable with *sensus proprius*) in the *Assertio* (WA 7, 96, 5). It appears there in a quote, but no indication is given as to what he may have been quoting. The bull of Leo X does identify Luther with heretics who interpret scripture according to their own wisdom rather than that of the church and the fathers, and that no doubt occasions Luther's response in his *Assertio*.

3. Joseph Lortz, *Die Reformation in Deutschland,* 3rd ed., vol. 1 (Freiburg: Herder, 1948), p. 402.

of the individual exegete and even the ambiguities of the tradition can be transcended, therefore, only by the "objectivitism" of the "collective," the church and the magisterium, culminating in the papal office. Those who persist in questioning the legitimacy of such claims to transcendence are usually suspected of subjective arbitrariness, i.e., disobedience to the church. This was the charge made against the Reformers — particularly Luther — and it persists down to the present.[4]

Sola scriptura is in the first instance a reaction to claims made to such transcendence on behalf of tradition and the magisterium, especially the papal office. It should be noted, however, that the *sola scriptura* was not just a Reformation doctrine or concern. It was abroad in the church long before the Reformation. As such, it was most often a subset of the same basic hermeneutical model indicated above. The difference is only that it finds the claim that human subjectivism, the *spiritus proprius,* can be transcended by a collective spirit or the papal office to be dubious. They are still only human. Thus it counters such claims with the insistence that scripture alone as divinely inspired word, not human words, transcends individual subjectivism and is therefore the sole and ultimate authority.

The problem with such a claim, however, is that as long as it remains simply a subset of the same hermeneutical model, *sola scriptura* becomes a defensive position over against tradition and magisterium. To bolster its case it has to make additional formal claims to inspiration, infallibility, inerrancy, sufficiency, etc. to claim divine warrant. As such a defensive position, however, *sola scriptura* is hard-pressed to hold its ground against the advances of critical study of the scriptures, the history of the church, and the growth of tradition. It is virtually platitudinous today to point out, for instance, that scripture is itself a product of "tradition," written by human authors in differing contexts. This ploy relativizes it, reduces it to the level of human words and tradition. Within the presuppositions of the given hermeneutic, therefore, a kind of standoff develops between a scripture-and-tradition position and a *sola scriptura* position, each disagreeing with the other about how human subjectivism and arbitrariness is to be over-

4. See, for instance, Paul Hacker, *The Ego in Faith: Martin Luther and the Origin of Anthropocentric Religion* (Chicago: Franciscan Herald Press, 1970). The book carries a commendatory preface by Joseph Ratzinger. The basic charge of subjectivism persists even in so positive an interpreter of the Reformation as Joseph Lortz. See Lortz, loc. cit. and also *Die Reformation als Religiöses Anliegen Heute* (Trier: Paulus-Verlag, 1948), pp. 144ff.

come and true objectivity achieved. Where does the divine Spirit enter the scene — in the books or in the office or both? To put it in its most extreme form, we end with a standoff between papalism and biblicism, each disputing what appear to be the exaggerated or inappropriate authoritarian claims of the other.

Even though the *sola scriptura* became one of the most prominent slogans of the sixteenth-century reform movement, its significance is not fully grasped until one engages the hermeneutical question. One must advance beyond the merely formal statement of the *sola scriptura* to the understanding of scripture as *sui ipsius interpres*. This claim presupposes a quite different hermeneutical model.[5] To make a long story short, it means that the roles of the text and the interpreter are essentially reversed. The interpreter does not remain standing simply as subject over against the text as object to be interpreted. Rather, in the engagement with scripture, it is the scripture that comes to interpret the exegete. It is the task of the exegete to allow the Spirit of the scripture, the matter itself, to speak. The exegete is put in the position of the hearer who is to let the Spirit speak through the scripture precisely by "getting out of the way," i.e., setting aside the subjective *sensus proprius*. In short, the scripture is not to be understood merely as the object upon which the exegete works, but rather as the means through which the Spirit works on the hearer. The concern moves beyond the question of what scripture means to what the Word does. The movement in the direction of the oral and living Word in this is unmistakable. Intensive occupation with scripture results in scripture asserting itself as living and active on the exegete — the model is the fire and the hammer (Jer. 23), which is living and active, sharper than a two-edged sword (Heb. 4). It clarifies itself and leads to, drives to, the proclamation. The means of transmission is proclamation — the Word as active. The exegete is a hearer, who upon being addressed and exegeted by the Word, becomes in turn a speaker or preacher.

In this model, it is also recognized that the greatest obstacle to true interpretation is the subjectivism, the *sensus* or *spiritus proprius* of the interpreter, i.e., the attempt to make the biblical story conform to others, to make it fit our culture and world. But it is not believed that this subjectiv-

---

5. For a more thorough explication of the issues raised briefly here, see the excellent article by Walter Mostert, "*Scriptura sacra sui ipsius interpres,*" chapter in *Lutherjahrbuch* 46, ed. Helmar Junghans (1979), pp. 60-96. Hereafter cited as Mostert.

ism is overcome either by the collective weight or activity of church or tradition as such, nor is it overcome by merely formal declarations about biblical authority or inerrancy nor, for that matter, by individual claims to possess the Spirit. Thus Luther, for instance, saw the claims both of the individual spiritualist and of the papacy to be of the same order: subjectivism — i.e., the formal claim to possess the Spirit outside of the external Word and thus the claim to stand above the Word and be the ultimate interpreter.[6] The insistence that scripture be heard as *sui ipsius interpres,* however, means that the problem of the subjective *sensus proprius* can be handled only when one allows the Spirit itself speaking through the Word actually to do it: to end the claims and needs of the old dying subject and call to life a new one who hears the promise. That scripture is *sui ipsius interpres* means that it establishes itself as authoritative over the hearer by *claiming* the hearer. In other words, scripture establishes itself as authoritative because it is a justifying, saving, and redeeming Word. "The authority, sufficiency, and revelational quality of the scripture is due, according to Luther, quite unpolemically and *a posteriori,* to the experience that Scripture imparted to him life, salvation, comfort, freedom — i.e., a new being in faith"[7] *Sui ipsius interpres* is simply the hermeneutical correlate of justification by faith alone. The *solus Christus* is important because it denotes the only possible attitude to the Word as *pro me.* In this light, formal claims made for extra-scriptural authority structures and/or formal declarations about biblical authority (inerrancy, infallibility, etc.) are constructs that in one way or another are simply a reflex of the needs of the subjective *sensus proprius.*[8]

What does this have to say about the question of scripture and tradition? First of all, as the formula itself asserts, the interpreter, whether as individual or as collective, is not accorded any independent or automatically privileged status as such. That scripture is *sui ipsius interpres* means that the problem of subjectivism in matters of interpretation cannot adequately be met simply by placing either the collective *spiritus proprius* or formal assertions of biblical authority between the individual subject and the text. If the subjectivism, the *spiritus proprius* of the inter-

6. See Luther's *Smalcald Articles,* Pt. III, Art. VIII, *Book of Concord,* ed. and trans. Kolb, Wengert, et al. (Minneapolis: Fortress, 2000), pp. 321-23.

7. Mostert, p. 70.

8. Mostert, p. 70.

preter is to be overcome, then it is the Holy Spirit speaking through the preached Word according to scripture who must do it. The Word of God, that is, must do it. To set an authoritative office or formal claim to biblical authority between the Word and the hearer is to introduce a foreign and legalistic element into the relation. It is the task of the interpreter to be a hearer of the Word, and having heard, to be one who speaks it again effectively.

Thus, *sui ipsius interpres* has to be seen as a critique of the place assigned to tradition in usual formulations. Tradition understood as an extra-scriptural institution that is to preside over the process of interpretation and put a check on the *sensus proprius* of the interpreter really leaves that *sensus proprius* basically intact. Like the law, it may restrain sin but it does not cure it. As long as the fundamental relation between text and interpreter remains the same no real change can occur. For even if the individual *sensus proprius* as a matter of fact comes to agree with, or submits to, the traditional institution, all that happens is that the subjective *sensus proprius,* in concert with the collective *sensus proprius,* finds a "meaning" in the text convenient to its own concerns. The subject remains the interpreter of the text; the text is not allowed to become the interpreter of the subject.

At the very least, this means that tradition as extra-scriptural institution claiming absolute or unquestioned authority over the interpretation would have to be rejected. The "and" in "scripture and tradition" cannot be a plus sign that elevates tradition to the same level as scripture or in actual practice, above it. If we are not permanently or irrevocably to install some particular instance of human or collective subjectivism over the scriptures, or even between the scriptures and us, then it would seem that we could best consider ourselves as the company of hearers of the Word, straining to hear what the Spirit has to say to us through the Babel of other voices — including our own discordant notes. The tradition, perhaps it could be said, is an account of what the company of hearers has diachronically heard, what we believe and confess, the intent of which should be to summon us to the task of listening ever more carefully and exactly, asking: Is this not what it says? As such it is to be taken seriously and even given a primary place in the discipline of listening. It is, you might say, a "hearing aid," but not itself the source or judge. It may be a "normed norm" *(norma normata),* but not a "norming norm" *(norma normans).* It must always be open to better hearing, and must stand under the scriptures.[9] Tradition properly understood does not exist to call attention to itself, or to insert itself between us and scripture (or even to call attention to its own "development" and growth), but rather to clear the way, to point us toward a proper hearing of the text.

The fact that scripture is to be understood as self-interpreting in no way means therefore that the interpreter has nothing to do. On the contrary, it makes the task of interpreting much more demanding and exacting. "The intensity of the exegetical work is directly proportional to the acknowledgment that scripture is *sui ipsius interpres.*"[10] Luther could specify it in *Assertions Against the Bull of Leo:* "So we must therefore strive, not to set aside the scriptures and norm ourselves by the human writings of the Fathers, but much more to set aside the writings of men and all the more persistently dedicate our sweat to the Holy Scriptures alone. The more present the danger that one might understand them by one's own spirit *(proprio spiritu)* the more this must be done, until at last the exercise of this constant effort conquers the danger and makes us certain of the Spirit of Scripture, which is simply not to be found outside of scripture."[11]

9. Thus, even though Luther accepted the *homoousion* of the Nicene Creed without personal reservation, he could also say (in "Against Latomus"), "Even if my soul hated this word, *homoousion,* and I refused to use it [because it was not scriptural], still I would not be a heretic. For who compels me to use the word, providing I hold to the fact defined by the council on the basis of scripture?" (LW 32, 244).

10. "It is well known . . . that polemically Luther had in mind the *sensus proprius* in the form of the Roman Catholic and enthusiast concept of Spirit. What he criticized thereby was that a criterion was introduced into scriptural exegesis that was foreign to the concern of scripture. Now in the context of Luther's theology as a whole the Roman concept of tradition and the enthusiast concept of Spirit are seen not just as isolated historical phenomena, but as historic appearances of the general human inclination towards *sensus proprius,* to enthusiasm. If Luther sets the self-asserting power of scripture against traditionalism and enthusiasm, one must see this in the overall view of his whole theology, which crystallizes around the self-seeking sinner after his own salvation versus the God who simply gives his salvation." See Mostert, 74.

11. WA 7, 97, 3-9.

The Irrelevance of the Modern World for Luther

When requested to say something about Luther's relevance for the modern world, I said, "No way!" Attempting to prove or persuade someone of the relevance of something is always too much of a defensive and losing battle. If you have to explain the relevance of something or someone, it's already too late. As Karl Barth aptly put it, those who set out to explain the relevance of Christianity to contemporary society will find themselves always running after the train that has just left. It's like trying to explain the relevance of love or marriage or sex to your beloved. If you have to explain it, the beloved is likely to say, "Forget it!" Today, we tend to confuse relevance with topicality. If something is relevant, it transcends that which is only of passing fancy or interest, and is thus lifted above a particular time or place to the level of universality. If it is relevant, it is always so. If it is meaningful only for a time and then goes out of style, it is topical; it pertains only to a *topos,* a place and time. It is like the "topics" on TV talk shows presented by people who incessantly blab and who have no expertise or authority whatsoever to do so. Such presentations are just as well forgotten by the time you wake up in the morning.

So, instead of trying to plead for the relevance of Luther for today, it might be more fun to turn the tables and talk about the irrelevance of the modern world from Luther's viewpoint. What do you suppose Luther would say about us were he to return? Admittedly, that is a speculative question. We cannot hope to do it justice in a few minutes, but maybe we can have some fun with it. So in what follows I will take the side of Luther and make some observations that might provoke our thought and questions. Of course, Luther would be amazed at the technological changes in the world, and we do not need to dwell on that. But what would he say about the spiritual state of the modern world? As is well known, he made a fundamental distinction between looking at the world according to human judgment *(coram hominibus)* and according to divine judgment *(coram deo)*. According to human judgment, we may indeed do what can be called good. But, is it good in the sight of God — as we say, "spiritually speaking"? A physician, for instance, may do much genuine good humanly speaking — healing people, saving lives, etc. But at the same time, he or she may be a money-grubbing egomaniac. And that's not good — at least not in the sight of God. So even though the world may have made tremendous technological progress, the basic question is whether there has been any remarkable improvement *coram deo,* in the judgment of God. That's what would concern Martin Luther.

Luther would find the modern world irrelevant right away because it no longer makes any distinction between human judgment and God's judgment. What is important is strictly human judgment — what others think of us, or what we think of ourselves, what we call self-esteem. Self-esteem, Robert Schuller says, is the "new Reformation." Feeling good about ourselves is the goal of life. Therapy, not theology, is the way to go. "St." Sigmund (Freud) is the real patron of the modern age. It seems nobody worries about God much anymore. God, if anyone thinks about him (her?) any more, is just love, love, love. God is a patsy. And so God just drops out of the picture for most folks. If God is just love, love, love, then no one need worry about him any more. What is important is not to get right with God, as they used to say in the old days, but to get right with ourselves. What is important is not to live the godly life, but to learn how to affirm one another in our chosen lifestyles. Whatever happened to God? Does anyone believe in God anymore, i.e., that God is living and that he is not only love, but above all, the judge? Does anyone believe that the ultimate question for our lives is not human judgment but God's judgment?

We could say that reducing everything to the level of human judgment is the contemporary form of trying to save oneself by good works. But, this move fails to allow humans the freedom they seek. After all, human judgment is a hard and cruel taskmaster. We ourselves can be as hard on ourselves as anyone. From watching my own children grow up, I sometimes think that hardly any are more cruel to one another than the young.

Perhaps that is one reason we hear so much talk about self-esteem. Children can be so devastated by their peers it's a wonder they ever recover. And, tragically, sometimes they don't. We hear it said that what moderns are searching for is not a gracious God, but a gracious neighbor, someone who cares. Good luck! The other has his or her own life to live. Besides, just when you get close, you may find out they have bad breath. "When a guy smells," the ads tell us, "it's such a turn-off." But that's just a prelude. Because one day the neighbor, the other, will desert you forever. To put it crudely, then they will really smell! What a turn-off!

What Luther discovered in reading his Bible, in his conversation and struggle, was that we can't be saved by works, no matter how highly they may be esteemed by human judgment. A world that thinks to do so is simply irrelevant. So when he heard St. Paul saying that it is not our estimate, not our judgment, but God's that matters, the "gates of paradise," he said, swung wide open. We are justified before God by faith alone, not by works. That, you will recognize, was the watchword of Luther's Reformation. We are judged righteous before God because of what God has done in Jesus Christ, not by our own deeds. What God wants from us is faith, and if the faith is right, the deeds will follow of themselves. What God wants from the physician, mentioned above, is to "keep the faith," as we say today.

Now, of course, it is just this claim, that in the judgment of God we are just because of the faith that Jesus awakens in us, that the world finds so absurd. Just before God, the ultimate judge, by faith alone? Is that not preposterous? But you see, that's just the point. It is preposterous to us as "old beings," what Luther and others could call the Old Adam. The point is that as Old Beings we are, so to speak, irrelevant. That is why it is fundamentally a mistake to try to make someone like Luther relevant to the modern age. The gospel of justification by faith alone is never relevant to this or any age. It is the end of the age, the end of the old, the death of sinners. God is not out merely to change, or even to convert old beings. This is not like a new paint or remodeling job. Faith in Christ is a death. God is out to put the old being out of its misery once and for all. Faith is not like choosing a new coat, or even a set of values. It is *being chosen*. And being chosen for the Old Adam and Eve is a dying because it means that God takes charge. But it is not just a death; it is also the hope of resurrection, a being grasped by a new life of love, hope, and care.

If one looks at the modern world from the viewpoint of such faith, a dying to the old and a rising to the new, there are many things one would find disappointing and perhaps finally irrelevant. Perhaps the first thing, strangely enough, that would have caught Luther's attention was the world's religion. Now, the world seems to think that it has separated religion from public life, its center for doing its business. It is quite self-deceived in this regard. In many ways, the modern world is very religious, as can be seen in our civil religion, various idols of pop culture, our utopian ideals of progress, our Romantic worship of nature and the self, and continued commitment to the institutional churches. Now, the fact is, Luther did not care much for religion. When you do not have faith, religion is what happens to you sooner or later. If you do not have faith in what God has done, then you have to do something about religion yourself. Then, in Luther's (and Paul's) terms, you fall under the law. Now law, here, does not mean just moral demands. It means that indeed, but being "under" the law means much more. It is something like our expression "being under the gun." It means that you are always in the position of chasing yourself, trying to fill the emptiness of your being, whether it be with pleasure, greed, sex, money, self-esteem, feeling, and sometimes even more "spiritual" matters like all the talk of spirituality and "new-ageism" — all the "gods" of modern religion. Perhaps Luther would have wandered about in our culture and said something of the same thing Paul said when he went to Athens: "I perceive that in every way you are very religious. But as I passed along I saw an altar without a statue, and it said, 'To an unknown God.' The one you don't know any more, this I proclaim unto you." And then, like Paul, he would preach the one who comes to us and who was crucified by religion and yet raised, the one who is the end of religion, the end of the old and the beginning of the new.

In spite of its religiosity, Luther would have found our age quite superficial — in Ernest Becker's excellent phrase, one that "tranquilizes itself with the trivial." Luther would find our age superficial because it has forgotten about or trivialized the darker side of life, the "enemies" we are up against when faith is lost: sin, death, and the devil. The modern age, of course, prides itself in having erased these enemies from our consciousness. With our science and technology, we have sought increasingly to control our fate. The enemies do not get much press any more — at least favorable press! But that only means that we are all the more susceptible and exposed to them. What the modern world misunderstands is that these enemies work best and are much more powerful when no one knows or calls them by name. The forces of darkness work best in the dark — they detest the light! They want the field all to themselves. Who, after all, knows what sin is anymore? Maybe it turns up in tabloids or movie titles as a synonym for illicit sex, something to entice you to spend your money. We don't sin anymore, we just succumb to certain diseases. Is sin, perhaps, located in faulty DNA? Sin, at most, is passive — something "they" do to us. We picture ourselves mostly as "victims." We are "oppressed," "alienated," and harassed. "They" are the sinners. We are not. If we could just get them to stop, we would save the world. Some time ago there was a cartoon in the *New Yorker* showing a group sitting in hell with the flames licking up around them, and one was explaining to the others, "What I'm in here for is no longer a sin." We seem to think that all we need to do to get rid of sin is to erase it or change the label. We live in a world of exchangeable labels. Somehow we think if we erase or change the label the problem will go away. So we go from "old folks," to "elderly," to "senior citizens," and finally perhaps to "the chronologically challenged." And before you know it, the problem has disappeared into semantics. This is all, of course, just cosmetics. It is terribly superficial — literally "over the face," a cover-up job. But, one day we will be seen, face to face. Luther, of course, would find all this horribly mistaken. A "theologian of glory" calls the bad good and the good bad. A "theologian of the cross" says what a thing is! The Bible tells us "if we say we have no sin, we deceive ourselves and the truth is not in us." For the gospel comes to expose sin, to name it, to call a spade a spade, not to disguise or hide it. It comes to show us what it is, so we can confess it and be saved. For if it is true that we can stand before God only by faith, only by the forgiveness of sin, then it is only sinners, not saints who shall be saved.

The modern world would be judged by Luther to be equally superficial, when it comes to the question of death. It is strange how much death we see about us — on TV, in the movies, on the streets, the escalating horror of spilled blood in one picture after another. On the other hand, death is often hidden from us. We hide the dead away in "funeral parlors." We may see the violent act of dying, but then they zip them up in a bag and take them away. I am not sure what to make of death in contemporary society: we seem to be both fascinated by it and repelled by it at the same time. But all in all, whether it happens before us in real life, or on the mass media screens, it seems — except to those few who knew and loved the dying ones — to be trivialized. It is not important. But, even though it is deemed unimportant, it continues to invade our lives all the more. Children shoot children in an argument over a jacket or a bicycle.

Of course, for Luther this would be frightening. He believed the Bible when it was said that death is the last enemy. In *The Denial of Death,* Ernest Becker claims that because we hide from and trivialize death we do not know how to live. It is our denial of death that calls the shots. Luther would find the modern world quite superficial and irrelevant on this score. Death must indeed be faced. It cannot be trivialized or hidden away. Indeed, Luther insisted, Jesus came to die for us, to take away the sting of death from us, so that we could begin to live. And the "big death" is first of all to believe that we are just before God for Jesus' sake. The "big death," the hardest death for us to take, is just the sheer gift of grace, the divine election. Physical expiration is indeed tragic and painful enough, but it's nothing like the election of grace, because that means that God takes control of our destiny.

Finally, Luther would find the modern world superficial and irrelevant because it has somehow forgotten or just overlooked the real adversary, the one who holds the power of death, the devil. If you ever read Luther you will discover that he talks a lot about the devil. We tend not to see it. We have a "blik" — we just don't see it. But the devil, the adversary, plays a vital role in his thought. To most of us moderns, the devil is largely disregarded. We find it curious for someone to believe in demons, or the devil. But, once again, that is just fine with the devil. As it has been well put, if there is a devil, then his cleverest trick would be to get us to believe that he does not exist. Because then, he has the field all to himself. The devil does not care whether anyone believes in him or not. And even if you do, he will destroy — like parents who beat their children to death. He wins.

What Luther knew, and what the modern world has forgotten, is that we are not up to defeating the devil. That is what Luther is about. Perhaps the greatest mistake is to think that there is *some* kind of neutrality in this battle. Humans are like a beast made to be ridden. Either God or Satan is in the saddle. We are the battleground. And it doesn't look good. But Luther knew that he could not fight Satan head on. He could only preach as guided by the doctrine of justification by faith alone. In spite of the modern world's irrelevance, triviality, superficiality, and its religious self-reliance, he would have continued to preach the same message. After all, it is a message that cuts both ways. It does comfort the afflicted. But even if there are no more of them, it afflicts the comforted. It exalts those of low degree and brings down the mighty from their seats.

Counter to modern assumptions that prioritize human judgment and deny the prospect and all-pervasiveness of sin, death, and the devil, the gospel promises a sure commitment of God to his people. Paul makes this clear: "For I am convinced that neither death, nor life, nor angels, nor rulers, nor things present, nor things to come, nor powers, nor height, nor depth, nor anything else in all creation, will be able to separate us from the love of God in Christ Jesus our Lord" (Rom. 8:38-39). It is this message, more than any other, which is relevant. It is the gospel promise — it alone — that effectuates the new life that we need.

ATONEMENT AND JUSTIFICATION: CHRIST UNBOUND

Caught in the Act:
Reflections on the Work of Christ

Already in the twelfth century Peter Abelard put the question to which we must at last attend in our thinking about the work of Christ, a question almost totally ignored by subsequent centuries:

> If [the] sin of Adam was so great that it could be expiated only by the death of Christ, what expiation will avail for the act of murder committed against Christ, and for the many great crimes committed against him or his followers? How did the death of his innocent Son so please God the Father that through it he should be reconciled to us — to us who by our sinful acts have done the very things for which our innocent Lord was put to death?[1]

In a moment of candor rare in the tradition, Abelard sees the death of Christ as a murder in which we are implicated. He wonders how such an act could be considered so pleasing to God as to "satisfy" him. The question is aimed, of course, at his great contemporary Anselm, primary architect of the view of the work of Christ that has tended to dominate western Christian thinking, the doctrine of vicarious satisfaction. Anselm, like subsequent thinkers, concentrated on the sin of Adam, arguing that it was so

---

1. Peter Abelard, "Exposition of the Epistle to the Romans," *A Scholastic Miscellany: Anselm to Ockham*, ed. and trans. Eugene R. Fairweather, *The Library of Christian Classics*, ed. J. Baillie et al., 26 vols. (Philadelphia: Westminster, 1953-69), vol. 10, pp. 282-83.

great an affront to the divine honor that only the voluntary sacrifice of the God-man could make satisfaction for it. But such thinking diverts attention from the brute reality at hand: Jesus, the innocent one, was murdered by us. The sin of Adam, Abelard avers, was indeed bad enough, but surely it was small potatoes compared to the sin of murdering the Son of God. "Had not this very great sin been committed, could he not have pardoned the former much lighter sin?"[2] Far from "satisfying" God's honor or wrath or justice or whatever, the murder of Jesus, Abelard thinks, would only make matters worse — much worse.

I. Theories Aside

The contention of this essay is that our thinking about the work of Christ today, like Abelard's remark, must become more concrete, more in accord with the "brute reality" as it is disclosed to us in the actual events. We need something more like a "smoking gun" approach to the matter, the consciousness of being "caught in the act." We need to be grasped more than heretofore by the realization that Christ's work is and remains always an act in which we are involved and implicated, which cannot be translated into convenient and quiescent ideas. Indeed, the fatal flaw in most thinking about the atoning work of Christ is the tendency to look away from the actual events, to translate them into "eternal truths," and thus to ignore or obscure what actually happened and our part in it. We interpret Christ's death as though it were an idea, a necessary part of a logical scheme of some sort, as though God were tied to a scheme of honor or justice making *him* the obstacle to our reconciliation. We exonerate ourselves, so to speak, by blaming the necessity for the cross on God.

So it seems at least, in most theories of atonement. In the so-called "objective" theory it is maintained that God needed the death of Jesus in order to be able to be merciful to us. God is the object of the atoning act. The demands of his law, or wrath, or justice had to be "satisfied." So we are exonerated because the cross was necessary to God. But the inevitable consequence of such thinking is that it doesn't finally reconcile us to God. If the cross is necessary to pay God, God will be pictured as at worst a rather vindictive tyrant demanding his pound of flesh or at best an inept subor-

2. Abelard, "Exposition," p. 283.

dinate caught in the same inexorable net of law and justice as we are. The theory intended to foster reconciliation actually contributes to further alienation. At bottom, that is what animates Abelard's question to Anselm. The persistent criticism of doctrines of vicarious satisfaction and substitutionary atonement since the Enlightenment has the same root. The picture painted of God is too black, too contrary to the biblical witness. If the death was *payment*, how could reconciliation be an act of *mercy*? Mercy is mercy, not the result of payment. If God is by nature love and mercy, why could he not just up and forgive? Jesus, it seems, forgave sins *before* his death. Why then was the death necessary? The logic of the theory threatens the very thing it wants to promote: the *mercy* of God. To quote Abelard again: "Could not he, who showed such loving-kindness to man that he united him to his very self, extend to him a lesser boon by forgiving his sins?"[3]

Yet the "subjective" theory of the atonement touted by Abelard and his latter-day followers shows that the question about the murder of the Son of God was not taken seriously by them either. It is used largely as a negative foil to discredit the idea that God is the object of atonement, that the death of Jesus could have a positive effect on God. The subjective view also diverts attention from the actual event by locating the "necessity" for the cross in Jesus' own inner life and devotion and the persuasive power flowing from his example, his faithfulness unto death. Thus, it would seem, God sent his Son to a shameful and painful death to provide an example powerful enough to entice us to be reconciled to him as a God of mercy and charity.

But what then happens to the question about the murder of the innocent one? Somehow it has been whisked out of sight again by the machinery of the theory. For could not the question just as well rebound on Abelard and his followers? How can God possibly be "justified" in sending his Son into this world to be cruelly murdered at our hands just to provide an example of what everybody already knew anyway? If the cross does not actually accomplish anything *new*, is not the price too great? Is not a God who would do such a thing fully as thoughtless and cruel as the God of vicarious satisfaction? Those who push the "subjective" view rarely entertain such questions. No doubt because of the terror and cruelty of the actual event as well as our implication in it, it has been quietly forgotten. Since it

---

3. Abelard, "Exposition," p. 282.

is "necessary" or at least understandable on moral or like grounds, we are (more or less) exonerated. We can sit back and admire the event that took place on Golgotha! It was so impressive!

Of late, those who have sought to avoid the debits of both the "objective" and "subjective" views have tended to take refuge in what Gustaf Aulén called the "classic idea" or "victory motif." Christ's work in incarnation, death, and resurrection is understood as victory over the demonic powers that enslave us. Instead of a merely "objective" change in God or a "subjective" change in us, Christ's work brings about a *new situation:* the demonic powers — sin, law, death, the devil — have been defeated; Christ has triumphed for us. No doubt there is much to be said for this view insofar as it seems to provide a better conceptual structure for considering Christ's work. Something actually new is said to be accomplished in the cross and resurrection, and God's mercy is not overly tarnished.

Yet we must ask how the victory motif fares in the light of our question. Once again the killing has been covered up. Jesus' death is somehow necessary to defeat the demons. We are exonerated because the demons did it. God, too, is exonerated in the process because he can appear as the hero of the piece, the mighty conqueror of the demons. Since he is not the obstacle to reconciliation (at least directly), he can appear more unambiguously as a God of love and mercy.

But the question is whether all this exoneration has not been purchased at too great a price: God loses some of his sovereignty to his dualistic adversaries, and the work of Christ is translated to a semimythical cosmic battle quite removed from our world. We should not forget that both Anselm and Abelard were well aware of the victory idea. What bothered them, however, was precisely the question of divine sovereignty over the demons. Why should the cruel death of Jesus be necessary to defeat the demons? Surely if God is God, he could just put the demons out of commission whenever he wished. The inadequacy of the victory idea as an explanation for the actual and painful death was the *very reason* for Anselm's question: *Cur Deus Homo?* If victory over the demons is all that is necessary, why the death? Why should God have to "stoop to such lowly things," or "do anything with such great labor," when he could, supposedly, just blow the demons away?[4]

Abelard also attacked the idea that the demonic powers provide nec-

---

4. Anselm, "Why God Became Man," *Scholastic Miscellany,* p. 110.

essary reason for the murder of Jesus. If the demons acquired the right to torment sinful humanity only by divine permission, the permission could simply be withdrawn — if God is God. After all, Jesus cast out demons and forgave sins only by fiat and presence.

> So what compulsion, or reason, or need was there — seeing that *by its very appearing alone* the divine pity could deliver man from Satan — what need was there, I say, that the Son of God, for our redemption, should take upon him our flesh and endure such numerous fastings, insults, scourgings and spittings, and finally that most bitter and disgraceful death upon the cross, enduring even the cross of punishment with the wicked?[5]

The victory motif, in short, could not provide adequate reason for the murder of Jesus. The Fathers, it should be recalled, had considerable difficulty with the question themselves. They vacillated and temporized, wondering whether the "ransom" was to be paid to the devil or not, just who had rights and who didn't, or whether God surrendered Jesus to death to deceive the demons or to deal fairly and honorably with them or whatever. The very indecision and ambiguity led, no doubt, to the ultimate demise of the view — at least in the west — and contributed to the ascendancy of Anselmian theory. In spite of its several advantages, the victory motif, too, stands somewhat embarrassed before the hard question of what actually happened: Why the murder of the innocent one? Even if the mercy and propriety of God is not overtly challenged, the question covertly rebounds on God again: If he is God, could he not have spared his Son the agony?

In sum, each of the major types of atonement theory tends to obscure the truth of the murder of Jesus in the very attempt to convey its "meaning" and "significance" to us. As a matter of fact and not just coincidentally, the theories seem to defeat their own purpose: they tend to alienate rather than to reconcile. In attempting to explain the "necessity" for the death of Jesus by taking it up in the schemes suggested, God's "reputation" is endangered, not enhanced. Why should a God who is by nature merciful demand satisfaction? Is a God who consigns his Son to an excruciating death just to provide an example of what everyone already knew really a "loving Father"? If God is God, could not the defeat of demonic powers

---

5. P. Abelard, "Exposition," p. 282 (emphasis mine).

have been accomplished without the painful death? In other words, "Was this trip really necessary?"

So we come back to our original question: Why the murder of the innocent one? What does that accomplish for us — or for God? What is "the word" of Christ? What does he actually do for us that God could not have done with greater ease and economy in some other way? The crucial and persistent question emerging from discussion of the various views seems always to be that of the *necessity* for the concrete and actual work of Christ among us. It is, of course, ultimately the question of the necessity for Christology at all. Cannot God just up and forgive and/or cast out demons? Or to use another current form of the question: Is there not grace aplenty in the Old Testament? Or in nature? Or in other religions even? Why Jesus? Why the *New* Testament?

II. The Brute Facts

If we are to get anywhere with these questions today, we shall have to begin by paying closer attention to the "brute facts" of the case, looking at the actual events as they have been mediated to us in the narrative itself to see what we can make of them. Perhaps this is to say, to use a distinction employed for the person of Christ, we should begin our consideration of the work of Christ "from below" (from our point of view) as much as possible before we proceed to discuss it "from above" (from "God's point of view") — realizing the problematic nature of such distinctions. The reason for insisting on such a beginning is not to invest theological capital in the distinctions as such, but simply to suggest that we have tended in the past to hurry by what actually happened here "below," with us and to us, to get to the theory, the perspective "from above." The theory has overrun the event. If we begin "from below" perhaps the impact of the work of Christ will emerge more naturally and directly from the narrative itself and we will find ourselves "caught in the act" in more ways than one — caught at it and at the same time caught by it. If we can begin in this fashion we might be better prepared, I think, to get some glimpses "from above," some indications (*a posteriori*, of course!) of why God could not or at least would not do it any other way.

Why could not God just up and forgive? Let us start there. If we look at the narrative about Jesus, the actual events themselves, the "brute facts" as they have come down to us, the answer is quite simple. He did! Jesus came preaching repentance and forgiveness, declaring the bounty and mercy of his "Father." The problem, however, is that we could not buy that. And so we killed him. And just so we are caught in the act. Every mouth is stopped once and for all. All the pious talk about our yearning and desire for reconciliation and forgiveness, etc., all our complaint against God is simply shut up. He came to forgive and we killed him for it; we would not have it. It is as simple as that.

We don't like, of course, to face that brutal simplicity because, I suppose, we are caught in the act, the act of being who we really are: sinners, fakes, liars, deniers, unbelievers. "But," as my students sometimes protest, "don't we really want reconciliation? Don't we seek it and desire it?" The best answer to the question, I like to say, is "Cock-a-doodle-doo!" No doubt, Peter "wanted" reconciliation. It's a nice "idea." He even swore that he would not deny his Lord. But the cock crowed. Too late! Caught in the act. So it is now. The cock has crowed. It is an act, an event, not an idea. It has occurred. It is too late for all our protestations. We treat "reconciliation," "salvation," and "forgiveness" as though they were things, ideas, lying on a shelf somewhere which God "provides," which we could want or not want and thus, perhaps, acquire or have more or less at will. No doubt, we might want salvation; but what of a savior? One who actually *works* it, *does* it to us. What shall we do about that?

Why was Jesus killed? It would seem from the actual narrative that we should be much more careful about saying that Jesus had to die because God, at the outset, was angry with us. There is indeed a sense in which we must say that Christ's work is to "satisfy" the divine wrath. But it is surely a mistake to say, to begin with, that Jesus was killed because God's honor or justice or wrath was the obstacle to reconciliation which had first to be "satisfied" *before* mercy could be shown. Surely the truth is that Jesus was killed because he forgave sins and claimed either explicitly or implicitly to do it in the name of God, his Father. When we skip over the actual event to deal first with the problem of the divine justice or wrath, we miss the point that *we* are the obstacles to reconciliation, not God. "Jerusalem, Jerusalem, killing the prophets and stoning those who are sent to you! How often would I have gathered your children together as a hen gathers her brood under her wings, and *you would not!*" (Matt. 23:37). *We* are caught in the act. We have first to come to grips with the fact that *we* did it. The victory motif also errs in this regard when it allows us more or less to drop out of the "drama" in favor of the demonic forces. Surely the view must be deepened to say (at the very least) that the demonic powers operate *through us,* their quite willing lackeys. As it was put in a Pogo comic strip, "We has met the enemy and they is us!" We did it.

No doubt, this is a sensitive issue especially today because of the quite mistaken move in the Christian tradition to blame the Jews for killing Jesus. We have exonerated ourselves not only at God's expense, but at the expense of the Jews. This certainly must cease. But it is hardly a gain theologically if we simply continue to exonerate ourselves by shifting the blame from Jews to Romans! There are no Romans left so we are not likely to hear much protest! But we will still have missed the point. Certainly if the death of Jesus is to have any point for us at all, we must start from the realization that *we — all of us —* did it and in countless subtle and not so subtle ways continue to do it. We are united in that, at least! The universal significance of the death of Jesus has its roots first of all in the fact that he is *universally rejected* and killed by us, not in a theory about how his death is of infinite worth or universally "satisfying." "The stone which the builders rejected has become the chief cornerstone" (Luke 20:17; Acts 4:11; 1 Pet. 2:7). Caught in the act!

But why did we kill him? It was, I expect we must say, a matter of "self-defense." Jesus came not just to teach *about* the mercy and forgiveness of God but actually to *do* it, to *have mercy* and *to forgive* unconditionally. It is an act, not an idea. That is his "work." That is the *New* Testament. He came to do "what he sees the Father doing" (John 5:19). Now we are, no doubt, quite open, generally, to the *idea* of mercy and forgiveness in God and his "heaven," but actually doing it *here* for God is quite another matter — especially if it is the absolutely free and unconditional having mercy and forgiving of the sovereign God who ups and has mercy on whom he will have mercy! How can one actually *do* that here? How can *this* world survive, how can *we* survive if mercy and forgiveness are just *given* unconditionally? The *idea* is nice, but what shall we do with one who *actually* eats with traitors, whores, outcasts, and riffraff of every sort and just blows away our protests by saying, "They that are whole need not a physician but they that are sick"? Actually *doing* it, giving it unconditionally just seems to us terribly reckless and dangerous. It shatters the "order" by which we must run things here.

We should make no mistake about it. One who comes actually to have mercy and to forgive in God's name is just an absolute and total threat to the way we have decided we must run things here. So either Jesus must go or we must. But how can we — mere dying beings — surrender all our plans and gains to him? So Jesus is "wasted" as an intruder. He is crucified between two other rebels against the order of the age, a thief and an insurrectionist. But Jesus is ultimately the most dangerous because his opposition is total; he gives unconditional forgiveness. He has the crazy conviction that such unconditional saving mercy is what God and his "Kingdom" are all about, and that it is the true destiny of human beings which will make them new and pure and whole and won't ultimately hurt them at all. He seems to think that there actually is "a river, the streams whereof make glad the city of God"! In short, Jesus is most dangerous because he actually believes in God and his Kingdom, and because he himself realizes it, does it among us. To consent to that would mean (just as he said!) for us to lose the life we have so carefully hoarded. So he must go. It is a matter of self-defense.

If we can approach the work of Christ in some such fashion "from below," perhaps we can begin to see that it is a matter of being caught in the act — caught, in the first place, in the act of being ourselves, our "old" selves. God is not the obstacle to reconciliation; we are. Those who advocated the "subjective" view of the atonement were at least right in that, I expect. God is, indeed, sheer unconditional love. They were wrong, however, in thinking that *we* would in any way be open to one who actually came to *do* that among us. Consequently, the idea that Christ's work is to effect a mere alteration in the "subject" by the example of his dedication is just another defense mechanism against the act, the *doing* of the divine love. It is translated into an idea or an ideal that serves ultimately just to reinforce the way we run things. The fact that we had to kill the Jesus who came to forgive exposes us for who we are. No mere subjective alteration will do for the likes of us. If we are to be saved by him, we must somehow be ready to receive what it is he comes to give. But that will take some dying. And that is the point. Not only are we caught *in* the act; we will have to be caught *by* the act.

III. Starting "From Below"

If we can begin as we have attempted, "from below," this will open, I think, new possibilities for suggesting how the work of Christ might look "from above." Anselm and the champions of the "objective" view were quite right in insisting that the ultimate reason and "justification" for the cross must lie in God. The persistent question through theological history has been whether God could not have done it in some other way. If he could have, the matter recoils on him. The cross is just too high a price to pay: "Father, if it be possible, let this cup pass from me. . . ." Ultimately, God must answer for the cross. No doubt, that is what gives the "objective" views their right and strength. Neither the persuasiveness of the example nor the defeat of demons — nothing exterior to God himself — provides sufficient reason for abandoning Jesus to his cruel fate. Yet to say that the cross was necessary to satisfy the divine honor or wrath or justice is also clearly suspect. The event of Jesus tells us that God's intent is simply to have mercy, that God is love.

But why then must Jesus die? Bearing in mind that this "must" is always *a posteriori*, not *a priori*, not an abstract, logical "must" determined beforehand but one that flows out of what the act itself accomplishes, perhaps we can say something about how it might look "from God's point of view." If what we have been saying about the murder of Jesus by us is at all the case, then God's "problem" comes more immediately into view. God's "problem" is not that he can't be merciful until he has been satisfied but rather that he won't be satisfied until he succeeds in actually having mercy on whom he will have mercy. God, that is, won't be satisfied until he succeeds in actually giving the concrete, unconditional forgiving he intends. As we can see from Jesus, God's problem is how actually to have mercy on a world that will not have it. The question for God is whether he can really succeed in getting through to a people that likes the *idea* of forgiveness but doesn't want an actual forgiver, a world that turns everything God purposes to do into a theory with which to protect itself *from* him. God's problem is just how actually to *have* mercy, how to get *through* to us.

If that is the case, then at least a couple of considerations follow. As long as God is not "satisfied," we exist under his "wrath." But he is not satisfied because we will not let him be who he wants to be: the one who actually forgives, does it unconditionally, has mercy on whom he will have mercy. His wrath is therefore his "jealousy," the obverse side of his intention to have mercy, to be who he will be. We are under his wrath not because of something so abstract as his "honor" or his "justice" to which "payment" must be made, but because we will not let him be who he will be for us: unconditional love and mercy.

The second consideration is that if this is the problem, *God can do nothing about it in the abstract.* Here is at least the beginning of the answer, it would seem, to why God could not do it in any other way. He cannot have mercy on us in the abstract. As abstraction he is always a terror to us, hidden, wrathful. The *idea* that he has mercy on whom he will have mercy is, as *idea*, the most frightening thing of all. We may twist and turn to change the *idea*, but all we will come up with then is that he has mercy on those who fulfill the necessary requirements. We just go out of the frying pan into the fire. The problem is simply that as abstraction God is absent from us and we are inexorably "under wrath." Even God can do nothing about that — except to come to us. If the problem is absence, the only solution is presence. The only solution to the terror of the *idea* of one who has mercy on whom he will have mercy is actually *to come* and *have* mercy. The *act* must actually be done. The only solution to the problem of the absolute, we might say, is actual absolution!

So God must come *to us* to have mercy. This God does in Jesus. But why must Jesus die? Why is not just the coming enough? The answer has already been given "from below," from our side. We will not have it. There is no "place" for the Son of Man to lay his head here. But what about "from above," from God's side? Why does God abandon him unto death? Why are the heavens silent at Jesus' cry? To attempt final answers to such questions "from God's side" is, of course, a risky and presumptuous business, but since we have suggested that previous attempts are suspect, we must perhaps make some tentative counter-suggestions at least.

Why does God abandon Jesus to be murdered by us? The answer, it would seem, must lie in that very unconditional love and mercy he intends to carry out in act. God, I would think we can assume, knows full well that he is a problem for us. He knows that unconditional love and mercy is "the end" of us, our conditional world. He knows that to have mercy on whom he will have mercy can only appear as frightening, as *wrath,* to such a world. He knows we would have to die to all we are before we could accept it. But he also knows that that is our only hope, our only salvation. So he refuses to be wrath for us. He refuses to be the wrath that is resident in all our conditionalism. He *can* indeed be that, and is that apart from the work of Christ. But he refuses ultimately to be that. Thus, precisely so as not to be the wrathful God we seem bent on having, he dies for us, "gets out of the way" for us. Unconditional love has no levers in a conditional world. He is obedient unto death, the last barrier, the last condition we cannot avoid, "that the scriptures might be fulfilled" — that God will have mercy on whom he will have mercy. As "God of wrath" he submits to death for us; he knows he must die for us. That is the only way he can be for us absolutely, unconditionally. But then, of course, there must be resurrection to defeat that death, lest our conditionalism have the last word.

Or we can put it another way. Jesus came to forgive sin unconditionally for God. Our sin, our unbelief, consists precisely in the fact that we cannot and will not tolerate such forgiveness. So we move to kill him. There is nothing for him to do then but to die "for our sins," "on our behalf," "give his life a ransom for many." For him to stop and ask us to "shape up" would be to deny the forgiveness he came to give, to put conditions on the unconditional. Thus he must "bear our sins in his body" — not theoretically in some fashion, but actually. He is beaten, spit upon, mocked, wasted. That is, perhaps we can say, the only way for him to "catch us in the act." The resurrection is, therefore, the vindication of Jesus' life and proclamation of forgiveness, God's insistence that unconditional forgiveness be actually given "in Jesus' name." To accept such forgiveness is to die to the old and be made new in him. His death is, therefore, our death. As Paul put it, Christ "has died for all; therefore, all have died" (2 Cor. 5:14). One should not mistake this for a "subjective" view of the atonement. We are speaking of the *death* of the old, not a mere *alteration* of the continuously existing subject. Christ's work is to realize the will of God to have mercy unconditionally, and thus to make new beings and bring in the new age. The "New Testament" is that since Jesus has been raised, this will is now to be proclaimed to all, actually done, delivered, given, to the end that faith be created, new beings created. Christ has died "once for all," all people, all time. To be sure, it is a dangerous message in this age. Either we kill it by our endless qualifications and conditionalisms (and thus crucify Christ again) or it kills us and makes us new in faith and hope and love. But having died once to sin, he dies no more! The deed is done!

IV. Why the Death of Christ?

In some such fashion perhaps we can get at least a glimpse of an answer to the "why" of Jesus' abandonment unto death. It must lie in God's immovable resolve to forgive, to have mercy on whom he will have mercy in concrete act, thereby to create new beings. Even though that seems an impossible project to "this age," it does begin in faith, and God, we are assured, intends to carry it to fruition. If that is the case, we can also suggest a somewhat different and, it is to be hoped, more acceptable sense in which Christ's work, as tradition has insisted, "satisfies" the wrath (justice, honor) of God. When faith is created, when we actually believe God's unconditional forgiveness; then God can say, "Now I am satisfied!" God's wrath ends actually *when we believe him,* not abstractly because of a payment to God "once upon a time." Christ's work, therefore, "satisfies" the wrath of God because it alone creates believers, new beings who are no longer "under" wrath. Christ actualizes the will of God to have mercy unconditionally in the concrete and thereby "placates" God. When, that is, we are caught in the act so that we are caught by the act, God reaches his goal.

Loser Takes All: The Victory of Christ

Nobody likes a loser. There is hardly anything worse we can say of a person today than he or she is a loser, a real loser. We want winners. We worship winners. We want to be winners — often at any cost. Yet, by our standards, Jesus was a loser.

The prophet of God saw it coming long ago: "He grew up before him like a young plant, and like a root out of dry ground; he had no form or comeliness that we should look at him, and no beauty that we should desire him. He was despised and rejected by men; a man of sorrows, and acquainted with grief; and as one from whom men hide their faces he was despised, and we esteemed him not" (Isa. 53:2-3). What the prophet saw came to pass in Jesus. In our eyes he was a loser, a real loser.

We don't like to have this said about Jesus. We like to think of him as a stunning attraction, a glowing, handsome, exemplary, winsome winner — one who fits perfectly with our "winner-takes-all" outlook on life.

We try by all sorts of trickery — religious and otherwise — to twist the story of Jesus and his cross so it will fit into our "winner's circle." Splinters from the cross will cure our diseases. The uncrucified Jesus will be our leader and example. The cross is painted on our battle flags or carried on crusades. Jesus is portrayed for all the world like a pro football player emerging radiant and glistening from the shower after the big win. He can even be our substitute winner so we can relax and equate piety with sloppiness. Everyone wants a winner.

But it is all false. Jesus cannot be made over by us into a winner. By our standards he was a loser. We have to face it.

I suppose it seems strange to begin an article on the victory of Christ like this — insisting that Jesus was a loser. But we have to see that, I think, in order really to get the point.

The victory of Christ, the triumph of Easter, is a note that is often lacking in our teaching, our preaching, and our piety. This is because we tend to think that there was nothing really vital at stake — either for him or for us. We think of him as a kind of supreme, unruffled, orthodox theologian, or plaster saint, who could not possibly lose anything and whose victory is consequently no real surprise. He is merely the illustration of an eternal truth.

Wanting a Winner

We seem to prefer ideas and images that are more neutral — not to say calculating and frozen — in talking about him. He is the "supreme example of morality" (what an icy thing to say about anyone!). Or he is the one who somehow transacts business with God behind the scenes and pays the debt we owe (as though heaven were some big credit union in the sky!). And since we think of him in this fashion, we do not seriously entertain the thought that he could actually be a loser. We want a winner. We want a sure thing. So we tend to miss the real nature of the victory. Easter is a once-a-year curiosity we may enjoy when it comes around but is soon forgotten and about which we have little to say.

This is why we have to face seriously the fact that Jesus was first of all a loser. Of course we do not like it! But the point is that he, this loser, "this Jesus whom you crucified," is the one whom God raised from the dead — precisely in the face of our dislikes! It is God who ultimately accomplishes the victory by raising Jesus from the dead. God audaciously turns the tables on us by raising up this one whom we judged to be a loser. In this strange fact lies hidden the mystery of Easter, the victory of Christ.

What is the nature of this victory? Whom or what does he defeat? Usually we say that it was a victory over "the enemies" — sin, death, and the devil. And this is true. But what does this mean? How does this affect us? Sin, death, and the devil still seem to abound. How can we say they have been defeated? Here we get to the really sticky point.

The victory of Christ is the victory of a loser in a world of would-be winners. He came into this world where we are all bent on winning at all costs. We have all gone the route of the first Adam, listening to the voice of the tempter: "You shall not die, you shall be as gods" (you shall be a winner!). So we fight and kick and scramble to get to the top — no matter whom we hurt or what we exploit to get there. But sin, death, and the devil are not just "out there" somewhere. They are operative through us.

Into this situation Jesus comes and goes the way of what we think is a loser. He refuses steadfastly to go the way of the first Adam, to try to be a god. He goes the other way. He decides to be a human being. He sticks to it to the end. "He . . . became obedient unto death, even death on a cross" (Phil. 2:8). This is his victory. The resurrection alone is not simply the victory. If so, it would mean he was our type of winner after all — that he "snatched victory from defeat" at the last minute like some of our championship teams in spite of playing a bad game. No, it was precisely by losing in a world of winners that victory becomes possible. For God shocks everyone by raising this loser from the dead. God vindicates his cause by making this Jesus to be Lord and Christ.

A Glimpse of Greatness

Perhaps now we can begin to catch a glimpse of the greatness of this victory. In a world of destructive, compulsive "winners," how else could he be victorious except by losing? How else could he get through to us? Over us and for us he finally has to be victorious — to put to death the "old Adam" (the winner-at-any-cost) so that we could be made new, be made human beings again.

He might have staged a different sort of show. He might have muscled his way to victory by some means more to our liking. But then he would never really have been able to change us. The power play, the hurt, the sin, the death would go on forever and ever. But now there is something else. There is the victory of this loser. To be sure, sin, death, and the devil are still around. Yet they have been defeated. God has raised Jesus from the dead. In the end this loser takes all. The victory has been won!

In Our Place

With this essay I will respond to the critique of the doctrine of the atonement as it appears in the essay by Joanne Carlson Brown and Rebecca Parker entitled "For God So Loved the World?" (hereafter: Brown/Parker). The essay appears in a collection entitled *Christianity, Patriarchy and Abuse: A Feminist Critique,*[1] and so wants to be considered a feminist critique of atonement doctrine. It has enjoyed considerable popularity in that role. The critique is essentially rather simple and can be identified in the opening words of the essay:

> Christianity has been a primary force in shaping our acceptance of abuse. The central image of Christ on the cross as the savior of the world communicates the message that suffering is redemptive. If the best person who ever lived gave his life for others, then, to be of value we should likewise sacrifice ourselves. Any sense that we have a right to care for our own needs is in conflict with being a faithful follower of Jesus. Our suffering for others will save the world. The message is complicated further by the theology that says Christ suffered in obedience to the Father's will. Divine child abuse is paraded as salvific and the child who suffers "without even raising a voice" is lauded as the hope of the world. Those whose lives have been deeply shaped by the Chris-

---

1. Ed. Joanne Carlson Brown and Carole R. Bohn (New York: Pilgrim Press, 1989), pp. 1-29.

tian tradition feel that self-sacrifice and obedience are not only virtues but the definition of a faithful identity. The promise of resurrection persuades us to endure pain, humiliation, and violation of our sacred rights to self-determination, wholeness, and freedom. Throughout the Scriptures is the idea that Jesus died for our sins. Did he? Is there not another way for sins to be forgiven?[2]

The basic thesis seems to be that the center of the Christian faith, the fact of the suffering and dying Jesus, is tantamount to a glorifying of suffering as such, and suggests an ethical model that "upholds actions and attitudes that accept, glorify, and even encourage suffering,"[3] leading to victimization and oppression, especially of women.

There are at least two dimensions to this argument that we will find helpful to distinguish for the purposes of our discussion. In the first place, there is a theological critique of the doctrine or doctrines of the atonement as such. Such critique is for the most part gender neutral and can be, indeed has been, made by men as well as women. In the second place, there is the claim that the very idea of a suffering and dying savior glorifies and encourages suffering, and that this legitimates and perpetuates victimization and oppression of women both in church and society. I will separate these two dimensions because I think I am more qualified to speak about the first than the second. However, there will be something to say about that second dimension if we begin with the theological critique first.

Hermeneutics of Moral Tropology

In the main, I agree with many critiques of the traditional doctrines of the atonement in Brown/Parker. I would want to dispute some of the details of interpretation of the various doctrines, but essentially, on a theological level, I find the critiques appropriate. I have made many of them myself beginning over thirty years ago now, culminating in the locus on "The Work of Christ" in *Christian Dogmatics*.[4] Brown/Parker punctuate with dramatic force what I have insisted on all along from a theological point of

2. Brown and Bohn, p. 2.
3. Brown and Bohn, p. 4.
4. Ed. Carl Braaten and Robert Jenson (Philadelphia: Fortress, 1984).

view: atonement theories as such do not actually dispel or end the fact that we live under wrath. As a matter of fact, they often intensify the sense of the wrath of God. The chief culprits here have been those theories that understand the death of Jesus as the "vicarious satisfaction" of what humans owe to God for their transgressions. The result is that on the one hand, God is pictured as a vindictive tyrant demanding his pound of flesh before he can be merciful and that we, on the other, must believe this kind of transaction if we wish to be saved. Such a view does imply, to say the least, that suffering is necessary to pay this debt and is therefore redemptive. The theory assumes a kind of built-in law of distributive justice that has to be satisfied. But wrath is surely thereby intensified because the mercy of God is eclipsed. Such a picture of God indeed repulses and alienates.

There are, however, some parts of Brown/Parker's critique of vicarious satisfaction with which I have difficulty. The idea that God's demand of Jesus' sacrifice is a case of "divine child abuse" is something of a stretch, more the sort of theological comment one would might expect from the Frugal Gourmet. After all, Jesus was not exactly a child: 33 was something more like middle age in those days. Indeed, John's Gospel, precisely to forestall such thought, quite pointedly has Jesus say, "No one takes my life from me, I lay it down of my own accord." In the vicarious satisfaction view, Jesus' sacrifice had to be voluntary. Jesus freely gave what he did not have to give. Only so could it be vicarious.

Also, Brown/Parker's understanding and critique of the place of blood in the vicarious satisfaction theory depends too much on a chain of inferences from ritual studies to carry the weight they want to put on it. Ritual studies, we are informed, have revealed that various forms of ritual bloodletting are imitations, by members of a male cult, of women's bodily experience. Circumcision, in some cultures, is spoken of as "men's menstruation." Therefore, the notion of flowing blood has its roots in cultural efforts by men to take unto themselves power that properly belongs to women. Men's imitation of women's bodily power has likewise almost universally been accompanied by the subjugation of women. Ritual exclusion of menstruating women and women who have recently given birth is a sign that sacred imagery has been stolen.[5] Such is the chain of inferences. Conclusion: The religious imagery of the atonement is founded upon the robbery and subsequent defamation/degradation of women's experience.

5. Brown/Parker, p. 10.

The religious imagery of Jesus' blood carries an implied, silent devaluation of women. However, can such a chain of inferences from religion in general really carry this much weight? Anyone who has been around the business of ritual studies knows that they can be used to prove almost anything! It is a risky enterprise to slip so easily from one religion to another and poke around in the phenomenology of religion in general to establish a case.

But even though the vicarious satisfaction view tends to be the major culprit, Brown/Parker insist that *every* theory of the atonement commends suffering to the disciple. The basic "hermeneutic" they use throughout — and we shall have to come back to that — is that of *moral tropology:* Christ is always understood solely as example. The Christian, they aver, is to be like Jesus. One is to imitate Christ, and that means first and foremost that one must accept an obedient willingness to endure pain.[6] Hence, in their reading of the "Christus Victor" theory, the believer is persuaded to endure suffering as a prelude to new life.[7] Even the "moral influence" theory, according to Brown/Parker, "is founded on the belief that . . . only an innocent, suffering victim for whose suffering we are in some way responsible has the power to confront us with our guilt and move us to a new decision."[8] Now the problem with moral influence theory, of course, is that it too operates with the hermeneutics of moral tropology. Thus, it is a set-up for the feminist critique. Christ as moral example becomes a precedent for the victimization of suffering minorities, the poor, and especially women, because their suffering, like that of Christ's, is used in sermonic efforts to move the victimizers to repentance. Victims are fodder for someone else's edification.[9]

Thus, the conclusion to which the Brown/Parker essay comes is that Christianity is contoured by an abusive theology that glorifies suffering. "Is there any wonder that there is so much abuse in modern society," they ask, "when the predominant image or theology of the culture is of 'divine child abuse' — God the Father demanding and carrying out the suffering and death of his own son?" Parenthetically, one may wonder here how much cogency this charge can carry. It would rather seem that serious con-

6. Brown/Parker, p. 10.
7. Brown/Parker, p. 7.
8. Brown/Parker, p. 12.
9. Brown/Parker, p. 12.

sideration of the atonement has been on the wane for at least a century now. In Protestantism, at least, the central figure is a gentle Jesus, meek and mild, the savior of Christmas and incarnation, not Good Friday and Easter. The latter has virtually disappeared from Christian pulpits. Could it not just as well be that abuse is on the rise exactly because of the demise of the doctrine? At any rate, for Brown/Parker the upshot is that "if Christianity is to be liberating for the oppressed, it must itself be liberated from this theology." But that means for them that "We must do away with the atonement, this idea of a blood sin upon the whole human race which can be washed away only by the blood of the lamb. This bloodthirsty God is the God of patriarchy who at the moment controls the whole Judeo-Christian tradition."[10] So the question with which we are left is whether there can be anything remaining that could be called Christianity at all. If atonement is thrown out, what is left?

Exposing Latent Antinomianism

Now it is time to ask what is going on here. As I have already indicated, fundamental problems surface on the level of hermeneutics for Brown/Parker. There is an adamant insistence in the essay on reading the text of Jesus' death and resurrection through the lens of a strictly moral tropology. Jesus' suffering can only be taken ultimately as an example, whatsoever view of the atonement one espouses. The fact that Jesus suffers and dies for any reason whatever can only be translated into the universal truth that "suffering" is redemptive. That being the case, the only way to participate in it is to suffer. This is the way such a hermeneutic always works: *the particular and one-time event has to be turned into a universal, and the universal always comes home to roost as demand, moral example, law.* That can only have one result: a theology of the cross becomes a negative theology of glory. If you cannot make it by succeeding on the glory road, at least you can make it by suffering and failing. One turns suffering and dying into a way that we might traverse, as a project we can undertake.

Now the interesting thing about such a hermeneutical procedure is that it does a couple of things simultaneously. On the one hand, it can lead one to see where the problems and pitfalls are. Thus, the critique of the

10. Brown/Parker, p. 26.

doctrine of the atonement can be sharp and incisive, as is the case here. What was supposed to be a blessing has become a curse. Instead of atonement, we find alienation. The law, so to speak, exposes the mistake. Indeed, it is quite proper to say that if Christianity is to be liberating it must be liberated from such a theology. But the problem is that as long as one cannot break out of the confines of the hermeneutic of example and imitation, one simply finds oneself on a dead-end street. The hermeneutic affords no escape. As the Reformers would put it, *lex semper accusat!* The law always accuses. It closes all loopholes.

Given the hermeneutic, the only possibility left is the antinomian move. One is driven to attempt an escape from the accusing law. This can take at least two forms. On the one hand, if one wants to stay within the Christian orbit, one might try a more covert form of antinomianism. One might try to "save Jesus" either by ignoring or rejecting the cross, the suffering and the dying (many theologies, not only feminist, do that — which, we should remember, was the Gnostic solution!) or by reinterpreting the suffering and the dying so as to make it into an example more worthy of our emulation — Jesus suffered at the hands of unjust oppressors for the sake of life and liberation. Thus, Jesus is really on our side, or "they" did it. The final sections of Brown/Parker recite a number of such attempts. But either way the hermeneutic sticks. Whether one ignores the cross and suffering or tries to make it more amenable, one does not escape the law. One simply goes out of the frying pan into the fire. So on the other hand, those who honestly sense this are tempted to the more overt forms of antinomianism. They will try to throw off the whole thing altogether and simply leave the church. Now that may be psychologically liberating, at least for a time. Who of us has not entertained such a delightful prospect — at least occasionally? But, it is only in the New Jerusalem that there is no temple. Thus theologically speaking, antinomianism of that sort is pointless. It is, you might say, a kind of premature eschatology. Indeed, antinomianism is about the only heresy that is impossible to pull off. We might leave the church, but the law will go with us. You can count on that. Perhaps Johnny Cash's song "Sunday Mornin' Comin' Down" catches that as well as any theological statement.

> On a Sunday Mornin' sidewalk,
> I'm wishin' Lord that I was stoned.
> Cause there's somethin' 'bout a Sunday

That makes a body feel alone,
And there's nothin' short of dyin',
Half as lonesome as the sound
As the sleepin' city sidewalk
And Sunday mornin' comin' down.

That is why Luther could speak of antinomianism as a drama played in an empty theater.

One can hardly expect to escape the law by leaving the only place where one should have a chance, at least, to hear the gospel. The fact that the gospel may not be heard there is, of course, a tragedy. But it is a tragedy not only for women, but for us all. In any case, unless one can take the imitation, the moral tropology, one is driven toward antinomianism, and that is a dead-end street. We do not escape thereby, we only go out of the frying pan into the fire. Theologically, of course, this means that we only demonstrate that unless we are positioned to take the atonement more profoundly, we shall not, in fact, escape the wrath of God.

This is quite amply born out by the various attempts at reconstruction recorded at the end of the Brown/Parker essay. We do not have time to speak of them all, but perhaps Brown/Parker's own reconstruction can serve as an indication of the direction in which they would have us move. Thus they say

> We do not need to be saved by Jesus' death from some original sin. We need to be liberated from the oppression of racism, classism, and sexism, that is from patriarchy. If in that liberation process there is suffering it will be because people use their power to resist and oppose the human claim to passionate and free life. Those who seek redemption must dare to live their lives with passion in intimate, immediate love relationships with each other, remembering times when we were not slaves. Our adventure into freedom is empowered by rejecting and denying the abuse that is the foundation of the throne of sacrifice.[11]

Such is the basic vision and demand. This, for Brown/Parker, is what it would mean to be a Christian. All one can say, perhaps, is wow! Good luck! In spite of the attractive idealism, it is a rather tall order. Would it

---

11. Brown/Parker, p. 27.

not entail a lot of the voluntary self-sacrifice that the essay seemingly
wants to avoid? Do we not hear in this the law's voice sounding once
again in rather uncompromising tones? At any rate, Brown/Parker hold
that in order for Christianity to square with their vision it would have to
be revised so as to meet a number of conditions. The article concludes
with a list which, as might be expected, is a curious mix of the good and
the bad, now raising legitimate criticisms of traditional views of atonement, now sounding just like, if not worse than, old moral influence ca-
nards.[12] Christianity must be "at heart and essence justice, radical love,
and liberation." Those are fine things, of course, but is this a renewal of
the old nineteenth-century search for the essence of Christianity? What
happened to the gospel and salvation? Jesus, we are told, must be thought
of as one, but not the unique, manifestation of Immanuel, his life exem-
plifying justice, radical love, and liberation. Quite so, of course. If Jesus is
merely an example, he is not unique. One might even find better ones: St.
Francis or Mother Teresa, for instance. Further, they say, Jesus did not
choose the cross but rather chose to live a life in opposition to unjust and
oppressive cultures, refusing to change his course because of threat. Thus,
Jesus' death was an unjust act, done by humans who rejected his way of
life and sought to silence him through death. But the travesty is not redeemed by resurrection. There is, of course, truth in saying that Jesus was
crucified by humans to whom he was an offense. That is the whole point.
But the implication in such thinking always seems to be that had *we* been
there it would have turned out differently. We, of course, would not have
been offended. But it is always dangerous to be self-righteous before the
crucifixion. So as it stands Brown/Parker's proposal is largely a restatement, albeit in Feminist garb, of the favorite nineteenth-century theme
that Jesus was crucified by "them" because of his faithfulness to his calling. And that ended in the holocaust!?

There is also truth in Brown/Parker's assertion that Jesus was not an
acceptable sacrifice for the sins of the whole world because God does not
need to be appeased and demands not sacrifice but justice. But one can
hardly agree without further ado to the claim that this means no one was
saved by Jesus' death. It seems also somewhat strained to claim that suffering is never redemptive and cannot be redeemed. One might agree that
there is no general rule setting up suffering as the way to redemption, but

12. Brown/Parker; what follows here is taken from pages 27-28.

one ought perhaps to be cautious in the face of the biblical evidence about saying it is never so. The cross, we are told further, is the sign of tragedy, revealing God's grief there and in every time and place where life is thwarted by violence. "Every tragedy eternally remains and is eternally mourned. Eternally the murdered scream, Betrayal." Really? That does not sound to me like a very pleasant way to spend eternity! Must the *ressentiment* last forever? Is this not a greater indication of living under wrath than the claim that the cross is finally the end of it?

In sum, being Christian for Brown/Parker means passionate dedication to all these goals, to challenge unjust systems political and ecclesiastical, to refuse to be victims or give in to the threat of violence, suffering, and death. Fullness of life comes in moments of decision for such faithfulness and integrity. Resurrection is radical courage. It comes not in actually being raised from the dead, but in the heroic refusal to give in to the threat of death. Jesus "climbed out of the grave" not when he emerged from the tomb, but rather in the Garden of Gethsemane when he stood up to the soldiers and refused to abandon his commitment to the truth in the face of the threat of death by his enemies. The resurrection happens therefore before the crucifixion. The resurrected one was subsequently crucified on Good Friday. But that would mean, of course, that there is no Easter. The dying is an act of supreme heroism. And that is the end of the matter. Even the resurrection is moralized.

Christ as Sacramentum

Such is the picture. What shall we say to it? Can the Lutheran witness speak with authority and power to the bitterness and resentment embodied in this essay? First, the Lutheran witness will have nothing to say at all unless it is permitted to make the kind of critical analysis already begun in this essay. According to the Lutheran witness, the theologian's true business and art is to make the proper distinction between law and gospel. The purpose of that, of course, is precisely so that we may learn to speak the gospel. Now, Brown/Parker are pretty good in spelling out how gospel has turned to law in traditional atonement doctrine. However, the essay seems quite oblivious to the manner in which it turns around and does with a vengeance the very same thing it is complaining about. The heroism it commends to us may at first entice and encourage, but in the end it can only lead, as with all law, either to presumption and tyranny or despair. If that is not recognized at the outset, there is perhaps little more to say.

That said, we turn to the basic question raised by the essay, the matter of suffering. Is suffering redemptive? Does God need or demand it as propitiation for human sin before God can be merciful? Must Jesus therefore step in as our substitute to satisfy the debt we cannot pay? But there is an even deeper question: If all these questions would be answered with a yes, would that actually bring about atonement? Are we actually reconciled to God? The essay rightly presses these questions. But what it indicates is the desperate need for a theology that insists on a proclamation that actually delivers atonement, that puts a stop to the voice of the law and brings an actual end to the menace of the divine wrath that hangs over us. This is that with which the root of the Lutheran tradition, as found in Luther, is concerned. Christ is the end of the law and wrath. But the heart of this claim is that it is only through the crucified and risen Christ that law and wrath have an end. Only as we are in him are we saved. Christ is the end, not theology or task forces or even essays like Brown/Parker's.

How so? Because Christ suffers and dies for our sins and is raised for our justification. He can, ultimately, do nothing but die for us. Were he to do anything else, he would only add to the law's voice and increase wrath. As gospel, Christ could not come among us to be a new lawgiver, to blow the whistle on us and say, "Come on now folks, be nice! Stop sinning!" Or, in the fashion of Brown/Parker, "live passionate and free lives in intimate and immediate love relationships, fighting for justice, radical love and liberation in faithfulness and integrity." Were that Christ's aim, he would only add to human misery. That has all been said before. "The law indeed was given through Moses; grace and truth came through Jesus Christ." So he can come among the likes of us only to be obedient unto death. "He never said a mumblin' word," as the spiritual has it. It cannot be said that Jesus' real triumph, indeed resurrection, occurs in the Garden of Gethsemane in his refusal to abandon his commitment to the truth even though his enemies threatened him with death. It might appear that Peter who drew his sword would be a better model of what Brown/Parker advocate. Jesus, however, healed the severed ear of the enemy and told Peter to put up his sword. If such heroism were the name of the game, he says, my Father would send legions of angels and we would have a real donnybrook! But nothing new would come of that. There would be no atonement, only slaughter. There is no way but to suffer and die. Jesus did not come to set in motion some new idealism, some new political scheme or inspire some new heroism. Rather, he came to die for us, to die at our hands, and so to save us.

Now what does this tell us about God? Does God need the death of Jesus? One must be careful here because the use of language in the atonement doctrine gets very subtle. God does not need or demand Jesus' death so as to be able to "change his mind" about us, to be moved from wrath to mercy. That is the mistaken assumption of at least some vicarious satisfaction theories. Rather, God sends Jesus because of his immutable resolve to have mercy, concretely *to do* the mercy that he is. Because God insists on having mercy even in and to a sinful world, he sends not another lawgiver but his only Son, the preacher of forgiveness. The Son, therefore, does "only what he sees the Father doing." He does mercy. God may be said to "need" the death of Jesus only in the sense that solely through Jesus can he actually *do* who he *is*. The death and resurrection of Jesus, therefore, ends the wrath of God in the creation of faith. Christ is the end of the law to those of faith.

In contrast to Brown/Parker's view, the "original sin" of the human race is precisely that it does not believe in a merciful God but rather in its own ability to control its destiny under law. We live inexorably, therefore, under wrath — not because God is naturally vindictive but rather because we refuse his mercy in order to keep our control. Thus Luther could say that on the one hand there is terrible reality to the assertion that we are subject to the divine wrath. It is there. It is real. But on the other hand, Luther would also say that the belief that God is wrathful as such is the devil's delusion. But, if it is a demonic delusion, we are in big trouble. We think such delusions are intellectual mistakes we can correct. But the truth is, we cannot handle demonic delusions. For that, we need the one who casts out demons. So we are back again to the cross. There the prince of this world is cast out. The death and resurrection of Jesus is the only way the wrath ends. Without that death and resurrection and its proclamation to us, the wrath simply goes on forever.

What does this say about the question of suffering? Does Christianity glorify suffering so that it would be fair to say that it is an inherently abusive religion? We have already seen that kind of move rests on questionable hermeneutical assumptions. One reads the fact that Jesus suffered to mean that suffering in general is supposed to be redemptive and so is to be imitated as a way. One moves from the particular verb "suffered" to the more abstract verbal noun "suffering." Christ's suffering is thus taken as an example. But precisely this kind of move is radically challenged by the Lutheran tradition. In the first place, Luther always followed the Augustinian rule that Jesus should never be taken as an example *(exemplum)* unless he is first received as a sacrament *(sacramentum)*. In the second place, the hermeneutic is wrong. Luther moved from morality to faith in his understanding of tropology and this was one of the foundation stones of his Reformation. Ebeling has summed this up by saying that for Luther, Christ tropologically understood is not *imitatio* but faith. Christ comes, then, not to be imitated but simply believed.

Third and most importantly, this all adds up to a radically different perception of our relationship to Christ. This is designated by Luther under the title of the "happy exchange." If the tradition is to speak with authority and power to the problems at hand, we shall have to reclaim this vital teaching. In his once for all and therefore inimitable suffering and death, he takes our place and gives us his. Once again, the language is subtle — so one must beware. That Christ takes our place is to be understood in a quite active sense. He invades the house of the "strong man armed." In the first instance, he takes our place away from us. He takes it like a conqueror takes a city. He will not let us have the place we have tried to claim. As it was said in the tradition, he *dies* in our place. The place of death is, so to speak, "used up." So he takes it from us. We cannot enter it anymore. St. Paul said: you *have* died. But in so doing Christ gives us his place. This is not merely substitution.[13] It is a happy exchange. Nobody likes to be substituted for. Someone replaces you and leaves you sitting on the bench grumbling that you can do it just as well if not better. So you are always trying to take your place back in one way or another — even if it kills you. That is an important feature of the Brown/Parker essay. They rightly reject substitutionary atonement but are then fated to doing it all over again themselves. They want the place back again. The fact is that we cannot just decide to throw off the hermeneutic of morality. We have to be delivered.

---

13. There is a subtle distinction here between "instead of us" and "in our stead" or "place." In the German it is the distinction between *statt Unser* and *an Unser Statt.* "Instead of us" implies substitution, replacement, as when a substitute replaces a player in a game. The one replaced is left without a place, so to speak, and can only try to get back in the game, claiming, perhaps, to be a better player than the substitute. "In our place" especially when taken with the idea of the "Happy Exchange" has the sense of exchanging a dismal and hopeless place for a joyous and hopeful one.

The demon has to be exorcized. That is what atonement is about. That Christ has died in our place means that he has literally done this. "We know that Christ, being raised from the dead, will never die again; death no longer has dominion over him" (Rom. 6:9). He has drunk the cup to the dregs. So now there is no place for us to be but in him. And that, certainly, is a happy state of affairs, is it not?

Is suffering redemptive? There is certainly no rule to say it is. If there were, it would only be a new law, a new way. We are not promised, however, a life free from suffering for the time being. Indeed, we are led to expect that anyone who sets out on the journey of faith in the gospel can expect to suffer. But as Luther always insisted, suffering may, indeed will, come, but is not to be sought. It is not a new way, a "negative theology of glory." Not the law, but Christ, crucified and risen, is the redeemer, the one who takes our place and gives us his.

Just one concluding thought: Since he comes among us and is killed by us, it is not possible or appropriate to speak about these matters as though it were a matter of "us against them." Whenever the moral tropology is at work, that is exactly what seems to happen. Jesus was crucified by "them," the "enemies," the ones who don't agree with "us." That seems to mean that had we been there, it would all have come out differently. That supposition is one of the greatest and most persistent and pernicious errors in atonement doctrine. If there is a source of *abuse* or misuse, that is it! We have to face the fact that it would not have come out differently, and that we all are implicated in our own way. So to raise a final question that is implied by this discussion: Can Jesus save women? No, he cannot. But then, he cannot save men either. Because he came, you see, to save the world. To save us all. He is no idolatrous, mimetic reflection of our ideals or power. Rather, he took our place — completely. He came that it might now be proclaimed: "There is neither Jew nor Greek, there is neither slave nor free, there is neither male nor female; for all of you are one in Christ Jesus" (Gal. 3:28). That is to say that either we shall be saved *together* or not at all.

Forensic Justification and the Christian Life: Triumph or Tragedy?

For at least a hundred and fifty years the doctrine of justification has been under attack from "within." Of course, it has always been under a certain amount of attack "from without," either from the world of "cultured despisers" or from Christian communions that do not find it so central to their perception of the Christian message. But it is perhaps somewhat surprising to discover that attacks from within Protestant, even Lutheran theological ranks, are hardly a novelty. Usually we are led to believe that it is only *Der Mensch von heute* who has gotten up the gumption to ask such "radical" questions. Karl Holl dates the beginning of such polemic contemporaneously with the rise of the so-called *religionsgeschichtliche Schule*. Paul de Lagarde summed up the resistance in 1873 when in opposition to Ritschl's attempt to revive the doctrine he wrote:

> The doctrine of justification is not the gospel, but a Pauline invention, born out of Paul's Jewish spirit. Even in Paul it is not the only or the most profound form of solving the question of a person's relationship to guilt. Nor is it the fundamental principle of the Reformation and today in the Protestant Churches is dead. And that with perfect right. Because the doctrines of justification and atonement are mythologoumena valid only for those who seriously acknowledge the ancient church's doctrine of the Trinity, which today is true of no one.[1]

1. Quoted in Karl Holl, "Sammlung Gemeinverständlicher Vorträge und Schriften aus dem Gebiet der Theologie und Religionsgeschichte," chapter in *Rechtfertigungslehre im*

The 1963 Declaration of the Fourth Assembly of the Lutheran World Federation in Helsinki hardly marked much of an advance over de Lagarde when it pronounced that "*Der mensch von heute* no longer asks: How do I find a gracious God? He inquires more radically, more elementarily, he inquires after God *schlechthin:* where are you God?"[2] As Ernst Wolf once remarked, that kind of thing had already been said around 1910 and 1920 when there was much less knowledge of what Luther was talking of than there is today and which Karl Barth had rightly characterized as "one of the most superficial phrases of our time." Nevertheless, Wolf continues, "it remains the expression of a profound ignorance of Luther in his radicality as well as a serious miscalculation of the 'radicality' of the man of today." For:

> Man is at all times fated to inquire after God, but the question about a God gracious to me is the only legitimate form of this question. If one inquires about God apart from the question of grace then the question comes to naught. For if the word "God" is to be meaningful and not merely a cipher for a world view it must disclose my relationship to God; it must at the same time be able to declare to me how the human being as human being is established by God.[3]

But if the doctrine of justification as such has not fared well in recent years, the doctrine of *forensic* justification has fared even less well. Here the attacks are at least as old as the doctrine itself, beginning with Osiander and continuing in various ways until the present. The ambivalence within Lutheranism in the attitude towards forensic justification has meant that seldom have Lutherans come to a clear or unified understanding of it or its significance for the Christian life.

It is not within the scope of this paper to conduct an apology for justification in general nor for forensic justification in particular. Rather, my task is to explicate as clearly as possible what forensic justification means according to the Lutheran tradition and what role it plays — or should

---

Licht der Geschichte des Protestantismus, 2nd ed. (Tübingen: J. C. B. Mohr [Paul Siebeck], 1922), p. 1.

2. Erwin Wilkens, ed., *Helsinki 1963* (Berlin & Hamburg: Lutherisches Verlagshaus, 1964), p. 456.

3. Ernst Wolf, "Luther — Mein Herr," chapter in *Motive des Glaubens,* ed. J. Lehmann, "Stundenbücher," vol. 93 (Hamburg: Furche Verlag, 1968), pp. 99f.

play — in the Christian life. In doing that I shall attempt to assess its origins in Luther and to explore some of the highways and byways leading from this seemingly troublesome doctrine. The thesis of the paper is that justification as it stems from Luther and as handed on in the tradition is "forensic" in character and must retain that character if one is to remain true to the tradition (though one might perhaps quibble with the term). Furthermore, however — and this is also part of the thesis, such "forensic" justification as one finds in Luther proposes a radical reorientation in the understanding of the Christian life which has not been appreciated by the tradition. The difficulties within the tradition, it will be maintained, have arisen because of the attempt to retain the forensic justification without the radical reorientation. The result has been confusion, if not paralysis, in attempting to relate justification to life.

Definitions

Forensic justification is here taken to mean that justification comes to the sinner from without by the judgment of God, by his "imputation," his "reckoning." It comes from the divine "forum," the divine "tribunal." As *actus forensis*, a purely "legal" judgment made solely on the part of God and his "reckoning" in the light of Christ, it is to be distinguished from an *actus physicus*, a judgment made on the basis of or entailing some physical, moral, ontological, psychological, or otherwise empirically verifiable endowment in the creature. To my knowledge, Luther himself never used the term "forensic" as such, but of course repeatedly speaks of "imputation" as the divine act through which righteousness comes to the sinner and does on occasion speak of the divine "tribunal."[4] It was Melanchthon, I believe, who first gave the term "official" currency when he spoke of "forensic usage" in the *Apology:* ". . . to justify signifies, according to forensic usage, to acquit a guilty one and declare him righteous, but on account of the righteousness of another, namely, Christ, which righteousness of another is communicated to us by faith."[5] From these beginnings, the concept devel-

---

4. WA 34 II, 140, 6. Elert notes, "But before the tribunal of God *(Dei Tribunal),* where He Himself is the Judge, where no judge, executioner or jailer sits, it happens that He is merciful and compassionate to sinners. Before Him no saints carry weight, but only sinners. . . ." See *The Structure of Lutheranism,* trans. Walter A. Hansen (St. Louis: Concordia, 1962), p. 105.

5. *Concordia Triglotta,* ed. F. Bente (St. Louis: Concordia, 1921), pp. 206-7.

oped into the *actus forensis* of the later dogmaticians. Heinrich Schmid sums up the view of the orthodox fathers thus:

> The effect of faith is justification; [1] by which is to be understood that act of God by which He removes the sentence of condemnation, to which man is exposed in consequence of his sins, releases him from his guilt, and ascribes to him the merit of Christ. Br (574): "Justification denotes that act by which the sinner, who is responsible for guilt and liable to punishment *(reus culpae et poenae)*, but who believes in Christ, is pronounced just by God the judge." [2] This act occurs at the instant in which the merit of Christ is appropriated by faith, [3] and can properly be designated a forensic or judicial act, since God in it, as if in a civil court pronounces a judgment upon man, which assigns to him an entirely different position, and entirely different rights. [4] By justification we are, therefore, by no means to understand a moral condition existing in man, or a moral change which he has experienced, but only a judgment pronounced upon man, by which his relation to God is reversed, [5] and indeed in such a manner, that a man can now consider himself one whose sins are blotted out, who is no longer responsible for them before God, who, on the other hand, appears before God as accepted and righteous, in whom God finds nothing more to punish, with whom He has no longer any occasion to be displeased.
>
> Through this act of justification emanating from God we receive, 1. REMISSION OF SINS. . . . 2. THE IMPUTATION OF THE RIGHTEOUSNESS OF CHRIST. . . .[6]

One can sense from Schmid's summation something of the beauty and precision of the father's views, but perhaps also something of the anxiety attendant on holding such views. The view is stated boldly, but they are anxious to protect such forensic justification from any "contamination" by a "moral condition" or a "moral change" in one so justified.

---

6. Heinrich Schmid, *The Doctrinal Theology of the Evangelical Lutheran Church*, 3rd ed., trans. Charles Hay and Henry Jacobs (Minneapolis: Augsburg, 1961), pp. 424-25.

The Systematic Problem

Whence comes the anxiety in the orthodox view? No doubt because the very term justification implies a legal or moral process. It implies a standard, a law, according to which the justice in question is to be measured. Thus the term "justification" *(iustum facere)* in its common usage can only mean to "make just" according to such a standard. Justification would have to mean, therefore, some sort of movement from the state of being unjust to the state of being just, a movement from the state of sin or guilt to the state of righteousness. The misdeed or fault could not co-exist with the righteousness. The medieval tradition had, therefore, been more consistent when it described justification as a movement from a *terminus a quo* to a *terminus ad quem* comprising (a) the infusion of grace, (b) a movement of the free will toward God in faith, (c) a movement of the free will in recoil from sin, and (d) the remission of guilt. Such movement "could be called" justification or remission of sins because every movement takes its species from its end, the *terminus ad quem*. Even though the "movement" may be instantaneous temporally, it can be understood only as a movement, a change in the moral subject from sin to righteousness, effected by the infusion of grace.[7]

The inevitable result of such thinking in terms of movement, however, has meant that the dogmatic tradition has been plagued with a problem, especially when justification is identified with remission of sins. In its simplest form it may be put thus: If justification comes at the beginning of the "movement" or process, it is a legal fiction. If, however, it comes at the end of the movement, it is superfluous. If one has already made the "movement," one *is* just and need not be pronounced so. Thus, one finds oneself in a position where "forensic" justification seems to be at odds with the very scheme it presupposes, and this antinomy is raised to its zenith and betrays its anxiety when it feels called upon to insist that it cannot entail any "moral" change or progress. With this notation we move on to Luther.

---

7. Thomas Aquinas, *Summa Theologica*, 12ae, esp. Q. 113, Art 6. In *Nature and Grace*, ed. A. M. Fairweather, *Library of Christian Classics*, vol. 11 (Philadelphia: Westminster, 1954), pp. 192-93.

Luther on Justification and the Christian Life
(simul iustus et peccator)

Luther's view of justification can be understood only as a complete break with the attempt to view it as a "movement" according to a given standard or law, either natural or revealed. For Luther the divine imputation meant a shattering of all such schemes. It does not come either at the beginning or end of a "movement." Rather, it establishes an entirely new situation. The fact that righteousness comes by imputation only, thus creating faith, means that it is absolutely not a movement on our part, either with or without the aid of grace. We can be candidates for such righteousness only *if* we are completely sinners. That means of necessity for Luther that in place of all schemes of movement from sin to righteousness, we must put the absolute simultaneity of sin and righteousness: imputed righteousness as a divine judgment brings with it the *simul iustus et peccator* as *total* states.

Thus already in his *Lectures on Romans* Luther finds no other way to understand Paul or the scriptures than in terms of the *simul*. Commenting on Romans 4:1-7, he maintains that the imputation of righteousness to Abraham and its connection with the forgiveness of sins can be understood only by propounding two theses:

(1) The saints are intrinsically always sinners, therefore they are always extrinsically justified; but the hypocrites are intrinsically always righteous, therefore they are extrinsically always sinners.

(2) God is wonderful in his saints (Ps. 68:35); to him they are at the same time righteous and unrighteous. And God is wonderful in the hypocrites; they are to him at the same time unrighteous and righteous.[8]

Luther leaves no doubt throughout the entire commentary that the most vital enemy of the righteousness of God is not so much the "godless sinner" as the "righteous" who thinks in terms of law and "intrinsic" moral progress. Such theologians think *ad modum Aristotelis* akin to Aristotle's *Ethics* where sinfulness and righteousness and the extent of their actualization are based on what a person does.[9] The gaining of righteousness can then only be real to the extent that sin is expelled. For such thinking, imputation could only be a legal fiction or "a manner of speaking" due to the

---

8. Luther, *Lectures on Romans*, trans. and ed. W. Pauck, *Library of Christian Classics*, vol. 15 (Philadelphia: Westminster, 1961), pp. 124-25.

9. Luther, *Lectures on Romans*, p. 28.

incompleteness of the process or "in view of its end." Against such thinking, Luther proposes a thinking *ad modum scripturae* in which the divine imputation is the creative reality which, by the fact of the imputation, unmasks the reality and totality of sin *at the same time*. It would make no sense for God to impute righteousness if we were already either partially or wholly righteous. It would make no sense for God to forgive sin if we were not actually sinners. Thus in order that "God may be justified when he speaks and true when he judges" the "human" way of speaking and judging *ad modum Aristotelis* must be rejected. Before the divine tribunal no saints but only sinners can stand![10] For Luther, "forensic" justification means a complete break with thinking in terms of schemes and processes — and necessarily so because the divine imputation is fully as opposed to human "righteousness" as it is to unrighteousness.

So, for Luther, the divine imputation makes us sinners at the same time as it declares us righteous. And Luther was insistent that these be understood as total states. But this requires a radical reorientation in thinking about the Christian life. If one persists in thinking in terms of a process, the *simul iustus et peccator* will of course turn to poison, perhaps at best a false comfort for lazy sinners. It becomes merely the word that no matter how hard we try, we have to settle for the fact that we will never completely make it because we are, after all, *simul iustus et peccator*. It becomes a counsel of last resort. But that would be to treat the *simul* as merely a rescue for the legal scheme in the face of failure — the way it has all too often been treated. Luther's insistence that the *simul* means two totalities is designed precisely to combat such thinking. The imputation of righteousness by God for the sake of Christ as a totality unmasks its opposite, i.e., all the schemes and pretensions of human righteousness, sin as a totality, and in that very fact attacks it. Sin as a total state can only be fought by faith in the total imputed righteousness. Anything other than that would lead only to hypocrisy or despair:

> The *simul* is not the equilibrium of two mutually limiting partial aspects but the battleground of two mutually exclusive totalities. It is not the case that a no-longer-entire sinner and a not-yet completely righ-

---

10. For an excellent recent treatment of this, see Leif Grane, *Modus Loquendi Theologicus: Luthers Kampf um die Erneurerung der Theologie* (1515-1518), trans. E. Groetzinger (Leiden: E. J. Brill, 1975).

teous one can be pasted together in a psychologically conceivable mixture; it is rather that real and complete righteousness stands over against real and total sin. . . . The Christian is not half-free and half-bound, but slave and free at once, not half-saint, but sinner and saint at once, not half-alive, but dead and alive at once, not mixture but gaping opposition of antitheses. . . .

Luther goes even further: that realm of judgment in which the situation of our being as sinner is so totally depotentiated, is nothing other than the Kingdom of the last things. In the final analysis it is this and the coming Aeon that stand opposed to each other in the *simul iustus ac peccator.* The person in Christ is the person of the new age. The judgment of God which proclaims this person as established over against the opposing earthly situation, is likewise the anticipatory proclamation of the new world. The faith which receives and grasps that new status in Christ is an eschatological event; it is ever and anew the step out of this world of the visible, tangible, given reality, the world in which the *totus peccator* is the reality, into the eschaton.[11]

It is precisely the divine imputation as total state that reveals the totality of sin, and it is only in the faith that accepts both that the true battle of the Christian life is joined. For the battle is not merely against sin as "moral" fault, but also against sin as "spiritual" fault, as "intrinsic" righteousness and hypocrisy. Only faith in the imputed righteousness of God is truly equipped to do battle here. Thus the understanding of the Christian life undergoes radical transformation.

Luther and the Question of "Progress" in Sanctification

What then becomes of sanctification? The *simul iustus ac peccator,* as total states, would seem to militate against any talk of "progress" in sanctification. And as Joest points out, there are indeed many utterances of Luther that would substantiate just that.[12] Sanctification is simply included in jus-

---

11. Wilfried Joest, *Gesetz und Freiheit,* 2nd ed. (Göttingen: Vandenhoeck and Ruprecht, 1956), pp. 58-59. In my opinion Joest's book is the best Luther study on this issue. Cited hereafter as Joest, *Gesetz und Freiheit.*

12. Joest, *Gesetz und Freiheit,* pp. 60ff.

tification since it is a total state. Sanctification is simply to believe the divine imputation and with it the *totus peccator*. For where can there be more sanctification than where God is revered as the only Holy One? But God can be revered as the Holy One only where the sinner, the real sinner, stands still at the place where God enters the scene. That is the place where the sinner must realize that his or her own way is at an end. Only those who stand still, who know that they are sinners and that Christ is for them, only they give God the glory. Only they are "sanctified."

From this viewpoint, the way of the sinner in sanctification, if it is a "movement" at all, a *transitus,* is a *transitus* from nothing to all, from that which one has and is in oneself to that which one has and is in Christ. Such *transitus* can never be a completed fact this side of the grave. Nor is it a continuous line that admits of degrees of approximation toward a goal. Rather, each moment can only be at once beginning and end, start and finish. In this regard, the Christian can never presume to have reached a certain "stage" in sanctification, supposedly surpassed or left behind for good, which then forms the basis for the next "stage." The Christian who believes the divine *imputatio* is always at a new beginning. *"Proficere, hoc est semper a novo incipere."*[13]

By the same token, however, this means that the Christian never has an endless process of "sanctification" ahead that must be traversed to arrive. Whoever has the imputed righteousness may know that he or she *has* arrived. But such a one would know also, of course, that this is not a goal he or she has attained, but ever one that is granted anew for the sake of Christ. In such a view, the life of the Christian in *transitus* is not, as Joest says, a continuous or steady progress, but rather an "oscillation" in which beginning and end are always equally near. In attempting to "diagram" it Joest presents it thus:[14]

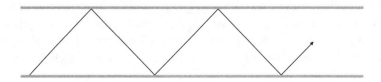

13. WA LVI, 486, 7ff. Quoted in Joest, *Gesetz und Freiheit*, p. 62.
14. WA LVI, 486, 7ff.

The bottom line represents the person *quoad in se (totus peccator)*. The top line represents the person *quoad in Christo (totus iustus)*. The zigzag line represents the *transitus*.

But this is apparently only one aspect of the picture. In many instances Luther does speak of a kind of progress, indeed, even of the Christian as one who is *partim iustus, partim peccator*.[15] He speaks of faith as beginning, but not yet the whole. Faith is not a perfect fulfillment of the law, but only the beginning of fulfillment. Indeed, what is still lacking will not be imputed for Christ's sake. Thus here the imperfection of our actual fulfillment of the law stands under the protective mantle of non-imputation. In such instances Luther speaks of faith in the imputed righteousness as the first fruits of the Spirit *(primitias spiritus)* which is not yet the whole. Such faith is the beginning because it is the beginning of the actual hatred of sin and its expulsion and the doing of good works. In faith, the law is fulfilled imputatively but thereafter is to be fulfilled expurgatively, for when the Spirit is given one begins *ex animo*, from the heart to hate all those things that offend the Spirit. Indeed, one begins to hate not only the things, but also to hate one's very self as sinner *(odium sui)* and to hope and long for the day when such will no longer be the case. Indeed, Luther can say that we are to do good works in order finally to become externally righteous and that it is not enough to have sins remitted by grace but that they are to be totally abolished eventually.[16]

What have we here? Has Luther contradicted himself? Has he gone back on everything said about the imputed righteousness as necessarily bringing with it the *simul* as total states? Some would say that in the heat of later battles with antinomianism and in disappointment with the moral laziness of the Reformation movement Luther, like Melanchthon, changed his tune somewhat. But the puzzling thing is that statements of this sort are present from the very beginning precisely in those passages where Luther has just propounded the *simul*! So others, looking at passages of that sort in the *Lectures on Romans*, opine that they are instances where he has not yet rid himself of remnants of medieval Augustinian *humilitas* piety! Without entering into the complexities of the debate spawned by such

15. WA 39 I, 542, 5ff. *"Lex promiscue docenda est tam piis, quam impiis, quia pii partim iusti sunt, partim paccatores."* Quoted in Joest, *Gesetz und Freiheit*, p. 65.

16. WA 40 II, 351, 27ff. *"Deinde operam dare debemus, ut etiam externe iusti sumus. . . . Peccatum per gratiam remissum non satis est. . . . Vellemus igitur non solum peccatum remitti, sed totum aboleri."* Quoted in Joest, *Gesetz und Freiheit*, p. 69.

opinions, it would seem safer to assume that because such material appears both early and late it belongs to the abiding substance of Luther's theology.

But how is one to interpret it? Does it mean that a notion of progress actually displaces all that has been said about "forensic" or imputed righteousness, the *simul,* and the *semper incipere?* This question is of course vital, so perhaps we should look more closely at a passage where such talk occurs precisely in the context of talk about the *simul.* Here we can do no better than to return to the *Lectures on Romans* itself and the discussion on Romans 4:1-7 where the *simul* was set forth. After setting forth the theses on the *simul* referred to above, Luther moves immediately to a discussion about concupiscence. He castigates the scholastic theologians for thinking *ad modum Aristotelis* that concupiscence is actually removed by something they call "grace." He says that he was entirely led astray by this "because I did not know that though forgiveness is indeed real, sin is not taken away except in hope, i.e., that it is in the process of being taken away by the gift of grace which starts this removal, so that it is only not reckoned as sin." And he goes on to say a bit later:

> Yet this concupiscence is always in us; therefore, the love of God is never in us, except in so far as grace has given us a beginning of it. We have the love of God only in so far as the rest of concupiscence, which still must be cured and by virtue of which we do not yet "love God with our whole heart" (Luke 10:27), is by mercy not reckoned as sin. We shall love God only at the end, when it will all be taken away and the perfect love of God will be given to those who believe and who with perseverance always yearn for it and seek it.[17]

What Luther seems to be saying is that thinking *ad modum Aristotelis* leads to an entirely false notion of human sanctification and progress. Then the notion of progress that it presupposes always remains intact. The only argument consequently can be about what one can accomplish according to such a scheme either with or without something called "infused grace." When, in order to exalt the supposed power of such "grace," it is asserted that concupiscence is actually taken away, it only succeeds in reaching the height of abstraction and nonsense. "Grace" is more or less a theo-

17. Luther, *Lectures on Romans,* pp. 128-29.

logical abstraction added to make the scheme "Christian." "Grace" becomes what Robert Jenson at one time aptly dubbed "the anti-Pelagian codicil" to the already existing scheme of what human powers are in fact supposed to accomplish.[18] But that is all the pious sublimation of natural desire, the "sanctified" self-centeredness that Luther knew all too well did not lead to actual love of God with the whole heart, but only to focus on the self and its concerns. It leads only to hypocrisy or despair. Faith born of the imputation of total righteousness, however, will see the truth of the human condition, the reality and totality of human sin; it will see that concupiscence indeed remains and that it is sin, but that God nevertheless does business with sinners. Such faith will see the fantastic magnitude of the divine act and actually begin, at least, to love God from the heart, to hate sin, and to hope for that righteousness which it knows full well it can never attain by any human powers either with or without what the Scholastics called "grace." Such faith makes a "beginning" precisely by believing the imputation of God which goes so contrary to all empirical evidence, and will cry to God "out of the depths," "wretched man that I am, who will deliver me," and actually "hunger and thirst after righteousness."

One must note carefully that when Luther speaks in this vein he is talking about actual affections: love, hope, and hatred of sin and "the body of death," not about theological abstractions. The radical nature of the divine imputation which sets the *totus iustus* against the *totus peccator* kindles the first beginnings of actual hope and love for God and his righteousness whereas before there had been only hypocrisy or despair. There is, I think, for Luther no contradiction between the *simul* and the *partim* once the divine imputation has blasted all thinking *ad modum Aristotelis* "out of the saddle."

But what sort of "progress" is here envisaged? Could it mean, perhaps, that the *transitus* in the life of the Christian is no longer simply a repeated "oscillation" between two extremes, and that under the impulse of the imputed righteousness one actually does begin to "improve" so that "non-imputation" covers what one has yet to accomplish? Could it mean perhaps that one does not have constantly to return to "point zero," and the *semper incipere*? Could the admonition, "become what you already are," find here its rightful home? Could one say that there is a certain

---

18. Eric W. Gritsch and Robert W. Jenson, *Lutheranism: The Theological Movement and Its Confessional Writings* (Philadelphia: Fortress, 1976), pp. 39ff.

"growth" of the sort where one would have a set of accomplishments behind one that provide a basis for the next step? Does one attain to a certain approximation of the goal?

Much as such a scheme might suggest itself by the language Luther uses, it does not apparently do justice to the full complexity of his thought. For such a scheme would suggest that progressive sanctification would mean progressive emancipation from the divine imputation. The more one progresses, the less grace one would need. *Iustitia imputativa* would be merely the starting point that one leaves progressively behind until it recedes into the background as an abstraction, perhaps even as a "legal fiction" compared to the "real" progress according to the scheme.

This, of course, cannot be. It would be a serious mistaking of Luther's intention that would be in danger of losing the whole thing. For Luther, the *iustitia imputativa* is not a mere beginning point that can be allowed to recede into the background. It is the perpetual fountain, the constant power of whatever *iustitia formalis* we may acquire. To look upon it as a stage that could be left behind or as something that we gradually would need less would be to deny it altogether. What this entails is that we cannot understand what Luther means by progress in "sanctification" unless all ordinary human perceptions of progress are completely reversed, stood on their head so to speak. The progress Luther has in mind is not our movement towards the goal, but the goal's movement in upon us. This has already been indicated in the idea that imputed righteousness is eschatological in character, and that a battle is joined in which the *totus iustus* moves against the *totus peccator*. The "progress" is therefore the coming of the kingdom of God among us. That is why for Luther "complete" sanctification is not the goal, but the *source* of all good works. *The way is not from the partial to the whole, but always from the whole to the partial.* "Good works do not make a man good, but a good man does good works." The *iustitia imputativa* is thus not a "legal fiction" without real dynamic, but a power, indeed, the "power of God unto salvation" that attacks sin as a total state and will eventually reduce it to nothing. It is always as a whole that it attacks its opposite in the form of both despair and hypocrisy. Good works are not "building blocks" in the "progress" of the Christian, they are fruits of the whole, the "good tree."

The "expulsion" of sin for Luther is thus quite the opposite of a morally conceivable process of sanctification. In such a "process" the person remains more or less constant and only the "properties" are changed. One supposedly "puts off sin" as Luther sarcastically remarks as though one were peeling paint from a wall or taking heat from water.[19] The sanctification that comes from and is identical with the *iustitia imputativa* does not offer a new "paint job." It does not, as Luther put it, merely "take sin away" and leave the "moral" person intact. Rather, it takes the person, i.e., the heart, mind, soul, affections, away from sin. There is a death and a new life involved that proceeds according to no moral scheme.

> Human righteousness . . . seeks first of all to remove and to change the sins and to keep man intact; this is why it is not righteousness but hypocrisy. Hence as long as there is life in man and as long as he is not taken by renewing grace to be changed, no efforts of his can prevent him from being subject to sin and the law.[20]

Any view of sanctification as a progress in "partialities," a changing of "properties," a mere "removing of sins," would be nothing but hypocrisy. Sanctification comes always from the whole, the penetration of the divine imputation into time, and thus involves the death of the old. The "beginning" is the "first fruits" of the resurrection.[21]

> Where he [Luther] is concerned to describe sanctification, he very often grasps at formulations that stand the natural-rational picture exactly on its head. For our question the following is the result: the progress of the sanctified Christian life for Luther is unconditionally a procedure *sui generis*. It can be compared with no immanent moral movement, with no continuous psychological development in the realm of the identity of the ethical subject with itself. Furthermore: wherever that progress takes place — whether in the beginning or farther on — it always happens as a whole. If it takes place extensively only in little steps, or in isolated actions against particular sins, intensively the whole is always there, the total crisis, the entire transformation of the person, death and becoming new is wholly present. . . . The expulsion of sin — which is really an expulsion of the person from sin — is therefore not a series of partial moments which follow upon and

19. Luther, *Lectures on Romans*, p. 194.
20. Luther, *Lectures on Romans*, p. 194.
21. Cf. Joest, *Gesetz und Freiheit*, p. 95.

expand the decisive turning or even prepare for it, but is the full turning itself which is always to be actualized anew.[22]

So, for Luther, the idea of progress must be stood on its head. The movement Luther speaks of is always a reversal of this-worldly conceptions. Sanctification comes from the whole and is always grasped as such. It comes from the *imputatio* which is the breaking in of the eschaton in our time.

> Just as the resurrection of Christ and with it the coming of the last things is not to be empirically measured, so also the progress in the life of the Christian cannot be psychologically measured. But just as certainly as the resurrection of Jesus Christ has really happened, and with it the coming of the Kingdom of God is real, so also is the progress a real one.[23]

Joest suggests that if one were to attempt to diagram such "progress" (which he realizes is difficult and questionable) it would have to look like this:[24]

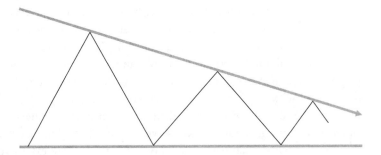

The way does not lead from below, the *totus peccator* line, upwards. Rather, the upper line symbolizing the totality of the righteousness imputed to faith descends toward the lower reality. The difference and opposition between the *totus peccator* and the *totus iustus* is not increasingly overcome from below, but rather from above, from the totality of grace. But the

22. Joest, *Gesetz und Freiheit,* p. 93.
23. Joest, *Gesetz und Freiheit,* p. 98.
24. Joest, *Gesetz und Freiheit,* p. 98.

"movement" does lead and strive towards fulfillment when by the power of the coming reality the *totus peccator* shall finally die and by grace alone be turned completely to love the God who gave it. *Then* we shall love as we are loved.

Some Reflections on the Subsequent Fate of Luther's Views

It seems virtually indisputable now that Luther's radical reversal was either not very well understood or else largely rejected by subsequent generations. The imputed righteousness indeed was accepted and became the talisman of the movement bearing his name in the form of "forensic" justification, but the radical reversal was not. We need not tarry here to ask where or why. Were his views too impractical for the young movement? Too subtle? Too radical to be grasped and made workable? Perhaps. At any rate, it seems that what happened largely was that Luther's followers for the most part did what he said could not be done: they attempted to mix the *iustitia imputativa* with thinking *ad modum Aristotelis*. What resulted, as Hans J. Iwand points out, was a theology that always carries within itself a profound inner contradiction.[25] Such a situation cannot, of course, produce very salutary results. Either the one or the other — the *iustitia imputativa* or the thinking *ad modum Aristotelis* will have to give way. History has, of course, largely relieved us of the necessity of speculation as to which.

It seems quite consequent, therefore, that virtually the first serious internal dispute should be about the place of law in the "system." Agricola, rightly sensing the impossibility of combining Luther's views with the place accorded to law by Melanchthon, tried to solve the problem by positing a temporal end to law. But this was a failure to grasp the eschatological nature of the *imputatio* and thus he also earned Luther's wrath. But the general result of such battles seems only to have been the solidification of the conception of human progress according to law as the "systematic" backbone of the "orthodox" scheme.

Once that occurs, however, the *iustitia imputativa* must be antiseptically removed from all contamination by the "progress" in sanctification.

---

25. Hans J. Iwand, *"Um den Rechten Glauben,"* in *Gesammelte Aufsätze,* ed. K. G. Steck (Munich: Chr. Kaiser Verlag), pp. 17ff.

It must become absolutely "forensic." Justification and sanctification must be stringently separated while at the same time one tries to insist that the latter must (may? will?) necessarily follow the former. But it becomes difficult to say exactly why. One lands willy-nilly back in the same systematic problem noted at the outset. Either the forensic justification makes the process unnecessary, or the process makes the justification a "legal fiction," a mere "anti-Pelagian codicil." So it is not strange that dispute should break out over whether "good works" were "necessary" or even "injurious" to salvation. When the eschatological reversal in Luther's views is forestalled by thinking in terms of immanent moral progress, justification threatens to become mere justification of the *status quo* so one must come down hard on the "necessity" of good works. But then the dynamic is lost. The "spontaneity," the *hilaritas* of faith, is nipped in the bud.

One lonely soul, Osiander, tried to remedy matters by attacking forensic justification itself. But the only tools he could come up with to do that were apparently carry-overs from mysticism: the indwelling of the divinity of Christ in the soul. He too failed to locate the neuralgic point and threatened only to make matters worse. Thus forensic justification became entrenched as the "objective" basis for faith, because of the merits of Christ, to be "subjectively" appropriated.

The increasing isolation of forensic justification as an "objective" fact could only mean that Lutheran divines were faced with the question of mediation all over again. Some way would have to be found to make the subjective appropriation of the objective fact conceivable as an *ordo*. One would have to provide, so to speak, a theological "shuttle service" between the objective and the subjective. The *propter Christum et per fidem* became a succession, a *reihenfolge* with the *propter Christum* the objective fact and the *per fidem* the subjective appropriation. As Wilhelm Dantine put it,

> the merit of Christ waits before the closed door of the heart like an immovable object, even though it carries in it the entire salvation of mankind. Only some action from within the heart can open the door and permit the salvation treasure to enter the existence of man. Even if one seriously takes into account the fact that faith was correctly evaluated as a gift of the Holy Spirit, did it not nevertheless lead to an understanding of faith as an independent means, and, finally, as the merit of pious inwardness? . . . One can also diminish the merit of Christ by appealing to the Holy Spirit, especially if one reduces this merit to a

dead, heavenly "thing" no longer capable of action as Lutheran Orthodoxy has already done. . . . This so-called objective fact of salvation thus really forms only something like a common foundation. It represents a basis on which the so-called subjective fact is only then able to begin the really decisive action. It almost seems as if God had to be reconciled anew through faith.[26]

The split between the subjective and the objective could only mean that the theologians would have to busy themselves with the question of "order," issuing finally in the so-called *ordo salutis*. The first steps were taken already by Melanchthon with the *notitia, assensus, fiducia* scheme where one moves from knowledge of the objective fact, through assent and finally to trust.[27] But such beginnings seem virtually to demand further refinement. How does "assent" and "trust" come about? How is it conceivable as an *ordo?* Apparently under the impulse of such questions the later dogmaticians (Calovius and following) developed the idea of the *ordo salutis* involving such things as the call *(vocatio)*, illumination, conversion and regeneration, mystical union and renovation. In doing this, according to Schmid, they

> seek to collect under one general topic, all that is to be said concerning what God or more accurately the Holy Ghost, does, in order to induce fallen man to accept of salvation through Christ, and what takes place in order to bring about the designed change in man.[28]

Even Schmid, whose love for the orthodox fathers is evident, is constrained to remark that "the introduction of an independent development of these conceptions led to an arrangement of the entire doctrine which we cannot call a happy one."[29] Among other things, it led to the fact that a fundamental distinction was made in Dogmatics between "the means of salvation on the part of God" (Word and Sacraments) and "the means of salvation on the part of man" (faith and good works), which means, again in Schmid's

26. Wilhelm Dantine, *Justification of the Ungodly*, trans. Eric and Ruth Gritsch (Saint Louis: Concordia, 1969), pp. 32-33.

27. Cf. Jaroslav Pelikan, "The Origins of the Subject-Object Antithesis in Lutheran Theology," *Concordia Theological Monthly* 21 (1950): 94-104.

28. Schmid, *Doctrinal Theology*, p. 407.

29. Schmid, *Doctrinal Theology*, p. 408.

words, that "we meet with especially this difficulty, that the full discussion is delayed so long."[30]

The attempt analytically to describe an *ordo salutis* was, of course, a tricky task, and the dogmaticians could not at all agree on the proper "order." But the net result of the endeavor seems only to have been that forensic justification eventually tended to get lost in the dogmatic woods. As Dantine puts it:

> its limitation to the territory of applied grace took increasing effect . . . and perhaps one will even have to conclude that here the old truth has again proved itself, according to which the greatest radiance is always followed by the deepest misery. . . .
>
> A contributing factor to this decline was, without a doubt, the particular development of the *ordo salutis* . . . into the scheme of which justification was squeezed as into a bed of Procrustes, there to lose its essential center and strength. . . . The Spirit, in Himself free and sovereign, was transformed into a front-rank man at attention, as it were, and the only consolation about this iron chain of interlinked divine operations was now that almost every dogmatician had a different notion of which order or march the living God should follow. At least a little freedom was left for the Holy Ghost, albeit only through the disunity of the dogmaticians! Later, a more and more penetrating interest in the proceedings and occurrences in the human realm was all that was needed to make a chain of religious occurrences in the human soul out of acts of a Spirit squeezed into a human scheme. Finally the whole order of salvation was transformed into a human process of development.[31]

For the orthodox fathers the problem of discerning the *ordo* was of course a purely analytic task, and such *ordo* was to be conceived as "instantaneous" and not as a temporal succession. But after all, Aquinas had said the same about his doctrine of justification, so one is once again back at the starting point. Once the move was made the way was open to the temporalization and indeed psychologization of the *ordo*. And it is difficult to escape the judgment that this is what indeed happened in at least some

---

30. Schmid, *Doctrinal Theology*, p. 408.
31. Dantine, *Justification of the Ungodly*, pp. 24-25.

forms of Pietism. A "dead" orthodoxy could be vitalized only in the same way an "arid" scholasticism could be appropriated (by mysticism, for instance): turn it into a "way" with a certain series of "steps" in the religious "progress" of the individual "subject."

From a reading of the history of modern Protestant theology, it is apparent that therewith the fate of forensic justification as an "objective" fact is more or less sealed. A temporalized or psychologized *ordo salutis* is all too easily either rationalized as a "pure practical religion" shorn of all "objective" and "theoretical" elements (Kant), or magnified into a religion of "pious feeling" (Schleiermacher), or elongated in a *Heilsgeschichte* (von Hofmann) and finally universalized into a *Geistesgeschichte* (Hegel). I realize that such judgment is somewhat facile and unsubstantiated, but it cannot be gainsaid that such was the course Protestant theology actually took. In all of that, forensic justification could not but get lost.

Some Conclusions and Ruminations

Justification, if it is to mean anything at all according to the Lutheran tradition, must be forensic in character. Lutheran orthodoxy and indeed Pietism is not to be faulted for maintaining that. That was their finest moment. The fact that it survived in much of the "churchly" tradition in spite of the "academic" tradition has been the sole redeeming feature of the former tradition. The problem is not with forensic justification as such. The problem arises because the tradition has not always fully grasped the radical reversal that Luther himself saw in imputed righteousness, and this led to an increasing isolation of forensic justification from the nature of the Christian life. The result has been either a conception of the Christian life that is at odds with its theology or a theology at odds with the actual course of the Christian life — a highly "unstable" situation, to say the least. If today we are going to "rescue" the significance of forensic justification for the Christian life, this can be done only by recapturing the radical reversal Luther saw as entailed in that explosive doctrine. This can be done only if we can proclaim and teach the radical "down-to-earth" nature of the Christian life — a life lived under the power of the "imputed righteousness of Christ" as an eschatological reality breaking into our time, exposing and attacking the totality of sin.

133

No doubt this will require some adjustment in our thinking about the relationship of law to the Christian life. I have not said much about that and cannot enter into a full discussion so late in this paper. But a few remarks can be ventured. There is no doubt that imputed righteousness bears a dialectical relationship to law. Precisely because imputed righteousness is an absolute gift which is the "end" and *telos* of the law, it establishes the absolute demand of the law as its counterpart. When one settles for less than the imputed righteousness as a total gift, as an eschatological reality, or fails to treat that as the basis for all true sanctification, one will quite likely also make accommodations in the understanding of law. This is the true root of all forms of antinomianism, either overt or covert. The law will have to be adapted to fit one's more or less paltry ideas of human "progress" and possibility.

For Luther, it was precisely the radical doctrine of justification that made possible and established the radical view of the law and the insistence that the law must and will remain "on account of sin" until the final end of the sinner and the appearance of the new being. This was the reason for his objection to Agricola's antinomianism. Antinomianism in one form or another wants to "solve" the problem of law by removing or "changing" it. Luther's insistence was that the law cannot be removed or changed by any mere theoretical arrangement. Rather, the sinner must be changed, and that "change" is from death to life by the grace of God. The objection to a so-called "third use" of the law would be of the same sort. There are of course many problems — semantic and otherwise — surrounding that concept, and I do not wish to go into them here. But the difficulty I see in the light of this paper is that a "third use" of the law proposes an alteration in the doctrine of law to correspond with the view of the Christian life as "change" and immanent moral progress. Nor, if one is seriously to maintain the imputed righteousness as the eschatological power of the new life out of death, can one speak of a "temporal" change in which the Christian "uses" the law in a "third" way. For Luther the sinner must die and be made new; the law is not changed. There can be no accommodations or alterations until the law is fulfilled. The sinner as *totus peccator* is thus attacked by law unto death until the new being arises who actually loves that law, that will of God. Luther thus knows of only two possibilities *vis-à-vis* law as an expression of the will of God. It is either an "enemy" or a friend but never a more or less "neutral" guide. Which is to say that the will of God for us is either law in the full sense of that word or gospel in the full sense of that word but never a "third" something which is neither.[32]

The same interpretation would apply to the New Testament parenesis. It can hardly be maintained that the exhortations of the New Testament taken *"ad literam"* represent any degree of attenuation of the will of God or his "law." If anything, the "stakes" are raised precisely because of the gospel. We are even exhorted to arise from the dead! How can we do that? It cannot therefore be a happy development from a "Lutheran" perspective when the attempt is made to subsume both the "you must, in order that . . ." and the "you may, because . . ." as subspecies under the genus "law."[33] The exhortations are either bad news or good news between which our actual life as *simul iustus et peccator* "resonates" until that day when Christ shall be "all in all," but not something in between.

To be true to a view of the Christian life rooted in the forensic justification of God one must then arrive at a different understanding of the relationship between law and the Christian life. One cannot view the Christian life *ad modum Aristotelis* as an ascent into the rarified air of what the world calls "the spiritual." Rather, it must be viewed as a descent, an incarnation, into the world in service and love. Luther tried to do this with his formula *conscientia in evangelio, caro in lege*. This corresponds exactly to the Christian life as *simul iustus et peccator*. The "conscience" is ruled and captivated by the gospel, the imputed righteousness breaking in from God's eschatological judgment. The "flesh," the empirical life I live in this age, remains however, *in lege*. And that in a double sense. Both in the sense that the law attacks "the flesh" as inimical to the will of God, and also in the sense that under the impulse of the spontaneity and joy fostered by the gospel in the conscience, the empirical life I live in this age is to become the actual "incarnation," the fulfillment of the will of God. Because of the gos-

---

32. Cf. Joest, *Gesetz und Freiheit*, pp. 190ff. Note: those biblical exegetes who believe themselves to be doing the Old Testament a favor by making its view of law something akin to the "third use" would, I think, from Luther's point of view, be courting a covert antinomianism. Thinking to construct an apology for the Old Testament and the law they succeed only in robbing it of its majesty and power, its "office." Here also I believe, lies the key to Luther's view of the Old Testament. For him there was nothing finally pejorative in identifying the Old Testament "properly speaking" with majestic, indeed, terrifying "law." Only thus could it gain a status and "office" worthy of and pointing to its counterpart in the New.

33. Cf. Joest, *Gesetz und Freiheit*, p. 200.

pel in the conscience, the absolute gift of the imputed righteousness and sanctification coming from God's eschatological "destiny," the Christian is free so that the true battle can be joined "in the flesh." The "new being" in Christ is not, for Luther, a "mystical theologoumenon" without substance, but is to be incarnated in "down-to-earth" fashion in the concrete *vocatio* of the Christian. In this battle, the law of God can be seen ultimately not as an enemy or as a mere emasculated "guide," but as a true and loved friend. For one should make no mistake about it. The law of God is to be and will be fulfilled. Not, however, by our powers, not by an immanent natural human moral progress, but by the power of the imputed, yes, the forensic righteousness of God.

Luther's "Ethics"

Invited to present on Luther's ethics, I tried to beg off. My reputation (which I covet and guard zealously) among friend and foe is that I am weak on sanctification. When questioned about this, I respond that since I have to work so hard to get people to believe in justification, I have no time to bother with sanctification! However, those of us who are supposedly weak on sanctification seem to be working the hardest! Throughout my professional life, it seems, I have been followed by people who are determined to clean up the mess left by my adamant insistence on justification by faith alone. As a matter of fact, I was recently interrupted while lecturing and awarded a T-shirt announcing my weakness in this regard! So now, in good Pauline fashion, I can boast in — even celebrate — my weaknesses. But our host managed to disarm my protests, saying that my weakness in this regard was the very reason why he approached me for this topic. So here I am, about to put it all on public display!

A Word against Ethics

My assignment is to say something about Lutheran ethics. Is there such a thing or is it an oxymoron? Some would ask whether there is, for Lutherans, such a thing as Christian Ethics. Is not ethics what Luther called the left-hand rule of God and thus just ethics for everyone? In any case, any talk about something as broad and general as Lutheran ethics would be difficult. Lutherans, like others, tend to disagree when it comes to ethics. But, let us assume for the sake of convenience that an ethic could be called Lutheran to the extent that it gets its fundamental bearing and shape from the thought of Martin Luther. So this will be largely an essay on Luther's ethics.

However, such an essay cannot begin without recognizing certain facts. Put audaciously, perhaps even irresponsibly, one might announce that the problem is that Luther does not have any ethics! Of course, much will depend on what one means by ethics. But if one is to take account of Luther's relation to the enterprise that goes by the name, it is necessary first of all to experience something of the shock and jolt his appearance on the scene entails. We must not rush in too soon and try to justify Luther before the all-conquering and all-seeing eye of ethics. He would not like that. It has been characteristic of the modern world to seek to reduce everything to ethics. To be considered "relevant" all doctrine must be justified before the bar of ethics. When the ethical lion roars, who can but fear? Luther, you might say, was not so afraid. No doubt in the end he has great significance for the doing of ethics, but we must begin by recognizing that Luther was not interested in ethics. He was concerned first and foremost about the eternal salvation of lost sinners. And ethics, at least as he knew it, hindered more than helped in that concern. One is saved by faith, not by works — and dare we say it? — not by ethics!

One would have to look long and hard through the indices of *Luther's Works* for a positive mention of what we call ethics, or for that matter, morals. Short of an exhaustive search, it seems that most instances in which Luther mentions ethics are negative. But why? It is largely because of his contemporaries' understanding and use of Aristotle. Ethics, in those days, primarily meant Aristotle's ethics. But the problem was not merely Aristotle's ethics per se, but how Aristotle was used in medieval scholasticism. So Luther attacked Aristotle furiously in his first public disputation *Against Scholastic Theology* (1517), where we find him defending theses such as the following:

41. Virtually the entire Ethics of Aristotle is the worst enemy of grace. This in opposition to the Scholastics.
42. It is an error to maintain that Aristotle's statement concerning happiness (foelicitate) does not contradict Catholic doctrine. This in opposition to the doctrine on morals.

43. It is an error to say that no man can became a theologian without Aristotle. This in opposition to common opinion.
44. Indeed, no one can become a theologian unless he becomes one without Aristotle.
50. Briefly, the whole of Aristotle is to theology as darkness is to light. This in opposition to the Scholastics.[1]

To what was Luther objecting? He was objecting not just to Aristotle's ethics as such, but rather a way of thinking that, when imported into theology, becomes the backbone of the system. Ethics, you might say, becomes the way of salvation. Already in his *Lectures on Romans* (1515) Luther had put his finger on the basic problem. He called it thinking *ad modum Aristotelis,* thinking in the manner of Aristotle. In simplest terms, this means that ethics provides the structure of the system; it defines the goal and the way to felicity, the key to the human story. The basic idea is that we become just and good by doing the good, by acquiring skill, habits, and virtue, just as people become builders by building and musicians become adept by practicing. To this, Christianity adds the promise of grace, and the theological virtues of faith, hope, and charity. Grace provides the gas, so to speak, to make the machine work. Ethics offers the fundamental meaning and structure, and grace makes it work. When Luther announced that one cannot become a theologian unless one parts with Aristotle, he pointed to the deepest and most fundamental problem in any theological discussion of ethics. It is the question of basic presuppositions. In those days they would say it was a matter of the tropology, the fundamental story of human life, or as we might put it, the "moral of the story."

Now, as we have already indicated, the problem is not just in the Aristotelian system or jargon as such, but in a way of thinking. It is therefore entirely possible to think in the manner of Aristotle using biblical concepts. Translated into biblical terms it goes something like this: God's original covenant with his people is a covenant of law and works. The law is the way of salvation: the law holds out the possibility, and grace comes along as the power to realize it. Grace is therefore an addition. In the medieval scheme this was explicit. At the very outset (before the fall) grace was a *donum superadditum,* an added gift enabling Adam and Eve to live as God commanded. The gift was lost in the fall and so must be restored to make

---

1. LW 31:12.

the system work. So it could be held that grace does not destroy but perfects nature. This sort of thing, for Luther, was a thinking *ad modum Aristotelis,* a mode of thinking defined by ethics. It is the worst enemy of grace.

What is necessary, Luther insisted, was an entirely different mode of thinking, an *ad modum scripturae* (in the manner of scripture), a fundamental change of the story. As early as his *Lectures on Romans* he remarks that the biblical story of the exodus had been interpreted (tropologically) to mean the exodus from vice to virtue. Now, however, it must be interpreted as the exodus from virtue to the grace of God! Grace must be the story. It is grace that determines the relationship between God, the creature, creation, and its destiny. Grace is what God is all about. Grace is what God is up to. And a graced creation is what God aims to arrive at.

What one must do, therefore, if one is going to think in the manner of scripture is first to change the tropology of the story, to disentangle grace from ethics, to dissolve the unholy alliance so that grace can stand forth as absolutely prior, and ethics can then find its own proper sphere. What actually should happen, of course, is that grace should free ethics from the impossible role it has been assigned so that it too, can take up its rightful task. Ethics is not the way of salvation. It is not, to use Luther's favorite image, the tree. It is the fruit of the tree. But we have to save that for later.

First, we must be clear that this move to thinking "in the manner of scripture" is by no means a simple one. It can never be a purely academic matter, as though one simply adjusts one's thinking to a new discovery or theory. If it were just a matter of changing our mode of thinking, all we would need (no doubt!) would be a good course in ethics taught by a seductively engaging professor! Indeed, that is often exactly the most fatal mistake of ethics! Thinking in the manner of Aristotle is not, for Luther, just an intellectual mistake. It is, rather, the result of temptation, a demonic delusion. We tend to disregard such talk. A demonic delusion, we think, is a small matter. It is to be taken care of by another dose of intellectual enlightenment. But for Luther, at least, if we are suffering from a demonic delusion, we have got big problems: we do not have the resources to handle such problems! Demons cannot be explained away. They only come back in a different form. Demons can only be exorcised by one who is stronger.

The root problem is that the creation has fallen for the serpent's false promise, "You shall be as God, knowing good from evil." The temptation is to believe that ethics, the knowledge of good and evil, deifies us, enables us to take charge of our destiny. As Karl Barth put it in a view Luther would share, "There is a definite content to the promise: *Eritis sicut Deus,* and to the concealed invitation to man to become the master of his own destiny. What the serpent has in mind is the establishment of ethics."[2] We think in the manner of Aristotle because our temptations drive us to do so. One thinks, theologizes, or philosophizes in these matters as one must. If we are not grasped by grace, then of course we must have recourse to the law and use some sort of ethics as the arbiter of hope. We have no other choice.

This being the case, any discussion of what we today might want to call Luther's ethics must begin with a word against ethics. Only if we begin with such a warning against ethics can we proceed — it is to be hoped with some safety — to say something positive. We must, that is, be *saved from* ethics before we can be genuinely ethical. So in what follows we shall use the familiar double-edged statement from Luther's treatise on the *Freedom of the Christian* (1520) as a framework to develop something of what Luther has to contribute to the question of ethics: *good works do not make a person good, but a good person does good works.*[3]

The Tropology of Death and Resurrection

Good works do not make a person good. For Luther, that kind of statement indicates first of all the limit of ethics and law. Perhaps we might paraphrase it for our purposes here: ethical deeds do not make a person ethical. There is a limit fixed which is absolute. It is simply not possible for good works to make a person good. Now why is that? For Luther it is not by any means a self-evident judgment. It is, rather, a judgment that comes from being gotten at, indeed, slain by the unconditional grace of God. It comes from being grasped by something absolutely new. The closest analogue perhaps is that it is like falling in love, which offers a new look at everything! Suddenly you see that so-called deeds "of love" do not make a lover. Just so, all understandings of life in terms of law and ethics are limited and come up against their end in grace. "For Christ is the end of the

2. *Church Dogmatics* IV/1 (Edinburgh: T. & T. Clark), p. 448.
3. LW 31:361.

law so that there may be righteousness for everyone who believes" (Rom. 10:4). The grace story is quite different from the ethics story. What grace establishes is a spontaneous and joyful relationship of love and trust. We have a hard time even describing it. About the best we can say is that it is a sheer gift. The point is that the story behind everything is not that of ethics but of grace and faith. To be saved is not merely to do good works, but *to be graced*. God wants to be related to us as a God of grace.

But now it must be seen for our purposes here that such a relationship can be betrayed or broken in either of two ways. God, you might say, has two problems with us: on the one hand, our immorality and on the other, our morality. The most obvious way the grace relation is broken is by our immorality, our unethical behavior, our misdeeds, our waywardness. We are all usually quite well aware of that. We all see the wrong of it. We have, as the saying goes, "fallen from grace." Might we take steps to repair the damage via our ethics?

Our misdeeds, however, are not the real root of the problem. They are just what the tradition called actual sins. There is a much more serious problem, what the tradition called original sin. It is much more subtle and inevitably hidden from us. The relationship is broken by the presumption of our ethical behavior, our morality, our good deeds, our insistence on doing it ourselves. The relation is broken because these too turn us quite simply against grace. They do not fit the story. The almighty God desires simply to be known as the giver of the gift of absolute grace. To this we say no. We say rather that we intend to make it on our own, that grace is "too cheap." Then the relationship is destroyed just as surely as it was by our immorality. Jesus seemed to think so when he announced that he had not come to save the righteous, but sinners, and that the first shall be last and the last first. That is why Luther could pronounce so boldly that almost the whole of Aristotle's ethics was against grace, or announce so confidently to Erasmus that God simply was not interested in his do-gooders or practitioners of self-reformation. Of course, such folk may well be more beneficial for society, at least in the short haul. The works in question are indeed "good." We must not lose sight of that. They look good, and do good, and are, by and large, in their effects, good. As Luther put it, they are righteous *coram hominibus* (in the sight of humanity, the light of human concerns). But *coram deo* (in the sight of God, the light of salvation and the divine will), they do not actually make a person good.

Good works do not make a person good. There is an inherent limit to what law and ethics can do. The law, that is to say, is not a remedy for sin. We always tend to forget this. The law may restrain us from doing evil deeds. It may even induce us to do good deeds. It may hold the world together while it is waiting for the gospel. But it does not save us because it cannot cure sin. It cannot fix the broken relationship. For all the good it does, indeed, maybe even *in* the good it does, it only makes sin worse. So said Paul, and Luther followed him in this. In Luther's terms, the old serpent's temptation is the problem: knowing good from evil seduces us into thinking we can use the law as a remedy for sin. It is a terrible mistake. The devil does not care how good or how bad you are. He just wants to destroy the relationship and eradicate grace. So he is very interested in ethics. If he can get us to believe that in ethics and law we possess the remedy for sin he has got us. Wherever God builds a church, the devil builds a chapel.[4] But Paul, the apostle of grace, exposes the subterfuge. The law, he insists, could not stop sin. As a matter of fact, it came in precisely to expose sin and even to make it worse so it would be shown to be sinful beyond measure. But that permits an opening for grace, because where sin abounds, grace abounds all the more.

This is the absolutely shocking and entirely unethical conclusion to which the story comes. Law — shall we say ethics? — and grace confront one another in a battle to the end. When they are pitted against each other on the same plane they simply cancel each other out. The legalist, the ethicist in us, for whom all the hope we have invested in the ethical tropology and the story of our goodness, is mocked by this outrageous turn of events. Paul himself puts the protest on our lips: well then, if that's the way it is, shall we not sin all the more that grace may abound? That is as far as ethics can go. It attempts to defend itself by reducing grace to an absurdity. It assumes, of course, that the question will have to be answered — as it usually is, by some sort of retreat or compromise. Shall we sin all the more that grace may abound? Well, not exactly. Because, after all, there is still the law and ethics. . . . Paul, of course, will have none of it. He moves to an *entirely different* tropology, an entirely different story, the story of grace as it flows from what has happened in Jesus Christ. "Are we to continue in sin that grace may abound? By no means!" Not because the law is still in control or comes back in some other form, but because the Christ story, the story of the triumph of grace through the death and resurrection of Jesus,

4. Ps. 101, LW 13:159.

takes over. "How can we who died to sin go on living in it? Do you not know that all of us who have been baptized into Christ Jesus were baptized into his death? Therefore we have been buried with him by baptism into death, so that, just as Christ was raised from the dead by the glory of the Father, so we too might walk in newness of life" (Rom. 6:2-4). Now *that* is the remedy for sin! We cannot get rid of sin. There is no ethical cure for it. The grace story kills the old to raise up the new. Since it is a whole new tropology, one can hardly resist the continuation:

> For if we have been united with him in a death like his, we shall cer-tainly be united with him in a resurrection like his. We know that our old self was crucified with him so that the body of sin might be de-stroyed, and we might no longer be enslaved to sin. But if we have died with Christ, we believe that we shall also live with him. . . . We know that Christ, being raised from the dead, will never die again; death no longer has dominion over him. The death he died, he died to sin, once for all; but the life he lives, he lives to God. So you also must consider yourselves dead to sin and alive to God in Christ Jesus. (Rom. 6:5-11)

This is how grace works, how grace announces and realizes itself. To think *ad modum scripturae* is to learn to think in terms of this tropology, to as-sume that what is behind it all is this story. It is not just playing with words. It is the death of us. But it is also the life of us. For if we have died with him, shall we not also live in him?

Luther was grasped by this story and set out to reshape the theology of the church and the understanding of salvation as well as ethics in its light. It might be argued, of course, that Luther did not complete so monu-mental a task as fully as one could hope. But it cannot be emphasized strongly enough, that what is at work in Luther's reforming work is a dif-ferent tropology. The presupposition for understanding scripture and ap-plying it is precisely the destruction of the old self who lives by the ethical trope and the calling forth of the new self who lives by faith. Failure to un-derstand this will only result in Luther being endlessly called into account before the bar of ethics and usually found wanting. Ours is still an age in which the moral tropology persists. Everything, it seems, especially in the church, has to be justified before the bar of ethics. Scripture is not relevant unless there is some more or less immediate social or ethical payoff. Again, when the ethical lion roars, who can but fear? So Luther will be judged by his supposed ethical sins. Justification by faith alone will come under immediate suspicion. One does not need proof because, for the moralist, it is simply axiomatic that it will lead to moral laxity, quietism, and neglect of sanctification and social ethics. That is because moralism is simply opposed to grace. Thus we find it impossible to change the story. Even if we get an inkling of the new story, we have to turn about and make sure it will not do any harm by adding the ideas of sanctification, the "third use of the law," and so forth. From the perspective of the "third use," you may indeed be saved by grace, but then you have to get really serious and attend to your sanctification. The law may have ended as a coercive force or an accuser, but now it comes back in a third way. The devil's real playground is where Christians are. Hence, the law is said to be a "guide for the believer." The lion of the law may indeed have lost his teeth, but now you just get gummed to death! In other words, you may indeed have gotten saved without effort, but now comes payback time. There is no free lunch. Or as the contemporary favorite rejoinder has it, grace does not come cheap.

So the old story comes back again. We just cannot seem to shake it. For Luther, of course, that was not surprising. For it is the serpent's story. It is our temptation. We cannot just change our minds about it, turn it off, or discard it like an old pair of shoes. We have to be saved from it. We have to die to it. Paul said it in winding up his argument in Galatians against Peter's backsliding vis-à-vis the law: "For through the law I died to the law, so that I might live to God." Or even more radically, "I have been crucified with Christ, and it is no longer I who live, but it is Christ who lives in me. And the life I now live in the flesh I live by faith in the Son of God, who loved me and gave himself for me" (Gal. 2:19-20). I can be saved from the serpent's story, you see, only when the Jesus story becomes my story. The grace story cannot be put in second place or shoved aside. So St. Paul concludes, "I do not nullify the grace of God; for if justification comes through the law, then Christ died for nothing" (Gal. 2:21).

Creation as the Arena of Ethical Action

A good person does good works. Now, after we have begun with a word against ethics, we can now turn to see what Luther claims positively for ethics. Here we can turn to the second half of his saying from the *Freedom of the Christian* (1520): a good person does good works. For Luther, this means that before there can be works that are truly good, there must be a good person. Even though a work may look good, and do good on a human scale *(coram hominibus)*, it cannot be considered good in the ultimate sense *(coram deo)* unless it is the work of a good person. If you feed the poor, that is indeed good. But if you do it to enhance your own status, you are just using the poor for your own benefit. Such work is not good ultimately. The biblical image Luther used tirelessly is that of the good tree bearing good fruit. The good tree cannot do anything but bear good fruit. It is natural and spontaneous. In other words, for Luther, the saved will do truly good works. That is, because one is saved, one can leave the question of self-enhancement both before humans and God behind, enter freely into the world, and do the good that appears good to do. One will feed the poor not to enhance oneself, but because it is a good thing to do for them. One will feed the poor to fill their bellies, not to gain salvation. So Jesus said, "But, when you give alms, do not let your left hand know what your right hand is doing" (Matt. 6:3).

But if the good person doing good works means doing it for the other and not to enhance the self, that means an entirely different arena is opened up in which ethics might find its rightful place, the sphere and community of the neighbor. If the story of grace is disentangled from law and ethics, they no longer cancel each other out, but each can find its proper place. Luther's attempt to work this out has come to be known in more recent years as the doctrine of the "two kingdoms." Much maligned, misinterpreted, and misunderstood, the doctrine has become a kind of catch-all for every possible complaint from ethicists and moralists for supposedly divorcing law and gospel, politics and faith, ethics and religion. Most of these complaints, however, may be legitimately directed at nineteenth-century misinterpretations rather than at Luther. So we need not go into that here, but will instead concentrate on understanding what Luther did say.

For our purposes, we can best proceed by saying that for Luther God has two plans of action for defeating the power of the devil, "two regiments," two ways of asserting his rule. The first and the ultimate plan is grace, the gospel, the unconditional gift of the Kingdom. To defeat the devil takes grace and leads to salvation. The second could be called a temporary backup plan, the law, or for our purposes, we could perhaps call it ethics. We need to look at these two modes of rule carefully because there is so much confusion about them.

First of all, we must remember that for Luther the enemy is the devil and all his works and ways. What Luther has to say on matters related to ethics is flattened out into rather dull business and ultimately distorted if you take the devil out of the picture. Most misunderstandings of the two-kingdoms idea stem from the fact that the kingdom of Satan is left out of the account. The kingdom of this world is then looked upon as a separate secular kingdom all by itself over against the religious kingdom. It is a static and dull picture. In reality, for Luther, it is better to say there are three kingdoms. The kingdom of God and the kingdom of Satan are locked in desperate battle over the kingdom of this world. Such a picture delivers something of the dynamic involved. The battle is treacherous. The devil, as we have already seen, is a very crafty foe. For the devil uses our finest efforts, the law, our best ethics, to destroy us, to cut off the relation to God, and drive us to despair, tyranny, or even death. So first and foremost we must be saved by God's grace alone. We cannot fight the devil. If our finest efforts are of no avail, what can we do? Whether we are good or bad we will only lose. As an old legend has it, if we take the sword to cut the devil in two, we only succeed in making two more of them. Occasionally, you read tragic stories in the newspaper about people who set out to drive the devil out of their children by beating them, sometimes to death. And so, of course, he wins. He does not care whether you fight against him in pious zeal or even scientific secularity, or with him in evil fury. He does not even care whether you believe in him or not. Either way he wins. So we can be saved from the wiles of the devil only by faith alone, by grace alone. God does ultimate salvation all by himself. He has to. The story of salvation is the story of grace alone: no mixture with law or ethics allowed here. Grace alone makes a good person ready to do battle with the devil. That is God's first and ultimate plan for undoing the work of the devil. It is, as Luther said, God's right-handed work, God's proper work, what was in the beginning, is now, and ever shall be!

But now, of course, a kingdom of grace has got to be just that, one of sheer grace, benevolence, promise, gift. It cannot be a matter of force or coercion, but simply an act of ultimate liberation. We can be a part of it only by faith, by being grasped by its own inherent power. This is where the big problem appears. The ethicist in us is afraid of grace alone: quietism, laxity, etc. Shall we sin the more that grace may abound? Now it is true: grace is a risky business. One way or another it can and will kill you as the old Adam/Eve so that the new being of faith can be raised. Since grace is given absolutely by divine power alone and comes in its fruition only in God's good time, we are turned around and sent back into world. We are enlisted for the time being in the battle against the devil for God's creation. We must attend carefully here because this is the point at which many mistakes are made. The first one would be to conclude that because the kingdom of God comes by grace alone, there is nothing to do. The opposite is true. Since the kingdom of God comes by grace alone, we are turned about into the world. There is a new world, the creation of God, the world of the neighbor, the other, to take care of. But the distinction here must be absolute. The Kingdom comes absolutely by God's power and grace — *sola*. If there is even the slightest hint of a human contribution to the kingdom of God, the old being escapes into its pious pretentions, disappears into the "kingdom" behind the walls, its ersatz version of the Kingdom. The old being, that is, thinks to escape into some sort of "eschatological vestibule," like a church, perhaps, or a monastery, or a desert cave. For Luther, that is not allowed. There is, you might say, a big sign on the kingdom of God that says: "KEEP OUT! GOD ALONE AT WORK! COMING SOON! For the Time Being, Mind Your Own Business!" It is not the Christian's business to bring in the kingdom of God in any way, shape, or form! If you try to do that you end only by helping the devil destroy it. This is why there has to be an absolute distinction. There has to be something like a two-kingdoms doctrine. It is for the sake of the gospel, not merely for ethics.

For Luther, the Christian is called to serve God in the world God has created, and not self, not devil, not vice, not virtue, but the neighbor. This, of course, is Luther's much neglected doctrine of vocation. Since one is not called to bring in the kingdom of God, one is called for the time being to serve God in creation, in the various dimensions of daily life — family, church, state. The point in saying that one is to serve God is to oppose the devil. People who complain that Luther has no proper doctrine of good works and sanctification or ethics always seem to forget this understanding of the Christian's calling. Perhaps because it is so utterly realistic and unromantic. But virtually everything Luther wants to say about ethics comes back to his doctrine of vocation. One is to serve God in one's occupation, in one's concrete daily life and its duties in the world. When I tell students that this first of all means that they should pay attention to being better students, they are often a little disappointed. They had more romantic things in mind like leading some protest, manning the barricades, joining in some romantic crusade or "social action" commission that sits about and cranks out resolutions on matters such as sex, to send to the synod. It does not occur to them that their first ethical duty is to be good students! Whatever call there might be for more extreme action, it must be remembered that Luther's idea is that first and foremost one serves God by taking care of his creation.

And this new arena for ethical activity, now disclosed as creation, what Luther sometimes referred to as God's left-hand rule, can never be taken simply for granted. Here is where a second mistake is often made. In the usual two-kingdoms doctrine it is assumed that the left-hand kingdom is just there, that it is a given, something much more evident than the kingdom on the right, which can't be seen and thus is more problematic. But that is once again to forget the devil. The devil for Luther, as for the New Testament, is the "prince of this world." Thus the world we see is not, as such, unambiguously the world as God created it. That the world nevertheless is, in spite of its distortion by the devil, God's good creation is grounded in a faith that is granted by grace. It is because one is saved by grace that one believes in creation. Creation as a sphere of ethical action, an arena for Christian vocation, is not simply a given; it is rather a gift. The good person, the one saved, is given creation back again as sheer gift, an arena in which to do the good. This is illustrated by the apparently apocryphal story about Luther's reply to the question of what he would do if he knew the world was going to end the next day. The answer was that he would go out in his garden and plant a tree. The story is well known but the point is usually missed. Since the kingdom of God is coming, there is nothing one can do about that — it's too late for prayers, piety, repentance, or acts of religious sublimation. But one is turned back into the garden so that when the good Lord shows up one might be found doing what God intended: taking care of the creation. Incidentally, he said the same thing about his marriage. The religious sensibilities of all Europe were shocked when right in the middle of the worst upheavals in 1525, i.e., the peasant's revolt, the debate with Erasmus, and the Reformation hanging in the balance, Luther went and got married. What began at the church door ended in bed. But, unperturbed, Luther replied that he had done it because he thought it would make the angels laugh and the devils weep.

Luther was an "apocalyptiker." He thought indeed that the world was about to end. But the effect of that was just the opposite from the usual. He was not led to forsake the creation, as has recently occurred with a sect in Korea, but precisely to turn back into it all the more. So he said of his mar-

riage that when the good Lord comes he was determined to be found doing "what comes naturally," obeying the command to be fruitful and mul-
tiply, in spite of all the nonsense perpetrated by popes, princes, peasants,
and ethical pundits. All that nonsense, you see, was for Luther the work of
the devil, the prince of this world. When the complaint was raised that he
was putting the cause of the Reformation in jeopardy, his answer, in effect,
was that this was precisely the cause. A good person does good works.
Good works are works done freely and joyously for the neighbor, in and
for creation.

But such a view cannot be taken for granted. Even our age now ap-
plauds the return to creation, but not as an arena for "good works"! It can
be held by faith only in the face of great trial and temptation. Our great
temptation, the devil's seduction, is always to desert creation, to be as gods.
Creation is never good enough. We are always on our way somewhere else,
to an idealist heaven where there is no change or decay or flesh or sex or
children and all that, or to a utopia, to Solla Salloo, where they never have
troubles, or at least very few. Creation is our steppingstone, and (literally)
devil take the hindmost. Thus, Luther could say that belief in creation and
the creator God is the highest and perhaps most difficult article of faith.

> For without doubt the highest article of faith is that in which we say: I
> believe in God the Father, almighty creator of heaven and earth, and
> whoever rightly believes that is already helped and set right and
> brought back to that from which Adam fell. But those who came to the
> point of fully believing that he is the God who creates and makes all
> things are few, because such a person must be dead to all things, to
> good and evil, death and life, hell and heaven, and must confess from
> the heart that he can do nothing out of his own strength.[5]

Note once again how this is true only if the ethical tropology has been displaced by the tropology of grace, death, and life!

For Luther, creation is the arena for ethical action. But now, when
one enters into the calling in this world, of course, one soon encounters
harsh realities. The Creator's sovereignty is disputed all along the line. We
encounter that "unholy trinity": the devil, the world, the flesh. In the opti-
mum case, if we were all "good persons," we would do good works freely,

---

5. WA 24, 18, 26-33.

joyfully, spontaneously. True faith needs no law, no coercion, no prodding. As Luther put it in the well-known passage from the "Preface to Romans,"

> Faith . . . is a divine work in us which changes us and makes us to be born anew of God, John 1[:12-13]. It kills the old Adam and makes us altogether different men, in heart and spirit and mind and powers; and it brings with it the Holy Spirit. O it is a living, busy, active, mighty thing, this faith. It is impossible for it not to be doing good works incessantly. It does not ask whether good works are to be done, but before the question is asked, it has already done them, and is constantly doing them.[6]

Again the entire thing is premised on a radical change, in tropology!

Ethicists, you can imagine, would charge Luther and the Reformation with hopeless naïveté because of such ecstatic outbursts. It is significant, and an indication of how much they miss the point, that here, for once, Luther the professional pessimist is charged with being just too optimistic about human possibility! Ethicists usually find Luther either too pessimistic or too optimistic. That good works do not make a good person is too pessimistic for most; but that a good person does good works is too optimistic. The contradictory judgments are simply a sign that they do not understand Luther at all. So, two things must be said. First, these statements about spontaneity are indeed seriously meant. They are a statement of the ultimate hope, the end, the goal of the creature, faith in creation. They are the light at the end of the tunnel. If they are not true, then of course there is no salvation for us. We would then be doomed to ethics forever. Heaven itself — frightfully enough — would be something like a meeting of the ethics section of the American Academy of Religion! Luther did indeed believe that faith would arrive somewhere, that the truly good would be done joyously and spontaneously, and ethics would not be needed. That has to be the light at the end of the tunnel. Christ is the end of the law to those who have faith.

Second, Luther was not naïve about this. He knew full well that the Kingdom has not arrived yet, and that our lives are not so driven by grace and faith as they should and eventually will be. He knew better than most that the Creator's sovereignty was disputed for the time being. "For still

---

6. LW 35:20.

our ancient foe, doth seek to work us woe, strong mail of craft and power, he weareth in this hour; on earth is not his equal," as we have it in his hymn "A Mighty Fortress." So there must be, for the time being, a second form of divine rule, a left-hand rule, an alien work. This is why it is appropriate to call it God's backup plan. There is the rule of law. There are ethics. As long as they are limited to this age, to their proper time, these can be and are God's blessing, the instruments by which the creation can be preserved and cared for until the Kingdom comes and their time will be over. To put it most positively, the world is held in readiness by the law until the Kingdom comes.

Thus Luther spoke of the "proper uses" of the law. The concept of proper use is always crucial for Luther's theology, whether one is talking about either law or gospel. It is in the use that the Spirit dwells, not in the thing itself. It is commonly agreed that Luther spoke explicitly of only two uses of the law: the political use — perhaps we could call it the ethical use — and the theological use. Again, it is important to get the nuance here. Luther was talking about the way in which the Spirit uses the law. It was not, for him, an ethical theory, but analytical observation. It was simply a statement about the way the law actually works in our lives. Politically speaking out there in the world, for the time being, law preserves order and restrains evil. It tells you to stop; you stop. Of course, you may choose to run the stoplight, but then you have to take your chances with the police and the violations bureau. It could cost you. So it works, most often, by threat, coercion, power, social persuasion and/or often just shame, that all-conquering threat: What will the neighbors think? H. L. Mencken said conscience is the little voice inside us that tells us someone may be looking! But it can also work by persuasion, conditional promise, by a kind of seduction or bribery. You eat your spinach, you get your pudding. Okay? Okay! You do your work well, you get your bonus! So it works, politically, ethically.

But theologically speaking, it judges us, convicts of sin. It even says: "Where are you, Adam?" It will cause us to reflect on why we think our agenda is so all-fired important as to endanger the lives of others by running the stoplight. It will do that — especially if we actually do harm to someone. This, for Luther, is not theory. This is the way the law actually works. It can't save us. It doesn't increase our faith or improve our disposition. I do not know of anyone who really learns to like to stop gladly at stop signs. But it does preserve us (first use) and awaken us so we can be saved; it keeps the devil, the world, and the flesh from being the ruin of us. As long as the law is not misused as a way of salvation, it functions as God's backup plan for combating the devil. When one enters creation one serves God through the proper use of law.

One must be very careful here, however, because, as we have seen, the minute one uses the law as a means for salvation, it is the "devil's whore," and faith, in Luther's colorful language, "loses its virginity"! However, such misuse of the law or ethics is not limited to the religious or ecclesiastical realm. The devil will see to that. The state or the social order can and most often does make the same mistake. It can set up a particular ideology or political program as the means to political and social salvation: a "thousand-year Reich," a "classless society," or "making the world safe for democracy." The result is the same. The devil wins. The state, for instance, can use the law to see to it that there is no longer Jew or Greek. But we all know what happens then. Whenever the law is used ostensibly to save rather than to take care of creation, tyranny takes over and someone dies. Paul was not indulging in empty talk when he called it the dispensation of death. Once again: the Kingdom comes by grace alone. The distinction between grace and law must be absolute. Only when that is so is law — as Paul put it — "established."

That is why law must be limited to its two proper uses. Although the argument is more subtle and complicated than we can do justice to now, one should be able to see why it is perilous to accommodate Luther's view with a so-called "third use of the law" as a friendly guide for the reborn Christian. There is no way yet into a state where the Christian can use the law in a third way. Such a view rests on presuppositions entirely different from those of Luther and, for that matter, Paul. It makes too many pious assumptions. It assumes, apparently, that the law can really be domesticated so it can be used by us like a friendly pet. Does law actually work that way? It assumes that we are the users of the law. We do not use the law. The Spirit does. And we really have no control over it. Who knows when it is going to rise up and attack with all its fury? Luther knew full well, of course, that in spite of all his piety he could not bring the law to heel. Indeed, even as a Christian, one needs to hear and heed the law — and the law will attack a Christian just as it attacks the non-Christian. One does not have the key to some third use. We do not live in an eschatological vestibule. Christians need the law in the same way non-Christians do. The idea of a third use assumes that the law story simply continues after grace.

Grace is just a blip, an episode, on the basic continuum of the law. Luther's contention is that the law story is subordinate to the Jesus story. The law is for Luther, as it was for Paul, an episode in a larger story, not vice versa. It is only grace that can bring the law to heel.

Conclusion

So, to conclude, when one is looking for a positive use for law in life and ethics in Luther's thinking, one should look to his understanding of the first use of the law, the political or ethical use, as the means by which the wiles of Satan are to be held in check while we wait for the kingdom of God. It is one of the great misfortunes of contemporary ethical thinking that people seem to know practically nothing any longer of this understanding of the uses of the law. Even in church publications we see all sorts of nonsense about how the gospel is supposed to have something to say about our ethical dilemmas. And the gospel just becomes synonymous with sloppy permissiveness. So sweet Jesus schlock reigns. The gospel does not have anything to say directly about such dilemmas. We must look to the proper uses of the law, and particularly the first use. We have all we need there; we do not need a third use!

How then does one come to know this law? For Luther, the law is natural to humans. It is written on the heart. He was, it could be said, a kind of "natural law" ethicist. But he was a nominalist, not a realist. That is, Luther did not believe that natural law was just a mimetic copy or imitative reflection of eternal law. In Luther's day most people who theorized about natural law really meant supernatural law, a built-in eternal and unchangeable order to things. For Luther, law is natural in the sense that it was built into the creation, simply a statement of the minimal requirements of daily life, a faithful and practical consideration of what works and preserves human society against the wiles of the devil. Faith frees you to use your head in the battle. The natural law, in that sense, was for Luther "written on the heart." To be sure, such law may be obscured by the fall. But in any case, for Luther, we have a restatement of such natural law in the scriptures, preeminently in the laws of Moses. Luther assumed, it seems, that since the Creator and the author of the scriptures, the Spirit, are one, there should be no fundamental difference between natural law and the law found in scripture. The touchstone for Luther's understanding of what is natural is therefore not a theory of natural analogy, but rather the Holy Scripture and the doctrine of creation. One cannot trust unaided reason without qualification. But where law is understood within and limited by the story of salvation, there it is, so to speak, naturalized. Indeed, the command to love God and the neighbor with all one's heart was for Luther natural law, as was also the Sermon on the Mount. The law is simply a statement of what created life should naturally be. If we don't know what that is, due to our fallenness, we must search the scriptures.

So, for Luther, if one is looking for answers to the question what should we do, for the time being, we will not be directed to our own feelings, or the art of learning how to affirm ourselves or one another in our chosen lifestyle, or whatever it may be. One of the things Luther polemicized against most regularly was the idea of self-chosen works — be they ever so pious. Rather, one must look to the commandments of God. The commandments of God are not given to make us pious, Luther insisted, but to lead us into the world of the neighbor to take care of it as creation for the time being. In this regard, we must realize that the law was made for humanity, not humanity for the law. Even if it happens, as it often does in this twisted world, that one should have to break one commandment for the sake of another, Luther's counsel would be to sin boldly, but trust in the mercy of God all the more bravely! In other words, go ahead and plant a tree in the garden of hope!

UNECCLESIOLOGICAL ECUMENISM

The Meaning of *Satis Est*

Much of the beauty of the Augsburg Confession (hereafter: CA) consists in that it means just what it says. In the question before the house in this session it says:

> Our churches also teach that one holy church is to continue forever. The church is the assembly of saints in which the Gospel is taught purely and the sacraments are administered rightly. For the true unity of the church it is enough *(satis est)* to agree concerning the teaching of the Gospel and the administration of the sacraments. It is not necessary that human traditions or rites and ceremonies, instituted by men, should be alike everywhere. It is as Paul says, "One faith, one baptism, one God and Father of us all," etc. (Eph. 4:5, 6). (Art. 7, translated from the Latin version, *Book of Concord*, Tappert, 32)

That is the catholic claim of the CA. The meaning is quite plain, and has been so from the beginning of the Lutheran Reformation until now. The *satis est*, especially when taken together with the next sentence stating that it is not necessary that human traditions or rites and ceremonies, instituted by men, should be alike everywhere, is clearly a setting of limits. It states what constitutes the true unity of the church, and limits what can be required of any church in order to be included in that unity. The confession asserts boldly that enough is enough, and that nothing more can be required for the true unity of the church.

We do not need to guess what Article 7 means. The texts are in good shape. We have all the sources any historian could desire. We have the writings of Luther, Melanchthon, and others relevant to the subject. We have the documents used as sources for the CA and plenty of letters. We know the historical context. The churches of the Reformation were accused of schism, breaking the unity of the church, because they had proceeded without Roman or Imperial institutional approval in undertaking certain reforms, especially in the Saxon Visitations. The CA is their "apology," as they often referred to it, in which they turn back the charge of schism. Even though they have undertaken several necessary steps to reform the church, thus indeed interposing certain discontinuities in existing institutional forms (traditions, rites, ceremonies, instituted by men), they have not broken the true and spiritual unity of the church, the Reformers claimed, because they seek only to proclaim the gospel and administer the sacraments which call that true church into being and give it its unity.

But one should have no illusions about what a drastic step this was for any understanding of the church and social life. It meant a renovation in practically every facet of existence. Just a list of what the "traditions, rites, and ceremonies" devised by men included is enough to indicate that:

> mandatory fasting; auricular confession; the veneration of saints, relics, and images; the buying and selling of indulgences; pilgrimages and shrines; wakes and processions for the dead and dying; endowed masses in memory of the dead; the doctrine of purgatory; Latin Mass and liturgy; traditional ceremonies, festivals, and holidays; monasteries, nunneries, and mendicant orders; the sacramental status of marriage, extreme unction, confirmation, holy orders, and penance; clerical celibacy; clerical immunity from civil taxation and criminal jurisdiction; nonresident benefices; papal excommunication and interdict; canon law; papal and episcopal territorial government; and the traditional scholastic education of clergy.[1]

But if the meaning is quite clear, what is the problem? When questions arise about the meaning of something so clear, our suspicions ought to be aroused. All too often that indicates that a move is afoot to make it mean

---

1. Steven Ozment, *The Age of Reform 1250-1550* (New Haven: Yale University Press, 1980), p. 435.

something other than it has been taken to mean all along. That appears to me to be the case in the current argument over the *satis est*. As is usual in such instances, the question of context is appealed to as the warrant for making the history say something other than what it clearly intends to say. If we wish to get at the question of the meaning of the *satis est* today, I expect we shall have to attend to such argumentation. To use an older distinction which I don't generally espouse but which may be helpful in this instance, the argument about the meaning of the *satis est* is not so much, perhaps, about what it *meant*, but what it *means*. It is not so much, that is, about what it meant back there, though that is inevitably involved, but perhaps more about what it supposedly means for us today — or even what we would *like* it to mean! It is helpful to distinguish these two things particularly in arguments where one appeals to context. With that in mind, we proceed to the question: What is the meaning of *satis est*?

The standard argument these days is the argument from context. The situation now, so the argument goes, is so different that the *satis est* is supposed to function differently from the way it did back then. This sort of argument has lately been raised to the status of what one supposes is virtual infallibility since it has been accepted as part of the supporting rationale for the ELCA statement on ecumenism at the churchwide assembly.[2] Since this is the voice of authority, we shall treat it as a classic statement of the argument about what the *satis est* means. The historical situation, the voice of the ELCA informs us, is now different from what it was in Reformation days. Then, we are told, the *satis est* was proposed to preserve an existing unity. Now, however, it should function, if at all, apparently, to enable us to move from visible disunity to greater visible unity and "full communion."

Just how the *satis est* is supposed to do that is never very clearly spelled out. Instead we are served a series of statements about the *satis est* that hardly follow from one another and seem virtually contradictory if taken according to their implied meaning. "Today," we are informed, "the *satis est* provides an ecumenical resource to move to levels of fellowship among divided churches." True. But only if the *satis est* is taken as a concept limiting what can be imposed upon churches as institutional requirements for unity. But that clearly is not what the argument is supposed to mean. For the next sentences indicate that the ecumenism statement has something quite other in

2. References are to William G. Rusch, ed., *A Commentary on "Ecumenism": The Vision of the ELCA* (Minneapolis: Augsburg, 1990), pp. 28-29. Hereafter: *Ecumenism: ELCA.*

mind. It moves immediately to try to remove the limits. "Article VII," it announces, "for all its cohesiveness and precision does not present a complete doctrine of the church. It is not in the first instance an expression of a falsely understood ecumenical openness and freedom from church order, customs, and usages in the church." What are such sentences supposed to mean? Clearly the drift seems to be that since CA 7 does not present a complete doctrine of the church and cannot be taken as pointing to a "falsely understood ecumenical openness," i.e., freedom from church order, customs, and usages, then we are called upon now to complete the doctrine of the church and take on, for the sake of visible unity, the orders, customs, and usages that the confessors declared could not be required. Instead, that is, of being a limiting concept, the *satis est* is taken to be something of a minimal requirement for unity, to which a number of other things could freely be added. This, of course, opens up the possibility of accepting the orders, customs, and usages that others may find to be necessary.

But it is hard to see what the next sentences are to mean in this new context. The "primary meaning" of the *satis est*, we are informed next, "is that only those things that convey salvation, justification by grace through faith, are allowed to be signs and constitutive elements of the church." The sentence seems a kind of grudging admission in the midst of the attempts to open things up, that the *satis est* does impose limits which cannot be denied. It seems a contradiction to the argument to this point. Then there is a kind of gratuitous reference to the fact that, unlike the sixteenth century, we must recognize the missionary situation of the church today. Another context is heard from. What that is to mean for the *satis est*, we are not told. Does it mean that in the light of the missionary situation we should be prepared to "loosen up" on the claims of CA 7? If not, why are such statements here? But then the statement returns to the subject by saying, "Yet Article VII of the Augsburg Confession continues to be ecumenically freeing, because of its insistence that agreement in the Gospel suffices for Christian unity." This is taken as warrant for the ecumenical method of bypassing insistence on doctrinal or ecclesiastical uniformity and looking instead to consensus on the gospel. Laudable enough. But what provokes interest is that "yet" with which the paragraph begins. "Yet" CA 7 continues to be ecumenically freeing. Why so, "yet"? Is that a reference back to the fact that the argument for openness, which took the *satis est* to be a minimum to which other things could readily be added, ran into a snag in the fact that "only those things that convey salvation" are allowed to be signs and constitutive elements of the church? So is the *satis est* to be rescued, finally, by a condescending "yet"?

The attempt to answer the question of the meaning of the *satis est* by an appeal to context thus seems to end in confusion. If it is now to function to help restore a lost unity, one can never be quite certain whether it is an enemy or a friend, an open door or a roadblock. If this is the more or less official position of the ELCA, we are in trouble. We are left not knowing whether our confessional position is a bane or a blessing. One even hears of snide references these days from highly placed ecumenical leaders, about "*satis est* Lutherans." Like Luther's drunk on horseback, the interpretation of the *satis est* falls off on one side, only to climb back on and fall off on the other. It vacillates back and forth between what it meant and what it supposedly means with no apparent consistency, with the general result that one is quite puzzled as to what it does mean for us today. The argument from context is used, apparently, to demonstrate that it should function differently today, but one is honestly at a loss to divine what that different function is. Perhaps the truth is that the argument actually tries to render the *satis est* irrelevant so it can no longer be an obstacle to our designs.

In what follows, I shall try my hand at expounding the meaning of the *satis est*. To do so, however, one must be considerably more careful about the question of context and therefore with the distinction between what it meant and what it means. It is, of course, a truism to say that matters were different then from what they are now. But then one must try to specify very precisely what those differences are. To begin with, it is doubtful that CA 7 assumes and therefore is designed to preserve an existing visible unity. After all, the confessors were being charged with schism — with having broken the unity of the church. But furthermore, just a little reading around in the writings of Luther indicates that he, and Melanchthon as well, was quite aware of the many ruptures in the visible or physical unity of Christendom. The words of Luther's great confession which stand behind much of the CA bear eloquent testimony to that:

> This [one, holy, Christian Church on earth] exists not only in the realm of the Roman Church or pope, but in all the world, as the prophets foretold. . . . Thus this Christian Church is physically dispersed among pope, Turks, Persians, Tartars, but spiritually gathered in one gospel and faith, under one head, i.e., Jesus Christ. . . . In this

> Christian Church, wherever it exists, is to be found the forgiveness of sins, i.e., a kingdom of grace and of true pardon. (LW 37:367-68)

One can find many other statements of the same sort in Luther and other reformers.[3] True, the "physical" disunity they see may be somewhat different from that which obtains today. It was not so much a matter of denominations as the church dispersed among different peoples or nations.[4] But differences there were, in traditions, rites, and ceremonies, as they put it, "instituted by men." Therefore, the task they saw was not that of attempting to preserve an existing physical unity, since that, quite obviously, no longer existed — if it ever had. The task, rather, was that of coming to a deeper understanding of the unity of the church in the face of such physical difference and dispersion. Thus they sought to grasp the *true* unity of the church which persists through all of its physical manifestations. And this true unity of the church could be grasped only in the light of the gospel of justification by faith alone. That is to say, the church and its unity could itself be nothing other than an object of faith, not of sight. The "invisibility" or better, "hiddenness," of such unity was not, therefore, simply a counsel of last resort, a taking refuge in "spiritualization" when all else failed. It was rather a matter of principle. It would make no difference at all to CA 7 whether there were one physical church or several. The true unity would still be an object of faith and not sight. If the church and its unity is to be an object of that same faith that justifies, then it cannot be an object of sight. That was not a counsel of despair. It was part and parcel of the good news itself.

There is a fundamental divide here between the church viewed from the perspective of justification by faith and the perspective of justification

3. See, for instance, M. Luther, "On the Papacy at Rome," LW 39:55-104 and "The Private Mass and the Consecration of Priests," LW 38:138-214. It is significant that Luther's most ecumenical statements about the unity of all Christendom come in the writings against the papacy!

4. Nevertheless, denominationalism has its roots very early on in the Protestant movement. See the interesting essay by Winthrop Hudson, "Denominationalism as a Basis for Ecumenicity: A Seventeenth Century Conception," in *Church History* 24 (1955): 32-50. Hudson points out that seventeenth-century divines found warrant for denominationalism in Calvin. But perhaps they could have found even more direct warrant in Luther's writings against the claims of Rome. See note 3, above. Furthermore, as Hudson points out, denominationalism was not what split the church, but rather an ecumenical strategy to bring it together once again.

by grace-wrought works. Where justification is by works the church must realize and manifest itself by its works in the world. It has, basically, two options. Either it must seek to make the world over and thereby dominate it, via necessary ruling institutions, or it must retreat from the world to its own holy enclave. The genius of Rome, one might say, was that it did some of both — in the papacy and its claims on the one hand and monasticism on the other. To equate the true unity of the church with such visible manifestation was simply to invite and perpetuate tyranny, or, in theological terms, put the Antichrist on the throne.

Where justification is by faith alone, however, the true church is revealed only in acts that set us free from the tyranny of law, sin, and death. So its only visible marks in this world are acts of ultimate liberation, primarily the pure preaching of the gospel and the proper administration of the sacraments, but also, as Luther would sometimes say, in other manifestations of liberation, ministry, bearing the cross, suffering, prayer, and so forth. The true unity of the church is therefore brought about by such acts of liberation from sin, death, and the power of the devil because they call into being a *communio* of those who believe in and hope for the ultimate triumph of this as yet unseen and unseeable "church."

In this light, the *satis est* was not part of an attempt to preserve an already existing unity. It was rather part of an attempt to redefine the true unity of the church in consonance with the gospel of justification by faith. Thus the confessors maintained, in the face of all the apparent physical and visible disunity, that nevertheless the true unity of the church persists by faith alone. Their apology therefore was that they had not destroyed the true unity of the church, and indeed that they could not. Consequently they insisted that for the true unity of the church it is enough to agree on the proper preaching of the gospel and administration of the sacraments. That was a statement of the limit imposed by the nature of justification by faith itself. A line was drawn by the gospel. Whatever traditions, rites, and ceremonies one might propose in addition must take their place this side of the line as strictly of human provenance. The *forms* devised by men to safeguard and deliver the gospel may, and perhaps should, vary. It is enough to agree on the proper doing of it. Enough is enough. That, I believe, is what it *meant*. And one should not serve up contextual hash to obscure that. But that cannot be the end of the story. Just what it *means* for us is, of course, the last, and most difficult question. So we must turn to that question to conclude this exercise.

What does the *satis est* mean today? It goes practically without saying that the context today is different from that of the original text. Critical interpreters are right at least in that. However, as pointed out, the real difference is not to be found on the level of the unity or disunity of ecclesiastical institutions. The major differences we have to attend to are more in the realm of theology and metaphysics. This is hardly the place to go into an exhaustive discussion of such matters, but if one is to draw out the meaning of the *satis est* for today, some judgments of at least a preliminary and suggestive sort will have to be ventured.

Theologically the most important contextual reality for the understanding of the *satis est* as well as ecclesiology in general today is the challenging and breaking up of nineteenth-century liberal and romantic continuities by the recovery of biblical eschatology. To this, Lutherans must also add the recovery of Luther's theology, especially the theology of the cross.[5] It is clear that originally the *satis est* marked an attempt to draw a line in order to protect the very nature of the gospel. To carry this through, the reformers used various distinctions in their thinking about the church: visible versus invisible; physical versus spiritual; sometimes (but all too rarely) hidden versus revealed; and above all, divine versus human institution. These distinctions did not fare well in the eighteenth, nineteenth, and early twentieth centuries. In one way or another, the transcendent (invisible, spiritual, revealed, divine) was collapsed into the immanent (visible, physical, human, moral). A similar fate befell the understanding of the church in both Roman and Protestant camps. The result was what Ernst Wolf characterized as the romanticizing of the church.[6] The church was taken to be a visible reality (a *gemeinschaft*, i.e., a commonality made — *geschaffen* — by human activity) which once — prior to the Reformation — united Europe, but now, because of its physical disunity, fractures it. Such romanticizing spawns a kind of ideology of unity: If we could put the church back together again, and perhaps restore its magisterial integrity, people would return to it. This ideology of unity fires much of the ecumenical pathos in the church today.

---

5. It is well to remember that the phenomenon known as "Luther's Theology" is really pretty much a twentieth-century discovery. The theology of the cross was virtually unknown until W. Von Loewenich's book on it in 1929, which was not translated into English until 1976!

6. Ernst Wolf, "Sanctorum Communio. Erwägung zum Problem der Romantisierung des Kirchenbegriffs," *Peregrinatio* (Munich: Chr. Kaiser Verlag, 1954), pp. 279-301.

But even though the collapsing of the transcendent into the immanent has come under heavy fire in virtually every other theological locus,[7]
the doctrine of the church seems to have escaped. Romantic notions of the
church have persisted and now take the form of the drive for visible unity,
koinonia, "full communion" and such grand things. The upshot is that the
old distinctions used at the time of the Reformation to protect the gospel
come under heavy fire and are often relativized if not rejected outright.
Should one not ask whether this relativizing or rejecting is not of a piece
with the general slide of the churches into the sociological swamp so vehe-
mently decried elsewhere?

The question before the house, therefore, is whether the *satis est* is to
be taken still today in some fashion as a part of our call to faithfulness, or if
it is just a piece of historical junk. We will be able to answer that question
confidently in the affirmative only if we recognize that it was groping — as
were all these Reformation distinctions — for what we today would call an
eschatological understanding of the church. The *satis est* pointed towards
an understanding of the church that takes account of the eschatological
distinction between the ages, this present old age and the future breaking-
in in the new. The *satis est* sets an eschatological limit to what can be
claimed by the institutional forms of the church in this age. When it asserts
that for the true unity of the church it is enough to agree on the right
preaching of the gospel and the administration of the sacraments in accordance therewith, it insists that the highest and final exercise of authority in
the church is the gospel which sets people free from sin, death, and the
power of the devil, thereby inaugurating the new age for faith and hope
and granting true unity as a gift. And since the preaching of the gospel of
Jesus Christ, crucified and risen, is the highest exercise of authority in the
church, the reformers always insisted, particularly against papal and episcopal claims, that Christ was the head of the church. He is the end of the
church and the promise of the new beginning, the new age, the kingdom
of God. Whatever the leadership of the church in this age, and however
necessary and useful it might be, it was strictly of human arrangement and
its forms could not be considered obligatory. The church, that is to say,
should be understood strictly as a this-age entity. What comes after the

---

7. One might hold, of course, that it is not only in the understanding of the church
that the theology of the nineteenth century is alive and well. That, of course, is true. But it is
also precisely our problem today.

church in this world, that for which the faithful hope, is the kingdom of God. And the kingdom of God comes by God's power alone in God's good time. There will be no church then, thanks be to God! The church lasts until the end of the age, and is its end.[8]

If the *satis est* is taken eschatologically, it means that the eschaton can be carried now only by the preached word and delivered sacrament. The eschatological word can only be, finally, its own warrant. If we grasp what Luther's theology is about we will see that at stake is a different understanding of how a truly "objective" reality is mediated. The eschatological word draws its objectivity from the fact that it is an "alien" word entirely from without, from God's future which is the end of us. It can live, therefore, only from its own inherent power. It does, indeed, need to be mediated, spoken and administered by humans exercising the office of such speaking and doing. One can even say that such an office is divinely instituted since God, by "providing the gospel and the sacrament," called it into being. But since it is an office announcing the end, it is self-limiting. It can only seek to get out of the way for the eschatological Kingdom. This is what the *satis est* means. It is a self-limiting concept. Therefore one can claim no more than human warrant for the institutional forms coined in this age.

And one should not look upon this self-limiting, pointed to by the *satis est*, as though it were something negative. As always, the eschatological limit saves the institutions of this age precisely by putting them to their proper tasks, making them truly historical. "Do we then overthrow the law by this faith? By no means, we uphold the law" (Rom. 3:31). Whenever the church claims something more than that, we have trouble. The trouble is just that law overcomes gospel. Indeed, if one of the churches claims to be the one church we will have nothing but trouble. History bears repeated witness to the fact that the drive towards visible unity in one visible church on earth is a dream most detrimental of all to ecumenism. The eschatological limit is transgressed and the figure of the Grand Inquisitor hovers in the wings. When the eschatological line is transgressed, the church begins to claim itself to be the unifying end of history, the fulfillment of history's meaning, and it "seeks to prove the truth of its message by the continuity

---

8. CA 7 says, of course, that the true church will last forever. However, the Schwabach Articles say it will last only until the end of the age. Here, as elsewhere, the Schwabach articles are better!

of its traditions, the 'validity' of its order and the solidity and prestige of its historic form."[9] The church, that is, begins to look upon itself as the visible incarnation of the invisible ideal church. It is simply not correct or appropriate to call opposition to such a position anti-catholic. It is not anti-catholic to believe that the one church is wherever the gospel is preached and the sacraments delivered. It is surely much more anti-catholic to claim that one institution is the one church now and forever. That is a transgression of the eschatological limit set down by the *satis est* which spells, in the end, tyranny.

What is the faithfulness to which the *satis est* calls us? If one looks at the matter in the light of the recovery of Luther's theology, perhaps we can avoid some of the endless debates of the past and needless debates of the present. What the *satis est* calls for is agreement not on a whole list of things or doctrines, but on the specific activity of teaching (preaching) the gospel and administering the sacraments according to that gospel. The debates of the past have generally gotten bogged down in arguments about doctrinal agreement — about "how much" is necessary. More lately the drive towards "visible unity" seems to incline its advocates to add some things by way of communal life and discipline. It is no accident that it was the Reformed theologian/ecumenist Lukas Vischer who coined the slogan, *satis est non satis est.* As a good Calvinist he wanted to add something about discipline and such. And even our bonny Lutheran theologians at Strasbourg seem to want to add things beyond the limits drawn by the *satis est.* They talk of the necessity of "lived unity" and such niceties — even statements to the effect that "to attempt to realize [sic!] the unity described in *satis est* without the relations of 'full communion' is to live in self-contradiction."[10] Whenever something gets added, the teeth of the law begin to show!

Is this not simply the same old game? Whenever the eschatological line is drawn in Lutheranism by the gospel and the sacraments, someone always wants to add something more. The gospel and the sacraments are never enough. Always, always, someone gets nervous and demands something more. The statements about adding things to the *satis est* list sound remarkably like the dreary business of the third use of the law, now applied to our ecclesiology. Those who refuse to add more "things" to the list are

---

9. Reinhold Niebuhr, *Faith and History* (New York: Scribner's, 1949), p. 239.
10. *Ecumenism: ELCA*, p. 111.

even accused of "satis est reductionism"![11] And, given the nervousness, such changes are consequent. Whenever the line is transgressed, the old being escapes. And where old beings escape the appointed end, the church has to take steps to bring them under control. The church becomes a surrogate for eschatology, a kind of eschatological vestibule! And that always turns out to be a prison.

The *satis est* calls us, surely, to believe and confess that the gospel and the sacraments are indeed enough. No doubt the irony of it all is that that seems precisely the hardest thing for churches and theologians to agree on. But what can be done about that? If we have listened to Luther, and learned anything at all from the recovery of his theology, I expect we will just have to say, "nothing!" It is simply not a matter of attempting to repair the supposed inadequacy of the *satis est* by adding or subtracting this or that. It is not a matter of a list of "things," doctrinally or otherwise. It is rather a matter of the specific activity of preaching the gospel — learning how to do that and sticking to it. If we don't know how to do that, or don't do it even when we know how, nothing can help us. No tinkering with a list of things and no bolstering of offices is going to help because the office is to preach the gospel. If one does know what the gospel is all about, one is certainly not concerned to play the game of expansionism or reductionism. If we are in trouble on this score, we are really in trouble. Nothing can be done about it except to do what the *satis est* is all about: to return to the preaching of the gospel and the doing of the sacraments with faithfulness until those who hear and receive have finally had "enough" and can consequently confess: *satis est,* I have had enough! What more could one ask?

---

11. Michael Root, "*Satis Est:* What Do We Do When Other Churches Don't Agree?" Unpublished paper read at the Convocation of Teaching Theologians of the ELCA, Techny, Ill., 1991, p. 27.

Lutheran Ecumenism:
With Whom and How Much?

According to several observers, we seem to have entered an ecumenical winter. Winter, especially in Minnesota, is when it is cold and slippery. Cars will not start, and even if they do, they run under protest and consume much more energy. Winter: that is when one is tempted to stay home and forget useless forays into the hostile atmosphere outside.

But why the ecumenical winter? Everything seems to be coming undone. The Anglican Communion is furious over Rome's official response to the final report of the Anglican/Roman Catholic International Commission I. At the same time, the Eastern Orthodox community is furious with Rome because of disputes over the fate of uniate churches in the wake of the collapse of the Soviet Union and because of Rome's unilateral appointment of Roman bishops on what the Orthodox consider their turf. Then there is the seemingly ubiquitous problem of proselytizing, Rome's ambition to evangelize territories left virtually secularized by Soviet antireligious policies. Even in Europe, things are not well. An ecumenist of no less a standing than Lucas Vischer is promoting a Protestant Conference under the auspices of the Conference of European Churches in the wake of John Paul II's recent assembly of the Synod of Bishops in Europe, apparently to counter the pope's call to re-evangelize (re-Catholicize?) Europe. So things are not well on the ecumenical front. All the classical sore points — papal primacy and presumption, episcopal jurisdiction, proselytism, and turf-claiming — are reentering the ecumenical arena with a vengeance. It's cold out there! How does it happen that the supposed symbol of unity causes so much disunity whenever it attempts to instantiate what it symbolizes? Is that endemic to the claims of the office or do we have to do just with the idiosyncrasies of the current pope?

Yes, it is bitter cold out there in the ecumenical world today. But I am from Minnesota. And in Minnesota we do not pay much attention to winter. We just put on our heavy parkas, boots, and gloves and arm ourselves with shovels so we can clear away what the storms leave and go about our business as usual. After all, if ecumenism is not just a passing fancy, not just a fair-weather pastime, we ought to learn to get on with it even in winter. In the words of the poet I remind myself when it gets really bad: "O wind, if winter comes, can spring be far behind?" So I would like to begin by venturing into the ecumenical cold and doing a little shoveling.

The Non-Issue of Mutual Recognition

First, I would like to begin by stating my personal opinions on ecumenism just to clear the air a bit. I speak from the limited perspective of a dialogue participant, not an "ecumenist." I believe in a policy of ecumenical openness with a concomitant theological tough-mindedness. Our biggest problem, here and in the church in general, is theological integrity. Basically, I have come to reject the principle of making exhaustive agreement in doctrine and polity a condition for intercommunion. From reading Luther and the Reformers, that is a quite un-Lutheran idea. Indeed, in most instances of churches confessing the triune God, there exists enough common ground for us simply to declare ourselves to be in the fellowship that already exists. This is especially true in those instances where we have had considerable dialogue and have arrived at mutual understandings. Certainly this is the case in light of the Lutheran/Reformed dialogue and the Lutheran/Roman Catholic dialogue. (The fact that Roman Catholics do not want to recognize such fellowship, since they reject the validity of Lutheran orders, is their problem. We need not give in to their views and play their game.) The high-water mark was when the fourth-round participants in the American Lutheran/Catholic dialogue studied the possibility of recognition, but met a stone wall. Since then it has been downhill. Now it is Lutherans who are expected to recognize Roman views on orders as valid.

Actually, Lutherans should think that the very idea that we are not in communion with other Christian churches is rather strange. To my knowledge, Lutheranism has never really "unchurched" anyone or declared anyone's ministry to be invalid. Lutheranism does not even have the ecclesiastical machinery for so doing. To assume that we are now going to put ourselves in fellowship with others, or that something is accomplished by "recognizing" their ministries, is to be tricked into playing the game according to Roman rules. In my estimation, this happens too much in ecumenical circles. It is assumed, for instance, that because those churches that insist on the "historic episcopate" and their concomitant sacramental ordination do not recognize, say, Lutheran ministry, then Lutherans in turn do not recognize episcopal ministry. Since I do not recognize you, you obviously have the same problem: you do not recognize me! That, of course, is not true. Lutherans may well have problems with it but, in order to make it seem as if there is reciprocity in the issue, Lutherans are supposed to go through the motions of "recognizing" their ministry. Or, in recent efforts to remove "mutual condemnations," the assumption seems to be that Lutherans have the same sort of problem in the issuance of condemnations as Roman Catholics do. So we go through the charade of lifting supposed mutual condemnations when, as a matter of fact, we do not really have any — or if we do, they are quite a different matter, administered by quite different ecclesiastical machinery, and serve a different purpose. Removing them is pointless — something like removing or ignoring imprecatory psalms from the Bible.

So, Lutherans should quit playing the game according to everyone else's rules and simply be about the business of stating what is the case according to our own lights. This is simply that Christ is the head of the church, that he makes Christians by grace alone through preaching and the sacraments. Since Christ creates the community, all human arrangements devised by denominations must be in the service of the head of the church and his gospel. The churches are of human provenance this side of the eschatological line.

However, the move to declaring fellowship cannot mean that our theological discussions are over. We still have a lot of snow to shovel. But that means that we would have to devise better means whereby it could begin in earnest. This entails that theological discussion would be best carried on within mutual recognition rather than as a condition for it. Further, it means that some form of conciliar ecumenism in which the denominations that recognize each other would agree to come together for serious conversation on theological, doctrinal, polity, and practice is desirable. For the time being, that kind of conversation would be the most advantageous.

Honoring Theological Differences

The question of serious theological conversation, however, brings us to the second point: theological tough-mindedness. After participating in a bilateral dialogue with Roman Catholics for some fifteen years now, I have come increasingly to think that the current method in ecumenical dialogue that seeks unity via theological convergence/consensus (the difference between the two seems never to have been cleared up) as a step toward some high-sounding goal like "full communion" is more or less theologically bankrupt. It leads ultimately to what could be called "repressive tolerance." When pressed incessantly as a method, it ceases after a while to kindle, promote, or foster useful theological discussion, but rather stifles it and soon seeks to repress it. Ecumenical officers move to shut it down. We get together to be professionally nice. What begins in the spirit of openness and tolerance soon closes down — in the fashion characterized by Allan Bloom in *The Closing of the American Mind*. This or that view will be designated as being "extreme," or perhaps "not representative," or "pre–Vatican II," or "too Lutheran" or some other grave theological sin. The message soon becomes: "you had better be tolerant, or else," or "if you don't back off you are just not serious about ecumenism." In the name of ecumenical tolerance and progress serious discussion is repressed. One who seeks to pursue difficult questions is something of a pariah. Documents that state issues sharply and cleanly have to be edited and toned down so as not to be too offensive. As Henry Chadwick once put it, the genius of ecumenical statements lies in their ambiguity — the art of stating things in such a fashion that no one could possibly disagree. Imagine: theology, which has been exhorted all these long years to strive for precision, is now, apparently, to cultivate deliberately the art of ambiguity! The drive today towards what is called "visible unity" becomes, under current conditions, an ideological crusade which seems — wittingly or not — only too ready to cut corners on the truth or even sacrifice it to reach its goal.

This attempt towards unity is driven by a specific ideology. It is the result of an alliance between Romanticism, politics, and theology coming out of the nineteenth century. Romantic yearnings for the good old days of the *corpus christianum* (by, for instance, Prussian unionists like Fredrik Wilhelm III, his jurist von Gerlach, as well as Stahl or Loehe, together with the church-historical judgment of Protestant converts like Friedrich Heiler who maintained that the Reformation shattered the church's unity and unleashed the wars of religion, destroying modern Europe's faith) have all colluded together to foist upon us an ideology of unity. Like all ideologies, this one functions virtually without question today. It is politically correct. It does not have to be argued for. We have uncritically adopted this Romantic view of history, ecclesiology, and the Reformation. We seem to have accepted the idea that once upon a time there was a pristine, pure *corpus christianum* whose unity was a kind of warrant for the faith. We have bought the idea that the shattering of this supposed unity is the reason for modern unbelief — that if we would put Humpty Dumpty back together again, people would flock home to the church. The Reformation used to be celebrated even in the secular world, particularly by the heirs of the Enlightenment, as the great triumph of the freedom of conscience over the imperialism and heteronomy of Rome and its power plays. No longer. Today, under the drive of the ideology of visible unity, the Reformation is more to be regretted than celebrated. All this is combined together to make up the general ideology of unity that seems to dominate the field without question. Denominationalism, which was actually the ecumenical idea that brought religious warring to an end, is now blamed for being the source of our troubles. Actually, of course, it is always the claim by one church to be the one visible church on earth that causes all the trouble to begin with. It could well be argued that the idea of "visible unity" is the most unecumenical idea the world has ever seen!

Given the weight of this ideological drive, legitimate theological questions and concerns tend just to get steamrollered. That means that we have to find some other way to proceed in a theologically responsible way. After all, does not the drive toward unity actually entice us to a kind of theological irresponsibility? The problem with repressive tolerance is that generally it spawns a gaggle of compromise statements that no one really cares much about, a kind of "middle kingdom" where all theological cats are gray. One spends a good deal of time cranking out such statements and then goes home and more or less forgets about them. At worst, the truth is obscured for church-political reasons. It is really a kind of subversion of the theological task when we, under the pressure of the ideological drive for unity, not only surrender the search for unambiguous speech, but indeed actually avoid it. A neat passage from the Robertson Davies novel *Fifth Business* indicates that sharper lay minds are onto this kind of business. Speaking of the church union in Canada, he says:

> In a movement that reached its climax in 1924, the Presbyterians and Methodists had consummated a *mysterium coniunctionis* that resulted in the United Church of Canada, with a doctrine (smoother than the creamy curd) in which the harshness of Presbyterianism and the hick piety of Methodism had little part. A few brass-bowelled Presbyterians and some truly zealous Methodists held out, but a majority regarded this union as a great victory for Christ's Kingdom on earth. Unfortunately it also involved some haggling between the rich Presbyterians and the poor Methodists, which roused the mocking spirit of the rest of the country; the Catholics in particular had some Irish jokes about the biggest land-and-property grab in Canadian history. During this uproar a few sensitive souls fled to the embrace of Anglicanism; the envious and disaffected said they did it because the Anglican Church was in some way more high-toned than the evangelical faiths, and thus they were improving their social standing.[1]

Perhaps such passages are an indication that the supposed scandal of our disunity is no greater than the scandal of our contrived unions!

Under the pressure of the ideology of unity we develop a kind of "middle-kingdom" language in which we finally end by saying things that we really ought not to say to one another or that are quite hard to take seriously or believe. For example, with regard to the recent Lutheran/Roman Catholic dialogue on Mary and the saints, the precariousness of the earlier round on justification with its dubious "convergence" between a Catholic idea of transformation by grace alone and a Lutheran view of the simultaneity of being just and sinful by faith alone was made apparent. The saints, for Roman Catholics, are those who are supposed to be pre-eminent examples of the way grace works. In effect, Roman Catholics want to claim that grace works so successfully in the lives of some that they immediately enjoy the beatific union and can be invoked to pray for us. Lutherans,

---

1. Robertson Davies, *Fifth Business* (New York: Penguin, 1977), p. 128.

skeptical about such religious success stories and subsequent claims to their eternal consequence, find the practice dubious, if not finally deleterious, to a sound conscience and the understanding of the way grace works. So then, what do we do? We move to a kind of middle ground in which Catholics say that Lutherans do not have to accept their teachings on the saints and Mary as long as they do not outright reject them. And Lutherans, for their part, are to promise not to accuse Catholics of idolatry in their faith and practice. And in that we are driven to saying to one another things we really ought not to say. It would seem to me that if Catholics really believe that the transforming power of grace can be so effective as to elevate at least some to immediate beatific vision, they ought not to be constrained to say that it is permissible for one not to accept it provided they do not reject it. Given the actual track record of the *magisterium* in such matters, and a good deal of actual practice on like matters, confidence in such assurances is not exactly unshakeable! Likewise, given the Lutheran stance, Catholics ought really not ask Lutherans to grant a kind of absolution in advance in which we agree not to raise the question of idolatry. Lutheran preachers should be concerned to sniff out and attack idolatry wherever it is to be found. No one should automatically exempt any Lutheran formulations, policies, or practices from such attack, and be asked *a priori* to do so for the sake of Roman Catholic practices. In sum, we end under the weight of a repressive tolerance that waters down what we want to say, dissolving it in the rhetoric of ecumenical ambiguity.

We have about reached the end of this line. The seeking of doctrinal convergence/consensus before unity leads more and more to theological irresponsibility, to deliberate obfuscation of language, and to the distortion of history so that it will not impair the impetuous drive toward the goal of "visible" unity — whatever in the world that might be!

What is needed is a different ecumenical method, a different way to exercise theological responsibility in a diverse, pluralistic theological situation at the same time that we pursue unity. We need to foster a collegiality as Christian believers that does not prejudice or prematurely shut down honest conversation about theological differences. That is why we can affirm that now there is enough agreement simply to declare ourselves in fellowship, but that that is not the end of the theological conversation, but rather perhaps the beginning of it in earnest.

Ecumenism as Confessional Integrity

Now let's consider the current situation in the ELCA. There is a kind of internal tension about the motivation and thus perhaps also the strategy for ecumenism in the ELCA. One might get at this by speaking of three factors: (1) ecumenism as an item in the agenda of political correctness, (2) ecumenism as ecclesial correctness (a cure for the threatened takeover by politically correct ideology), and (3) ecumenism as theological or confessional correctness. It may be a bit strained to see them all in terms of "correctness," but the characterization will do for now.

(1) *Ecumenism as Political Correctness.* The majority of folks in the ELCA who support ecumenism do so because it is simply a part of the politically correct agenda engendered by the spirit of the age which — as Kierkegaard once put it — seems to hang over us like a marsh gas, and is reflected in *The Lutheran* and other church publications. The Commission on a New Lutheran Church (of which I, alas, was a member) was dominated, it is fair to say in retrospect, by politically correct ideology and rhetoric. Ecumenism was simply another item on the list. Like quotas, inclusivism, social justice, peace, tolerance, openness, affirming anything and everything, etc., the case did not need, really, to be argued, but just accepted as a given. One paid lip service to theology or theological integrity, but it was not particularly important. And remains so for the majority of ELCA members today. Hence, when the statement on ecumenism came before the churchwide assembly, it was overwhelmingly approved. Why? Because it is politically correct — just like hosts of other statements set up for vote. It is somewhat amusing, therefore, when our ecumenical leaders take that vote to be an overwhelming affirmation of their policies. The majority, I expect, do not really care about the policies at all, and would be rather shocked if they realized what they had voted for.

(2) *Ecumenism as Ecclesial Correctness.* On the other hand, there are those in the church who have turned to ecumenical rapprochement with "catholic" Christendom, particularly Rome, precisely as a cure for the erosion of substance brought on by PC-ness and attendant follies that appeal to mainline Protestantism. Such folks look to the restoration of the historic episcopate, the authority of the magisterium, and sometimes even papalism, precisely to stop the ravages of such things as PC-ness. *But this means that the first view of ecumenism is really diametrically opposed — at least in motive — to the second view.* One wonders how, in the time to

come, this is going to shake down, and what it will mean both for the church and for ecumenism. Those who espouse the second view are often very vocal in castigating the first, even accusing them of apostasy, heresy, and such matters. And the frictions between the leaders of the church and those in category 2 are becoming more and more evident.

(3) *Ecumenism as Confessional or Theological Correctness.* Meanwhile, there is a third approach or faction which is driven by a somewhat different motivation. This can be generally characterized as a concern for theological and/or confessional integrity. Unimpressed, if not untouched by ecumenism as PC-ness on the one hand, and unconvinced if not antithetic to Roman institutionalism on the other, as the way to go for either pragmatic or theological reasons, this faction has been most concerned about preserving confessional integrity in the ecumenical venture. Needless to say, I would place myself somewhere in this third category. But, it seems, that is a kind of precarious place to be. You are likely to get caught in the crossfire between the other two factions. Those who understand ecumenism as PC-ness will accuse you of being particularly parochial, perhaps a victim of an "upper Midwest virus" — as one of our erstwhile bishops put it, or just not being "with it," and other political and social crimes. On the other hand, those favoring the Roman touch in matters ecclesiastical are likely to be scandalized by too much openness to denominations other than those blessed (afflicted?) with the historic episcopate. So one will be accused of being "mainline Protestant," or denominationalist, or sectarian (virtually the same thing!), or some other lesser breed. One might even be accused of having no ecclesiology! (I can boast that I have a pin that says in red letters: "Beware! This man has no ecclesiology.")

My chief concern in all this is for theological and confessional integrity. What the Lutheran communion has to contribute to the ecumenical church is its understanding of what the preaching of the gospel of Jesus Christ and the administration of the sacraments as gospel is all about. If we lose that, or decide that we need to compromise it in order to pursue a will-o'-the-wisp called "visible unity," we have no reason for being. Admittedly, we need to stress more strongly than before the teaching office of the church and assert its gospel and its significance in no uncertain terms. But frankly it is strange that when I try, in my calling as a theology professor, to do just that, I get accused of overdoing it! Why is it that all those who are always complaining about the teaching office object when somebody actually tries to do it? What is going on here? I can hear someone saying, "Move over, Forde, and let a bishop do it! You have no credentials!" I am re-minded that Carl Braaten in one of his recent essays speaks of the fact that people will no longer accept or tolerate confessional theology. They won't buy it. So, what should we do? His answer: We need a *magisterium* to shore up things, and should perhaps back off a bit on justification to gain ecu-menical approval. To my mind, backing off from our confessional position in order to gain the historic episcopate is tantamount to selling out to mainline PC-ness. Why should we bother to be inclusive if we have noth-ing worth saying to all the people we include? In both cases the gospel is lost. I do not see any reason to keep the Lutheran Church going if we are going to give up on the gospel that brought it into being. I do not believe in sacrificing theological integrity just to preserve the institution. That is why I believe that the only way ahead for the time being appears to be some sort of conciliar ecumenism in which confessional integrity can be preserved while the theological conversation continues.

Satis Est: The Eschatological Factor

The major problem in much of this is the relation of ecclesiology to escha-tology. That ecumenism as PC-ness tends to collapse the kingdom of God into the church hardly needs to be argued. It is just another version of the liberal Protestant identification of the Kingdom with the church. That ecumenism as ecclesial correctness tends in the same direction is perhaps a more subtle, but certainly no less serious, claim. But the attempt to claim more than human authority *(de jure humano)* for its institutional forms is a violation of the eschatological limit. The *Augsburg Confession,* article 7, specifies that limit when it says that for the true unity of the church it is enough to agree on the preaching of the gospel and the right administra-tion of the sacraments. The preaching of the gospel is always the ultimate and the highest exercise of authority in the church: the authority that sets people free from sin, death, and the power of the devil. That is why the Re-formers and Confessors insisted that Christ was the head of the church, and that there could be no other. The church, that is to say, must be under-stood institutionally to be strictly a this-worldly entity. What comes after the church in this world, that for which the faithful hope, is the kingdom of God. There will be no church there — thank God! The church lasts until the end of the age, and that's it! The *Augsburg Confession* 8 speaks of the church as lasting forever. But Schwabach says only till the end of the age! As in other things, the *CA* must be interpreted by Schwabach. Whenever the church begins to claim something more than temporal human warrant for its institutions we have trouble. The eschatological line is transgressed and the figure of the Grand Inquisitor, even Antichrist, heaves into view. The church begins to claim itself to be the end of history, the fulfillment of history's meaning, and "seeks to prove" the truth of its message by the continuity of its traditions, the "validity" of its orders, and the solidity and prestige of its historic form. The church, that is, begins to look upon itself as the visible incarnation of the invisible ideal church that now, supposedly, hankers after visible unity. But that just spells tyranny.

Now, much more could be said here on matters of ecclesiology. My point is simply that claims to authority beyond the merely human — and even claims for what is supposedly "historic" — are a transgression of the eschatological limit and as such a threat to the gospel itself. They should not be tolerated. For the true unity of the church it is enough to agree on the preaching of the gospel and the administration of the sacraments according to that gospel. That is a very broad ecumenical program. It is time we should get on with it.

What does the *satis est* mean? It seems to be rather obvious when one reads *CA* 7 against the background of its predecessor documents, the Schwabach and Torgau Articles. Since the Lutherans had been accused of schism in going ahead with their reform programs, they wanted to make a basic statement about church unity, about what is schismatic behavior and what is not. To do this they invoke a fundamental distinction between what is divinely instituted, so to speak, and what is humanly instituted. The one holy church, they say, will be and remain forever. But that church is not defined by hierarchical arrangements, bishops, territories, buildings, or anything of that sort, i.e., not by any of the ordinances or ceremonies of men, and prescinding from such ordinances and ceremonies, or changing them, does not and cannot destroy the unity of the church. Rather, the church is to be defined and located in terms of a quite specific activity. It is the assembly where the gospel is preached (in purity) and the sacraments administered (as gospel). Where that occurs, there is the church, and that is sufficient *(satis est)* for its unity. Now it seems that the unity they are here talking about is not what ecumenists today like to talk about as "visible unity" (whatever that is!). It is what is often called the "spiritual" unity of the one holy Christian church throughout all time of which they speak, the unity of that church which is the object and result of faith and not of sight. What can be seen is not the object of faith — not "seeing is believing" but "believing is not seeing." What can be seen is not to be believed! It does not have to be believed, because it can be seen, namely, law! Hence, the adjectives "hidden" and "revealed" are to be preferred to "visible" or "invisible," since they are much more appropriately eschatological and indicative of what the Lutheran view is about. Nevertheless, it is, of course, true, as our ELCA statement avers, that *CA 7* is not a complete doctrine of the church. But then one must first look back to the Torgau articles particularly in this case, and behind them to Luther's *Confession Concerning Christ's Supper* (1528), because they stand behind the words of *CA 7* and are the eventual source even of the very wording. It is just historically irresponsible to ignore such facts and becloud the issues by hinting that we should first go elsewhere to learn what they mean, or that we can impose any meaning on them we wish.

The ELCA ecumenical statement invokes the *satis est* in two instances: one in the brief historical background section and the other just before the conclusion to the policy statement where it is cited as warrant for the statement's view of "full communion." In the historical statement it is averred that the situation today is quite different from that in 1530. At that time, it is said, *satis est* was invoked to preserve unity. Now it must be invoked to reestablish a lost unity. But is that really the case? It is hardly the case that in 1530 the visible unity of the church was still quite intact. Did not the emperor call the Diet precisely to patch up an empire shattered by disunity, ecclesiastical and otherwise, so as to be able to meet the challenge of the Turks? At that time, the Lutherans were accused of schismatic behavior because they did not knuckle under to what they considered human ceremonies and ordinances. They defended themselves by insisting that only divine ordinances (gospel and sacrament) are necessary for unity. They would not submit to anything more. That was the limit. Is it really all that much different now? Is it not the case that Lutherans and other Protestants are considered schismatic because they will not accept what they consider to be purely human ordinances: papacy, historic episcopate, and the like? Does not the *satis est* raise exactly the same question now as then? Is preaching the gospel and giving the sacraments enough? One may, indeed, decide they are not. But then one has to come flat out and say that *CA 7* is wrong and not doctor the history to obfuscate what is being said. And if one wants to say it is wrong, then one will have to look to oneself as to how one is going to prove that and convince the church of it! If there is to be a policy that somehow wants to call the *satis est* into question, then there has to be a serious discussion of the matter, not just an attempt to throw historical sand in our faces.

It is at least dubious on the basis of *CA* 7 and its actual historical background, therefore, without further ado to claim that "full communion" as the ecumenical goal of the ELCA is consistent with the *satis est*. That is the second instance in which the *satis est* is invoked by the ELCA statement. If the *satis est* maintains that human ordinances (beyond preaching the gospel and giving the sacraments) cannot be conditions for the unity of the church, then it would seem quite contrary to set additional (human) requirements as conditions for such "full communion." (Full communion is a very slippery term, of course, so it is hard exactly to know what to do with it.)

But now, just what is it materially that the *satis est* finds to be "enough"? What is it talking about? What is it (following the Latin version) that we are to "agree" *(consentire)* about? Once again, there is no great mystery here. What we are to agree about is the activity of preaching the gospel in its purity and administering the sacraments accordingly as gospel. Here it seems that we have made matters a good deal more complicated than we should have. We get all tangled up in questions of doctrine — arguments about the correctness and completeness of our doctrines *about* the gospel. But the question here is not one of doctrines about the gospel, not whether we must insist on "the gospel and all its parts," the whole corpus of Christian doctrine and the doctrine of scripture to boot, all down pat before we have got "enough." Instead, the question is one of the pure *preaching of* the gospel and right *administration of* the sacraments. It is an activity that is enough for the true unity of the church: preaching and administering the gospel as gospel. Now, if that is the case, what is intended by the adverbs and qualifying phrases — "purely," "rightly," "in conformity with a pure understanding of it," and "in accordance with the divine word" — that govern the preaching and the administration? In light of the Reformation tradition, this also is not terribly complicated. Pure preaching of the gospel means simply a preaching in which gospel is not confused with law. In our terms, pure preaching is simply gospel preached as *unconditional promise*. Right administration of the sacraments, in accordance with the divine word means, then, sacraments also given as gospel, as unconditional promise, according to the scriptures and not bought and sold as sacrifices, votive masses, and all the traffic of medieval piety. In a real sense, it would seem, the distinction between human ordinances and ceremonies carries through also in the designation of what constitutes pure preaching and right administration. The gospel and the sacrament, that is to say, are God's gifts, and to offer them properly is not to take them captive to human arrangements, ordinances, and ceremonies, which would only enslave people, terrify consciences, and not liberate. The gospel and the sacraments are, we might say today, God's eschatological gifts and are not to be obscured by human perfidy. To ask for anything more than the pure giving of such gifts as a foundation for the true unity of the church is in itself already a perversion, already a confusion of law and gospel, an attempt to elevate human ordinances over and above the sheer gift, an attempt to construct a human device that transcends the eschatological limit. It cannot be done. *Satis est.* Enough is enough.

Now if it is such pure preaching and right sacramental administration that is enough for the true unity of the church, it is also important to note that for the Reformers this was by no means an exclusive claim. That is to say, you will look in vain in the Reformers for the claim that they were the only ones who were doing this — that they were the only ones who preached the gospel purely or administered the sacraments "rightly" in the sense meant by *CA 7*. Even in his most vitriolic attacks on the papacy (as antichrist!) Luther never argued that the gospel and sacraments or the forgiveness of sins were absent. In *On the Papacy at Rome* (1520) Luther sets the question:

> Whether the papacy in Rome, possessing the actual power over all of Christendom, as they say, is derived from divine or from human order; and, if so, whether it would be a Christian statement to say that all other Christians in the whole world are heretics and schismatics — even though they adhere to the same baptism, sacrament, gospel, and all articles of faith in harmony with us they do not have their priests and bishops confirmed by Rome or, as is the case now, buy them with money and let themselves be aped and mocked like the Germans. The Muscovites, the white Russians, the Greeks, the Bohemians and many other great nations in the world are some examples — all of them believe like us, baptize like us, preach like us, live like us. . . . I have held and still hold, that they are neither heretics nor schismatics; perhaps

they are better Christians than we are — although not all of them are, just as not all of us are good Christians.[2]

Or in the *Confession Concerning Christ's Supper* (1528) which is the immediate background in Luther for *CA* 7:

> This [one, holy, Christian Church on earth] exists not only in the realm of the Roman Church or pope, but in all the world, as the prophets foretold. . . . Thus this Christian Church is physically dispersed among pope, Turks, Persians, Tartars, but spiritually gathered in one gospel and faith, under one head, i.e., Jesus Christ. . . . In this Christian Church, wherever it exists, is to be found the forgiveness of sins, i.e., a kingdom of grace and of true pardon. For in it are found the gospel, baptism, and the sacrament of the altar, in which the forgiveness of sins is offered, obtained and received. Moreover, Christ and his Spirit and God are there. Outside this Christian Church there is no salvation.[3]

The Confessors did not claim that they were the only ones doing the kind of preaching and administration necessary to call the church into being and constitute its unity. What they did object to, however, most strenuously was that someone should demand of them something more than such preaching and, moreover, deny to them the right to preach the gospel on the basis of the fact that they did not knuckle under to these demands. The significance of pointing to all sorts of other Christians in the world is simply to say that if Rome cannot deny to these others the claim to being Christian, how then can they deny it to us? In other words, how can one possibly claim that variation in human ordinances and ceremonies ruptures the unity of the church? *Satis est* therefore simply marks a limit beyond which one can make no demands and beyond which one cannot accuse anyone of destroying the true spiritual unity of the church.

Now if one puts this together, it is apparent that the *satis est* is a very broad and open ecumenical principle. If the Reformers are saying that Rome cannot charge them with schism or with destroying the true unity of the church, then it would seem to be only consistent that they too cannot

2. LW 39:58.
3. LW 37:367-68.

charge others with schism or destroying the true unity. It is on this basis that it is consistent to make the claim presented at the outset that unless we are willing to declare these others schismatics and heretics (no gospel preaching, no sacraments) then we cannot but declare ourselves to be in fellowship. But this does not mean doctrinal agreement. It means the doctrinal and theological discussion must now begin. And the discussion, no doubt, will have to be about the extent to which human ordinances and ceremonies obscure the pure preaching and right administration.

Gospel-speaking and sacrament-giving mark, therefore, an eschatological limit to ecclesiology. They are the highest exercise of "authority" in the church, the marks of the church in this age. The church, though hidden as an object of faith, is nevertheless revealed in acts of eschatological liberation. The divine ordinances are those that convey and have as their ultimate aim the redemption and liberation of sinners. The constant temptation of the church is always to transgress, to overstep, the eschatological limit, to set itself up as a kind of "eschatological vestibule," a sacramental *Zwischenbereich*, perhaps even as a sacrament itself, a diachronic extension of the incarnation in time. When that occurs, there is a blurring of the eschatological limit, a tendency to vest its purely human offices with sacramental, indeed divine, sanction. The divine right of popes and bishops mirrors other political attempts to transcend eschatological limits, such as the divine right of kings. Backed up by the theology of Pseudo-Dionysius (of course in the Middle Ages they did not know he was "pseudo" so his writings had great authority), the earthly hierarchies reflected and exercised the authority of the heavenly. The human ordinances and ceremonies pick up divine weight and transcend the eschatological limit. When that is the case the preaching of the gospel as liberating word is in effect transcended. The eschaton, so to speak, is postponed (as an old graffito had it) due to the lack of trained trumpeters!

This blurring of the eschatological boundary is responsible for much of the confusion in ecumenical policy today and is, unfortunately, reflected in the ELCA statement. In the *Zwischenbereich* all sorts of ecumenical double-talk develops which simply confuses matters. Again, take the matter of "visible unity." Early on in the ecumenical movement there was a fundamental shift from the attempt to create unity to the goal of discovering and manifesting the unity we already enjoy in Christ. Suddenly now, that is not enough. Now we are supposedly obligated to achieve or create "visible unity." But, what is that? What is it that we are supposed to see? How does our unity in Christ become see-able — when we get a bunch of be-mitered bishops hugging each other? That may be better than bishops going to war against each other (as they used to in the days of the *CA!*), but still it does not make the unity visible. The unity of the church is an article of faith, a gift of the gospel, an eschatological reality, and as such cannot be visible in this age. In this age a visible unity becomes nothing but law. It is set before us as either a demand to be realized or something that is, in the very pious terms of indicative/imperative language, both gift and task. Spare us such platitude! I believe in the true unity of the church, but I surely cannot see it. I cannot see it even within my own communion (what crazy theology and practice we have to put up with!), let alone between communions. And the success of the ecumenical movement, however desirable and necessary, is not going to make the unity of the church one whit more visible. In a policy statement we need to speak with some precision and clarity about these things. Like the old LCA statement, we ought to distinguish clearly between union and unity or between our fellowship with one another (which admittedly needs improving) and the unity that is given in Christ.

The same thing is true with such muddled concepts as "full communion," supposedly now the goal of our ecumenical striving. But what is it? Is it the *communio sanctorum* of the creed, an object of faith, an eschatological reality coming upon us from God's future in Christ, or is it a goal to be reached by our pious strivings? Once again, current ecumenese seems deliberately to blur the lines and cultivate ambiguity in order to further its own ideology of unity.

When one steps back and takes a look at the whole, one sees that the drive towards consensus has created a kind of mythological middle kingdom in which deliberate ambiguity is practiced, blurring the lines and turning all theological cats gray. One puts together this-worldly adjective and eschatological substantives like "visible unity" or "full communion" and so quite thoroughly confuses rather than sheds light on the issues and problems before us. A policy statement ought not to do that. It ought to define and clarify issues so we know who we are and where we intend to go.

Postliberal Lutheranism: Gospel, Church, and Ecumenism

But now, the most serious shortcoming of the so-called policy statement is that it has no vision either of the contribution of the Lutheran Church to the ecumenical church today or of the eventual mission of the church. Fascination with the ideology of unity and the subsequent consensus *Schwärmerei* leads to a kind of theological myopia and timidity that insulates against a forthright statement of what Lutherans have to contribute today. Rather, the ELCA statement on ecumenism seems more geared towards what we ought to be prepared to give up — more interested in selling the farm than in contributing from its bounty. What, after all, do Lutherans have to contribute to this postliberal, postmodern age? Well, what is it that keeps a postliberal Lutheran catholic? What keeps me, for instance, in the catholic faith, ties me to the trinitarian confession of the church catholic? It is not the magisterium or its authority, not bishops or their alleged "historic episcopate" or "apostolic succession" or the dream of some sort of "full communion" or "visible unity" under the auspices of all of that decadent ecclesiastical furniture. What keeps this postliberal Lutheran catholic is precisely the most radical facets of the early Lutheran Reformation, such matters as the "theology of the cross," the anthropology emerging from the arguments about the "bondage of the will," the hermeneutics of "letter and spirit," and "law and gospel." These are some of the things we have to contribute. These are the kinds of things that will fortify the church against the acids of decadent modernity of which many are so concerned today. Yet these are the very things that never get discussed in ecumenical circles. Dialogues seem to shy away from them like a horse who has seen a rattler. Our ecumenists seem to be dedicated to the ideology of unity spawned by the Romanticism of late nineteenth-century ecclesiastical politics and the drive towards consensus rather than showing interest in what Lutherans might have to contribute theologically. This is a dubious and questionable road to take, to say the least. Lutherans actually have something of value to say, and it is not a proper or faithful move to leave it all behind to enter the middle kingdom where all cats are gray.

We Lutherans have a contribution that is a vital understanding of what it means to preach the gospel and to give the sacramental gifts. The claim that this is enough for the true unity of the church is itself already based on an understanding of the gospel and the sacraments as the last, the eschatological word, beyond which nothing else can be demanded. To ask for something more as necessary is already to call the gospel into question. At the very least, we need to come to some clear understanding of this. If the church must have a policy statement, then it had better be a clear one that affords us and the *oikumene* some real guidance in the days ahead.

The Catholic Impasse: Reflections
on Lutheran-Catholic Dialogue Today

One of the major hindrances in ecumenical discussion is the apparent difficulty in isolating, not to say understanding and expressing, fundamental
differences, or knowing what to do with them when we do find them. We
do well enough, it would seem, on well-known, historic differences, those
that have become virtually clichés through time, but we falter badly when
it appears that time and chance may have opened rifts that could be even
more serious. We continue to talk about the legitimacy of diversity, but
when the crunch comes we revert to searching desperately for what we
might call a "consensus" or "convergence" on ancient difficulties. Not long
ago I was invited to participate in an ecumenical conference that purport-
edly was to attempt breaking new ground by talking about fundamental
differences rather than the usual piecemeal convergences. But it soon became apparent that both sponsors and participants were wary of conversation about serious differences and so relapsed into the usual bromides
about convergence. We seem somehow to be afraid that serious investigation of differences will impede or even throw the movement into reverse,
perhaps foster a return to the era of hostile polemics. One who wants to
talk about such differences is usually regarded as something of a pariah.
But surely that is myopic. If the ecumenical movement has accomplished
anything in our time, it certainly ought to be that we have come to know
and trust one another enough to speak honestly, and that it ought to be
possible to find ways to live together nevertheless.

I am of the opinion that the ecumenical movement will not make much more meaningful progress until it tries to put its finger on fundamental differences, and then faces anew the question of what to do about them. Reluctance on the part of many Christians to join or support the movement wholeheartedly stems from the suspicion that differences have not really been faced, but rather just "papered over." Instead of being confronted, challenged, and, it is to be hoped, enriched by differences, dialogues usually end somewhat lamely with bland consensus statements that rarely excite or please and tend soon to be forgotten, sometimes in the very next round of the dialogue itself! Those concerned about the movement, therefore, need to probe deeply into and speak openly and honestly about what they believe such differences to be.

The nagging question before the ecumenical movement is why, after all the effort, time, and money spent on the dialogues, and the convergences and the agreements, we still do not appear to be much closer together. Participation in one such dialogue for some fifteen years now has suggested to me that we need a different strategy. We have likely done about as much as we can in pursuing agreements and convergences on discrete topics. Results tend to be more or less predictable and for that reason disappointing because they don't seem to light any fires or bring us closer together.

Impatience with the meager results of dialogue has led, apparently, to various attempts to bypass the logjam, practically or theoretically (*Facing Unity*, BEM, the Fries-Rahner proposal, in *Unity of the Churches*, etc.).[1] Diversionary tactics, however, seem to attract momentary attention but soon fall into a certain oblivion. The most recent of such attempts in the Lutheran-Episcopal dialogue demonstrates something of the futility of such tactics. The dialogue published a statement titled *Implications of the Gospel*,[2] which is aimed apparently at transcending differences by making a common statement on all manner of topics, dogmatic and ethical, in a language and form that deliberately avoids traditional disagreements and vocabulary. The statement is nicely done in many ways, but it is hardly

---

1. *Facing Unity*, published by the Lutheran World Federation, 1985; *Baptism, Eucharist, and Ministry*, Faith and Order Paper No. 111, World Council of Churches, Geneva, 1982; Heinrich Fries and Karl Rahner, *Unity of the Churches*, trans. Ruth and Eric Gritsch (Philadelphia: Fortress, and New York: Paulist, 1983).

2. *Implications of the Gospel*, Lutheran-Episcopal Dialogue, Series 3, ed. William A. Norgren and William G. Rusch (Minneapolis: Augsburg, and Cincinnati: Forward Movement Publications, 1988).

likely to be of much help precisely because it studiously avoids dealing with basic differences and thereby will likely only engender petty new ones. Suggesting that such documents be presented to the respective churches for "reception" seems virtually to have the effect of proposing a species of new common creed. But surely we don't need that!

Trying more seriously to get at fundamental and/or root differences, I suspect, might point us in the direction of new strategy. Are there still, or perhaps particularly *today,* some differences of a more fundamental sort than those that come to light in discussion on individual topics? If there are such, can we live with them? The purpose of such an attempt would not be merely to magnify differences and distances, but rather to see whether we might not discover even deeper levels of understanding and mutuality once we understand the differences.

It has been my experience in dialogue that the impetuous drive to convergence can often hinder rather than help understanding. After all these years in the Lutheran–Roman Catholic dialogue, for instance, I am still not certain we understand each other very well, or at least as well as we might. For one thing, we do not understand our individual histories since the Reformation very well and so operate often with stereotypical ancient formulas. For instance, it seems apparent to a Lutheran that Roman Catholics know next to nothing about the way in which Lutheranism (and its theology) was decisively shaped by battles with other reform movements or by its response to the Enlightenment. It has taken me, at least, some fifteen years to discover the extent to which Roman Catholics are still concerned about questions that Lutherans believe they have already answered in the context of arguments with the Reformed and the "enthusiasts." It is surprising (and disappointing!) for Lutherans to discover that in spite of all the evidence to the contrary in such battles, popular instruction — sometimes even on a seminary level — has taught Catholics that Lutherans are "subjectivists." Roman Catholics will likely say the same sort of thing about Lutherans. Most Lutherans know little of what such things as Jansenism or the Modernist movement meant for Roman Catholicism. Consequently we often find ourselves arguing about ancient formulas and stereotypes that, while indeed still reflecting differences, can obscure as much as disclose what is at stake.

This lack of understanding our own histories can also have the effect of obscuring the real nature of the argument and the passions that impel it. Given what I know of the history and current state of Lutheranism, for instance, while ostensibly arguing with my Roman Catholic counterpart I may in fact be arguing as much with ghosts out of the Lutheran past or even perceived present perils within my own house. That is to say, my argument is likely to be shaped as much, if not more, by the subsequent history and the perception of present "danger" as it is by the ancient break. In the meantime, what has happened to the basic differences? Have they grown deeper or come to express themselves in more radical fashion to meet new challenges? We have not paid sufficient attention, I think, to the extent to which the dialogues themselves uncover or even generate differences hitherto only dimly perceived. To be sure, some differences are lessened by seeking consensus. But others may only be "papered over" so as to make further understanding unlikely. To this, I believe, we have to attend more carefully in ecumenical discussion. This essay to honor one of the leading spirits in the ecumenical movement is intended as an experiment in that direction. It aims to pose the question about fundamental differences by speaking of what might be called an impasse in the discussion between Lutherans and Catholics. I call it rather boldly "The Catholic Impasse" because it involves one in questions about what makes and preserves the Catholic faith in our time. Pursuing such questions in a short essay of this sort is risky, no doubt, for it will have to venture into a "no man's land" of more or less free reflection without the benefit of the covering fire of footnotes to protect from the usual academic sniping. But so it is when one enters uncharted territory, and it is hoped that the venture will be worth the risk.

To begin in useful fashion today from a Lutheran perspective our question should be something of a self-examination: What makes and keeps a contemporary, postliberal Lutheran catholic? Why do I confess, cherish, preserve, and teach the catholic faith today? Why should I be interested at all in being a "catholic" believer? If I understand matters at all, it would seem that I do so for reasons that seem to me to be quite — indeed, fundamentally — different from those I see generally operative in the Roman Catholic Church. If that is the case, we have to do with something of a fundamental difference as it appears today, and not merely with ancient difficulties. If we probe such difference I expect we might be closer to understanding one another. But we need to unpack our question more fully to get at what is involved therein.

What is a contemporary, postliberal Lutheran? To frame something of an answer we have to back up a bit, at least as far as the Enlightenment.

What we say in an essay of this sort will of necessity be cast in broad and perhaps oversimplified generalizations, but that is unavoidable. How did the churches react to the break in the history of the West called the Enlightenment and its social and political aftermath? In broad terms, the reaction was of two sorts: resistance or accommodation. For both Catholics and Protestants the resistance took the form of a defensive hardening of lines against the Enlightenment "erosion" of the biblical and apostolic faith. At its apex, the hardening of lines took the form of rallying behind infallibilism: papal infallibility in the case of Rome and biblical infallibility or inerrancy in the case of Protestants. The threatened erosion of apostolic or scriptural truth by Enlightenment criticism could best and most safely be countered by outright refusal to consider the argument. The fact that both Catholics and Protestants reacted with something of the same tactic indicates that both operated with pretty much the same hermeneutical principles: the authoritativeness of the Holy Words rests almost exclusively in their ability to signify something on the order of "metaphysical" truth: i.e., "true doctrines." Where criticism erodes this ability or where the proper interpretation of the words is questioned, additional authoritative support is needed. Thus the resort to infallibilist claims, either ecclesiastical or scriptural. On the other hand, those who found the criticism of the Enlightenment convincing or inescapable believed that some attempt at accommodation was the only course open. Among Roman Catholics such attempts earned the name of "Modernism." Among Protestants it was called Liberalism. Broadly speaking we shall take "liberalism" in this essay to mean attempts to "liberate" from ecclesiastical or biblical authoritarianism by grounding faith elsewhere in "natural," human religious experience.

But now, for the most part, the great move toward accommodation has lost its steam or run off into sand. It was quashed in Roman Catholicism by the put-down of Modernism and superseded or upstaged in Protestantism by theological renewals of this century broadly characterized as "Neo-orthodoxy." One can, of course, debate whether the move to accommodation has in actual fact played itself out. Modernism may have been quashed, but certainly its questions linger and continue to shape current Roman Catholic theological debate and trouble ecclesiastical practice. Liberalism may no longer be fashionable among Protestants but it has left its mark. Indeed, one could argue that it has triumphed altogether in many theological circles, or perhaps even that matters have proceeded quite beyond accommodation to a capitulation complete enough to shock even an old-time liberal! But the latter case serves perhaps as much to punctuate our judgment as refute it. The age of accommodation is over. One has either to find some way back to the catholic faith or sell out altogether to whatever one may glean from the vestigial remains of the general religiosity of the age and its surrogates.

But now to return to our question. Where does Lutheranism stand in all of this? What makes and keeps a postliberal Lutheran catholic? What brings a postliberal Lutheran back to faith in the triune God, the divine/human redeemer, the atonement, the resurrection, the church, i.e., the main corpus of traditional catholic doctrine? Most assuredly not the magisterial authority of an infallible ecclesiastical office or assertions about the inerrancy of an infallible scripture. And not, certainly, just romantic nostalgia for the safety of a lost conservative haven. The Enlightenment has swept all that away. It is when we pose this question in the light of recent history that we arrive at what we have termed "the catholic impasse" and begin to locate what would likely have to be considered a "fundamental difference" today.

To state the impasse at the outset, it has been my experience that precisely that which makes a postliberal Lutheran catholic is that which makes most Roman Catholics exceedingly nervous and what they appear most concerned to reject. The "postliberal Lutheran" is, of course, something of a shadowy, if not menacing, figure on the contemporary scene, perhaps not yet clearly defined, often a puzzle to both friend and foe, usually mistaken simply for a hard-line conservative confessionalist or orthodoxist. But that is seriously to misread the situation. It is a post-Enlightenment, postliberal position. A postliberal Lutheran is one who has been through the options spawned since the Reformation and realizes that they have all been used up. Least of all does infallibilism or reactionary conservatism of any sort provide an answer. In any case, Lutherans have always been uneasy with infallibilist solutions to faith's questions. Even where they have flirted with the ideas of scriptural infallibility they have had some anxiety and suspicion that it might be contrary to a gospel appropriation of the scriptural message. But attempts to ground faith in "natural religious experience" of some sort are also perceived finally to undercut the gospel as well and do not finally liberate. Thus the postliberal has been driven to reach back beyond the confessional, "orthodox," and liberal settlements and compromises of the post-Reformation era to the roots of the Reformation protest, particularly in Luther himself. What attracts the postliberal to Luther and the Reformation is precisely the most radical dimensions of the message that give promise of new possibilities beyond used-up options. In particular, one has to point to such things as what it means to be a theologian of the cross rather than a theologian of glory,[3] the argument against nascent humanism in *The Bondage of the Will,* and the significance for hermeneutics of the arguments about letter and spirit, law and gospel. None of these things, it is to be noted, are discussed in any depth in ecumenical dialogues. When the issues are raised, they usually meet with stony and studied silence. Indeed, it is significant, and a mark of the impasse here, that Roman Catholic theologians mostly show a marked preference for the more irenic and even innocuous formulations of Melanchthon in such crucial instances. But the irony is that the "Melanchthonian trajectory," if one may call it that, does not lead back to the catholic faith, but rather in the direction of Reformed Christianity and finally liberal accommodation. It is precisely Luther's radical stance that grounds and preserves the catholic faith and recalls the postliberal to that faith today. The fact that this is ignored in ecumenical dialogue means, in effect, two things. First, that whatever voice a postliberal Lutheranism may have is effectively silenced, and second, that reactionary infallibilism or liberal accommodation of some sort remain practically the only ready responses to the Enlightenment in the church. Contemporary Christians, Catholics or Protestant, are confronted with the choice of either capitulation to authoritarianism or a kind of liberal accommodation to the fads of the age.

What is it in the theology of Luther that attracts a postliberal and impels a return to the catholic faith? In the trade one has grown used to the idea that it is something peculiar to the theology of the young Luther that fascinates. That is shortsighted if one knows what one is looking for, but we need not argue that here. What is it? One could say many things or approach the matter from several different angles. Here, however, it will have to do to say it is simply the peculiar realization that the proclamation of the gospel when rightly done as the "word of the cross" itself cuts the ground out from under previous ways of doing theology, and does it more

---

3. It is important to state the matter in terms of the being of the theologian rather than abstractly in terms of "a" or "the" theology of the cross. It is difficult if not impossible to write "the" theology of the cross. It is rather a matter of how the theologian operates, what theology is for, what one does with it.

surely and radically than the Enlightenment ever did. The Enlightenment attacked the church and its God, you might say, but left autonomous man more or less intact. Luther, however, attacked autonomous man in the name of God and his Christ. He saw that as the heart of the matter. In joining the battle with Erasmus he addressed the world yet to come. In this sense one finds in Luther a critique in the name of the gospel more radical than that of the Enlightenment while at the same time detecting a proposal for a different way of being a theologian and doing theology. It is the recognition that the proclamation of the gospel is an absolute end to the old and its ways and a new beginning, a putting to death of the old and a calling of the new into being in faith.

If we are to set the impasse of which we speak clearly in focus, there are at least two things to be noted about such claims in behalf of a postliberal Lutheranism. First of all, it is the *right proclamation* of the gospel that does the deed. Proclamation of a quite specific sort is mandated, one that succeeds in being living, present-tense gospel declaration that ends the reign of law and sin. That is, not Bible reading, not teaching, not meditation, not some supposed direct or immediate mystical experience or encounter with "the spirit," however valuable such things may be, but concrete person-to-person address is the only vehicle for a communication that could be called gospel. Paradigmatically it finds its most direct expression in its liturgical forms: "I absolve you," "I baptize you," etc., and in that finds its roots in the catholic faith. And if one follows the "theologic" of such pronouncements one realizes they can only be made in the name of the triune God.

Second, it is crucial, particularly for Roman Catholics, to see that in the Lutheran view such proclamation absolutely requires a proclaimer. This, if anything, has become more clear for the postliberal than it was even for the Reformation age or certainly for subsequent Protestant optimism about the possibility of "finding God" somewhere. The postliberal recognizes that all the other options seeking to ground faith in religious experience, mediated via either "enlightenment" or via immediate experience of whatever sort, are used up because there is no gospel there. If there is to be anything called gospel it must be proclaimed and therefore requires a proclaimer. Or, as the *Augsburg Confession* puts it, by the very fact of providing the gospel and the sacraments, "God has instituted the office of preaching" (Art. V). Roman Catholics from the beginning seem to have feared that Lutherans were "subjectivists" proposing an unmediated gospel. But this is clearly not the case, or at least would have been clear had more notice been taken of bitter battles with the "spiritualists." If faith comes by hearing, there must be a speaker, indeed, a word from without — what Luther called "the external word." The sacraments punctuate this inescapable externality. Precisely in that sense they *are* the gospel.

If that is understood, it is apparent that too much time has been wasted on the question of mediation as such. There should be no disagreement over whether or not the gospel is mediated. Indeed, I should think it could be agreed that it is of the very essence of the catholic faith that it insists on the concrete mediation of God's saving gifts. That is not where the impasse comes to light. It appears rather when we begin to ask *what* in fact is mediated and how that *what* affects and shapes the mediation and the "office" through which the mediation takes place. In a recent reflection on the U.S. Lutheran-Catholic dialogue, Karl Peter put the matter thus:

> There are, as I see it, genuine differences between Lutheran and Roman Catholic members of the dialogue when it comes to assessing creaturely mediation and cooperation in the ways in which Christ's grace reaches human beings. Two different approaches are taken — motivated at least in part by diverse hopes and fears. Lutherans have a fear that the truth of Christ's unique mediation will be compromised and hope to avoid this by criticizing any function, form of worship or piety, office or person that looks like a pretender in this context. Roman Catholics fear that Christ's unique mediation will thus be made needlessly fruitless and hope to avoid this by stressing the truth of the manifold cooperation to which that mediation gives rise as his grace is communicated to those in need of it.
>
> I suspect that we are dealing here with what ecumenists today might call a fundamental difference. I doubt that it will ever be completely eliminated. But could such a difference exist in a more united church — could it be a difference within one faith rather than of diverse faiths?[4]

While Peter's statement does accurately reflect differences that surfaced in the dialogue they are stated too formally, I believe, to get at what is at stake. It is not simply the bare uniqueness of Christ's mediatorship versus human

4. "A Moment of Truth for Lutheran-Catholic Dialogue," *Origins* 17 (31): 541.

cooperation that reveals the "fundamental difference," but the question of how what is mediated reflects back on the mediation itself and the offices that carry it. For the "office" is precisely to proclaim the gospel of Jesus Christ that sets believers free. What is to be mediated is the freedom in Christ that comes through the death of the old and the rebirth of the new. The gospel of that freedom is consequently the highest exercise of authority in the church. To place something above the proclamation of that gospel would be simply to subvert it. The mediation, therefore, though absolutely necessary, is such that in the very act of mediation it limits itself. I am tempted to use an image from the television show "Mission Impossible" where the "team" receives its instructions via a tape or record that then announces that it will self-destruct in a number of seconds. The mediation is such that it seeks to remove itself once it has done the mediation. It seeks to set people free, that is, to get out of the way for the Christ it proclaims. "He must increase, I must decrease." Eschatologically speaking, the mediation is such that it limits itself to this age and ends itself precisely by its witness to the new age, the kingdom of God. The office does not seek to call attention to itself and impress its "subjects" with its institutional grandeur and perpetuity, but to commend all to the Christ who is the sole head of the church. It does not seek to subjugate people to itself, but to place them securely in Christ, who shall be all in all, and so to work itself out of a job. The peculiarity of this office, therefore, consists precisely in the recognition of its penultimate character and so in its announcement of the end of all offices. Where it claims more than that it betrays itself into the hands of law. It may be claimed with some justice that this office is the "highest," but that is so only because, so to speak, it is the last office to close!

Now perhaps we are in a position to speak more directly about "the catholic impasse." One way to put the matter is in terms of the old question about the concreteness and objectivity of the church's message. John Henry Cardinal Newman voiced a common Catholic complaint when he called Protestantism a great abstraction divorced from the actual flow of history. Perhaps there is some truth to that if one has in mind a Protestantism that hides behind the inerrancy of scripture and seeks only to repristinate the past. But the real question is what constitutes or guarantees true concreteness and "objectivity" in the church. Can claims made about the institution do it? A postliberal Lutheran is not likely to find such claims attractive or convincing. What attracts, however, is simply the power of the gospel proclaimed as the word of the cross. The theologian of the cross is aware of a quite different sort of concreteness and objectivity: that of the quite alien and external word that puts the old subject to death to raise up the new. Perhaps one can say that it is only in death and the promise of new life that we come up against that which is truly and irreducibly "from without." And only so is it truly "objective." In this light, institutional claims to objectivity fall short of the mark. At best they preserve a kind of continuity under the law, and if not limited, put the gospel in jeopardy.

So we have to ask, in conclusion, whether we do not arrive at what appears to be a real impasse over the grounding of the catholic faith. What attracts and holds a contemporary postliberal Lutheran to the catholic faith is the very things that a Catholic is likely to reject — or at least has done so to date. Is this a real impasse? Is it permanent? Or if so, can we live with it together in the same church? Whatever our personal answers may be, only time and the will of God will tell. However, it is to be hoped that precisely in attempts such as this to probe what seem to be real differences, equally real and deep commonalities hitherto unnoticed will come to light. Certainly in this essay the insistence upon the mediation of God's saving gifts in Christ Jesus our Lord and the necessity for the mediation of those gifts objectively and concretely in the living present reveals a bond in the catholic faith that, it is to be hoped, unites us more deeply the more we understand the difference. If that is the case, the essay will have reached its goal.

SERMONS

God's Rights

Am I not allowed to do what I choose with what is my own?

Matthew 20:1-16

"Am I not allowed to do what I choose with what is my own?" That is the unsettling word that closes in upon us in this familiar parable. It seems to be about rights. We hear a lot about rights these days: "inalienable rights" to life, liberty, and the pursuit of just about anything one might hanker after. Human rights, civil rights, right to life, right to bear arms, gay rights, gray rights, minority rights, women's rights, children's rights, animal rights — you name it, someone demands it or is demonstrating for it.

But now, like a bolt from the blue, a comet from some undiscovered realm, another right announces itself, projects itself smack into the middle of the payday lines of life: God's rights. Some came early, some late, and they all got the same — regardless. Is it not preposterous? Whoever heard of such a thing? And if that was not bad enough, the protest just gets the back of the hand: "Am I not allowed to do what I choose with what is my own?" How can we possibly accept that? Does God have the right to intrude, to butt in, on our affairs like that? For that matter, does anyone believe in God anymore — or at least a God like that? Oh yes, we tell ourselves that we do. We tell ourselves that God is, in general, love, and as such can be safely filed away in the back of the drawer. At best, God hovers in the background or just beyond the horizon of our important, busy lives.

God is a cipher whom we flatter with our favorite and most innocuous names. Can *God* actually intrude in this fashion? Yes, we talk rather grandly about "first article" concerns, but mostly that turns out to be about us, after all, not the Creator.

But here it is otherwise. God plants himself squarely — looks us straight in the eye and declares: "Am I not allowed to do as I choose with what is my own?" God's rights. The Creator's rights! What rights? We are not left to wonder: "Do you begrudge me my generosity?" God claims the right to be generous, to intrude, to butt in, if you will, not only to be gener-ous, but to give everyone the same. He risks the right to break up the whole show, to say something new, to start something new. And I expect that is what really galls us. As the Greek has it here: "Is your eye evil because I am good?" It is not the idea of generosity as such. Generosity is a nice idea. We are all for that — as long as it remains an idea. If God would just stay in heaven with the idea, or at least be fair about it and give payment where it is due, or be universal about it — be love in general — we could live with it. But actually to come, to intrude, to be generous to someone in particu-lar — to give to those lazy ones the same as me, and just claim the right to do so — that is surely too much.

Yes, it is indeed preposterous. Except . . . except, of course, if it is our only real chance. Except if it *is* true. For if we are honest, what chance do we have, other than the sheer generosity of God? What chance do we have if all the laborers do not get the same? Where would we be if we got what we deserved? What chance do we have if God doesn't assert his rights, re-mains in heaven, and is just love in general? "Am I not allowed to do what I choose with what is my own?" Could it be that is our only chance, our one and only real chance?

But where does that leave us? What is it that this God who claims such a right actually chooses to do? It would be a cruel trick if, after all this talk about God's right to do as he chooses, God actually does nothing after all. So we come to the heart of the matter — one last preposterous move. God has chosen that a word be spoken to you, a word that levels everything and puts an end to the old game and starts something new. It was a great risk. The world did not approve of this parable. This is not strange, for it is indeed awful — it meets no "need" of ours — so that we killed the one who told it. But *God* approved and raised him from the dead so the word should again be spoken, activating his Kingdom. "Am I not allowed to do what I choose with what is my own?" That's the way it is with God's grace

— it's wild! It is God who has brought us to this, so now there is no way around it — I *must* say it: "You are God's own! You were claimed as God's own in baptism. God did what he wanted, did what he chose — with you. And if you have forgotten that, hear it again. Come and taste it. God claims the right to butt in here-and-now and permits his word of grace to be said to you: *I declare unto you the forgiveness of your sins!* There it is. Isn't that preposterous? Something absolutely novel? Not an ideal, not a generality, but a meeting, a new word, God's choice to do something here and now. You have heard it, there it is. How do you know there is a God? Through this!

Now perhaps you may be a little bit disappointed: Is that all there is? Should there not be something more? Have we not heard that before? As we like to put it now and then, "Do we always have to be talking about salvation? Is there not something beyond that?" Particularly since we have gotten ourselves off to the holy ministry or seminary we might like to think that grander things are in store. Well, we need to recall that this parable was told particularly for religious folk. They all got the same, you see. There isn't any more. God has invested everything just to arrange this sort of meeting, to intrude, to break in and do a new thing, to speak to you. To make new beings — called into new life from that which was not — creatures who actually rejoice at this seemingly unjust arrangement. God is not out just to be generous in himself but to *do* this to us, to make us new out of his generosity. The generosity itself spells the end of the old, kills the protester, brooks no resistance, and thus it saves, and makes us new. Isn't that fantastic? Is there anything more? There is, perhaps, only that parting warning shot across the bow for those who don't see: so the last will be first and the first last. We might comfort ourselves that being last is better than nothing, but it is a dangerous slight.

So we end where we started: God's rights. "Am I not allowed to do as I choose with what is my own?" You are God's own. Think on that! Isn't it wild? Don't you see? All *our* schemes and projects are over. And maybe, just maybe, if we catch a glimpse of what that means, all those other arguments about rights would begin to fall into place.

So, anyone for the vineyard?

Exsurge Domine!

Arise, O God, plead thy cause;
Remember how the impious scoff
At thee all the day!
Do not forget the clamor of thy foes,
The uproar of thy adversaries
Which goes up continually!

Psalm 74:22-23

The opening line of our text, if you recall, reminds us that the man whose birth and baptism we commemorate today was excommunicated by "the Holy Catholic Church." The words from Psalm 74 are the opening words of the Bull of Pope Leo X threatening Martin Luther with excommunication: *Exsurge Domine et judica causam tuam.* Martin Luther was indeed excommunicated and, as we all know, he has never been reinstated in spite of occasional nice, ecumenical things said about him every now and again. This is not said in acrimony and certainly not to incite some fresh hatred against the Catholic Church or anyone, but only that we might get our bearings in trying to talk about this man. Perhaps we have grown too cozy with him through the years. We have thought, since we do bear his name, that he was somehow ours: our champion, our hero, our saint, our authority in our rather petty ecclesiastical chauvinisms and jealousies. Perhaps he is even our fate, and to that degree we may even come to resent him as our plague or oppressor, from whom we can never seem to escape — and even if we do we simply lose our identity. But he is not ours. He can't be domesticated. His unrevoked excommunication should remind us, especially now, that we find it convenient or at least politic to agree more often with the sort of things against which he argued so bitterly. He is a more or less permanent outsider, or at least expendable, the odd man out in most theological and ecumenical dialogues. I have been through enough of them to know that. Those ready to go the whole way with this man are very few and far, far between. He is, in that sense, at least, a heretic. Whether that is because he is too big or the church too small is the question that hangs in the balance.

Exsurge Domine et judica causam tuam! Old Pope Leo had it right on that score at least. It is a question of the *causa,* the cause — indeed, ultimately God's cause not Luther's. Only the problem here is that we run into a man whose course of life, because of the concrete circumstances, became so identified, so possessed (and this is the right word: possessed) by the cause that it is very difficult to separate the man from the cause. His life in a peculiar way became the mirror, the vehicle of the cause, and he saw it. Luther's cause, we should not forget, was the gospel of Jesus Christ, justification by faith alone without the works of the law and what happens when someone finally hears that. Shocked and scandalized, old Pope Leo, vicar of Christ, head of the church, could only call for help: "Arise, O Peter, and in the name of the pastoral charge committed to thee from on high, put forth thy strength in the cause of the holy Roman church, the mother of all churches. . . . Arise thou also, O Paul, we beg thee, who has enlightened her with thy teaching. . . . A wild boar has invaded thy vineyard!"

Yes, that's probably about it! A wild boar, charging, snorting about and uprooting everything — making havoc of the supposedly serene, ancient, venerable, nicely trimmed vineyard. Wild, undomesticated, Luther was not what the world or the church would call a saint. In itself, of course, that is not unusual. Most of us aren't! But the shocking thing was, no doubt, that he didn't think that was important to aspire to, or even possible, given the circumstances at least. And that was just his "heresy." He himself said it at Wörms: "I confess that I have been more acrimonious than befits my religion or my calling. For I do not pose as a saint, and I am not disputing about my own life but about the teaching of Christ." There wasn't time to be a saint. There were more important things to do. He was just a man, caught in the web of his own circumstances, who sought only to be faithful to his concrete calling and do to it with all the élan and gusto he could muster. He sought only to live as though God justifies sinners for Jesus' sake. That was his "heresy," and in a way the "catholic" world has never quite understood or forgiven him for it.

Arise, O Lord and judge your cause! Yes, that must still be the plea, I expect, when we talk about Martin Luther. He knew what he was up to. He knew full well that it was something of a scandal and his polemics something of an offense, not only to his enemies, but also to his more faint-hearted friends. When it was said that Philip Melanchthon was a fine example of the greatest moderation in negotiations for the cause, he replied, "The little fellow is a godly man . . . his intention is not bad . . . but . . . he hasn't accomplished much by his method. . . . I think . . . that my way is still the best. I speak right out and scold my opponents like schoolboys. For a knotty stump requires a tough wedge." Indeed. How else shall one strike at the root of the pious pretension of a world that pays lip service to the ideals of sainthood and uses it as a cover for its nefarious business? His advice to a timorous Melanchthon was that scandalous letter (August 1521) in which he said,

> If you are a preacher of grace, then preach grace that is true and not fictitious; if grace is true, you must be a true and not fictitious sinner. God does not save fictitious sinners. Be a sinner and sin boldly, but have faith and rejoice in Christ more boldly still, for he is the victory over sin, death and world. . . . This world is not the dwelling place of righteousness, but as Peter says, we look for a new heavens and a new earth in which righteousness dwells. . . . Do you think that the price that was paid for the redemption of our sins by so great and such a Lamb was so small (that sin could tear us away from him)?

But that is "heresy" is it not? Arise, O Lord, and judge your cause!

There is about the man a kind of reckless and tempestuous *hilaritas*, the joyousness of a faith willing to risk anything for the cause. Peter Mosellanus, writing on his impressions of the Leipzig debate, paints an interesting picture of Luther:

> In daily life and manners he is cultivated and affable, having nothing of the stoic and nothing supercilious about him; rather he plays the man at all seasons. He is a joker in society, vivacious and sure, always

with a happy face no matter how hard his enemies press him. You would hardly believe he was the man to do such great things unless inspired by the gods. But what most men blame in him is that in answering he is more imprudent and cutting than is safe for a reformer of the church, or than is decorous for a theologian.

"More imprudent and cutting than is safe for a reformer!" Yes, that is the problem. "A joker in society." Imagine that! Eric Gritsch has recently published a book entitled *Martin, God's Court Jester!* An apt title in many ways. Part of Luther's heresy, we can aver, was to introduce some laughter into the church, a kind of rollicking, Rabelaisian sense of humor. He was imprudent enough to think that much of the folly of church and world was more deserving of laughter and even ridicule than of serious discussion. The best cure for the devil was to fart in his face! He could dare to laugh at what the world calls serious and weep over what it finds ridiculous. He was a relentless exposer of pious pretense, one of the few people in the history of the world, as Norman Brown could say, who refused to sublimate. Here's old Duke Henry of Braunschweig/Wolfenbüttel, for instance, posing as a defender of the faith and writing tracts about it, a man who kept his brother imprisoned to extend his power, was rumored to have burned towns to the ground for the same reason, and even kept a mistress secreted in one of his castles to "meet his needs." Luther advised him, "You should not write another book before you have heard an old sow fart, and then you should open your trap with awe and sing, 'O you beautiful nightingale, now at last I hear a word that is for me!'" More imprudent and cutting than is safe for a Reformer of the church! Or is it? But what should one say to such people? Arise, O Lord, and judge your cause?

In the midst of the tempestuous events of 1525, the debate with Erasmus, the Peasant's Revolt, when the Reformation cause was hanging in the balance and Luther thought things were so bad the world was about to end, what did he do? He got married! Is it not preposterous? Could there be a more "heretical" response to fears about the end of the world? His friends were appalled and feared he would wreck the cause completely. Ah, but what *was* the cause? That is the question. He said that if the world was going to end then he ought perhaps to be found doing what the good Lord created him for, taking care of creation, and that he would do his part to the end no matter how much the pope, the princes, the peasants, or the whole world refused to do theirs. What was the cause, if not becoming

God's creatures? He said he thought it would make the angels laugh and the devils weep. But the world then apparently couldn't laugh. Perhaps even today, if for quite other reasons — or are they at bottom somehow the same? — the angels will have to laugh alone — if, indeed, even *they* have anything to laugh about anymore!

Arise, O Lord, and judge your cause. We have learned, since historical fate has saddled us with Luther's name, to try to make our feeble excuses for him, launder him, somehow to make him a saint to relieve our embarrassment. After all, we can excuse that in him for that was only human. It was due to the nature of the times and we in our day know so much better, and so on and so on. But, he would neither want to be excused for that nor countenance our excuses. I expect, at bottom, we find him upsetting and offensive because it is really *we* who are being attacked! So he lived, so he believed, and so he died, scribbling a note saying, "We are beggars, that's for sure!" The cause was the gospel. In the crucible of his particular circumstance, he would tolerate no opposition to that in whatever form, be it legalism, license, hypocrisy, or even what the world calls sainthood — from whatever source, be it pope, priest, humanist, Jew, Turk, prince or peasant, or whatever favorite cause, however legitimate humanly speaking. Should one, can one, risk that? Not if you want to be a saint! He couldn't and didn't want to play the game. God, not popes, or popular opinion, or majority votes make saints, he said. God makes them by his judgment — his grace alone. He is the judge, after all. That means, of course, that Luther neither wanted nor expected to be imitated. Luther is not a general rule, a universal example, a law. He fought, as Aarne Siirala put it, simply for the right to be Martin Luther, creature of God, believer, preacher of the gospel. He figured that if the good Lord was going to have him he would have to take him just as he made him, warts and all. Perhaps, if we could ever get that straight, we might get some clearer vision of what the cause is and where it might take us today. For, is it not true that somehow it always seems safer for us to sink back into something like the pious ideals and high-sounding assurances of the Pope's Bull? Luther, you know, threw it in the fire, burned it to ashes with the words, "Because thou hast destroyed the truth of God, may the Lord consume thee in these flames!"

"The theologian of glory," he said once, "calls the bad good and the good bad. The theologian of the cross says what a thing is." Somebody has to tell it like it is. Even if just for once! What about you? Arise, O Lord, and judge your cause! Amen.

Hidden Treasure

The Kingdom of Heaven is like treasure hidden in a field,
which a man found and covered up, then in his joy he goes
and sells all that he has and buys that field.

Matthew 13:44

There are two basic dreams we have about life. The first is very common
and respectable. We are not ashamed at all to subscribe to it. It is the dream
of "making it," the dream of making something of our lives, of being a success at something or finding our niche, of providing care for our own, and
perhaps even becoming prominent, well known, well liked, respected, a
good person, a successful pastor, making a name for ourselves, maybe even
"making a bundle." It is a dream that drives us in everyday life, beats the
drum to our ambitions, and stirs our moral fiber. Everything is relatively
ordered, scheduled, expected, nailed down. Or at least we try to make it be.
In itself, it is not a bad dream. That is the way things run in this life. That is
what spurs us on. But sometimes, perhaps even all too often, it becomes a
wild, wild, dream. We begin to think it leads to God. We begin to think we
can make it all the way to him — do enough, believe enough, grit our
teeth, and decide. It turns into the fantasy whispered in the ear of our first
ancestors: "You shall not die, you shall be as gods." "You can make it." And
then we are had. Everything, even our theology, will be put in the service of
that dream. Then we are lost.

But there is also a second dream. It is a peculiar kind of dream, a secret sort of dream, one about which we are half embarrassed, a little bit sheepish. It is the dream that some day, somehow, out of the blue, in utter contradiction to the stark realities of "actual existence," my "ship will come in." Perhaps an unknown rich uncle will die and leave me a million bucks. Maybe I will win a lottery and get a free ride from here on. Maybe I will discover a cache of old bills in the attic. Maybe I will win a dream home or a hundred dollars a month for life. After all, the come-on says, "Your number may already have been drawn, and you are not obligated to buy a thing." I know it's silly, but nevertheless I sneak down to the mailbox with the coupon or the card, hoping no one will see me, and I drop it in just in case. I've never won anything before, but who knows? Maybe this time it's my turn. I can hope, can't I? The dream is there somewhere. We may hide it, forget it, repress it, but it's there!

Now Jesus tells us that the kingdom of heaven answers to that second, silly, embarrassing little dream of ours. Imagine that! The kingdom of heaven is like *that*, like treasure hidden in a field that a man stumbled onto. That's something of a shocker! It would certainly seem more likely that the kingdom of heaven should be likened to that first dream, that of "making it." Certainly that is much more serious and preferable! For that dream is much more sensible and, of course, much more manageable. For then we could get everything all arranged with God. We could get our schedules all worked out. We could look matters over at our leisure and decide about things heavenly. We could perhaps postpone that decision or draw closer to it at will, perhaps even conjure up an experience or two according to our liking, get all our traffic with God down to manageable dimensions. Isn't that a much more practical way to think of it?

But the trouble is, it's not like that. It's like treasure hidden in a field onto which one fine day you just stumble, something you can't stage-manage at all. In a way, you can't even decide about it. After all, wouldn't it be rather silly to get up in the morning, look in the mirror and say to yourself, "Today I've decided to find some hidden treasure"? Our parable assures us it is not like that at all. It isn't planned or scheduled or managed — at least, not according to *our* plans or schedules. It just happened to the man "out of the blue." He just stumbled onto it. He didn't do anything for it. He didn't work for it, he didn't earn it; he just stumbled onto it!

But, you say, doesn't that leave the whole thing "up in the air," unstructured, something we can't ever get our hands on? We sputter all sorts of questions in our frustration. In the first place, if the kingdom of heaven is like treasure hidden in a field onto which someone just stumbles, doesn't that make the whole thing seem too easy, too cheap? The lucky stiff! He didn't deserve it! He just stumbled onto it! Why him? Cheap grace? Perhaps, in a sense, not at all. Because the man in the parable gave up everything for it. In his joy he went and sold *everything* to get that field. He blew it all for that one thing. Everything that he had been up to now was over. He was a different man. And note well, it was in his *joy* that he went and did that. Cheap? Not cheap; but *FREE!* It set him free — free to sell out everything he had.

But, you say, if the kingdom is like that, like treasure hidden in a field, doesn't that make it arbitrary and capricious? Maybe. But how else can you talk about an absolute, sheer gift? If it were not like that, where would be the surprise? Where would be the joy? If it were not like that would you be willing to sell all? You would no doubt want to hold back some of your bargaining power, perhaps go on the installment plan with all sorts of consumer protections built in, maybe even ask for a free trial period. But you see, you can't do business with the kingdom of heaven that way. It is like treasure hidden in a field. It is sheer, unexpected, undeserved, absolute gift.

Even when all that is said, we are faced with the fact that the mystery grows even deeper. For when the man found the treasure, he covered it up. Why? It might appear to us that his behavior was slightly unethical — he covered it up so he could buy the field before the owner discovered the treasure, or before someone else had a chance at it. But that is not the point. Quite probably, the man's action is related to the very nature of Jesus' parables. The parable hides even as it reveals, so that the dull-hearted and those whose ears have grown fat shall hear but never understand, see but never perceive. The treasure is hidden and it stays that way, even upon being found. For if it were not so, we might contrive to turn even the finding of hidden treasure into some kind of general rule. You see, we will try anything to control the dream and bring it to heel. We will do everything we can to convert the second dream back to the first. If it got out that the man found treasure, it would not be long before everybody would be out there rooting around messing up the poor man's field! We try everything in our power to set up some general plan by which the kingdom of heaven might be domesticated. If that could be done, we might end this little talk with a stirring summons for you to go out and find your hidden treasure. You would be encouraged to keep on plodding along faithfully, plowing your field, in the hope that some day, somewhere, you will find your hidden treasure! But that is impossible! It *is* hidden treasure, and it *stays* that way.

But if that is the way it is, what can we do finally with this parable? What, ultimately, can be said? I can't give you a plan. I can't set you up with a schedule. I can't send you on a treasure hunt. It would seem as though I had talked myself into a corner. Am I not reduced finally to silence? No! For there is only one thing left I can do. I can only *give* you the treasure. I can only say: Repent, for you have stumbled onto it today, *here and now.* For I say unto you, your sins are forgiven for Jesus' sake. *There it is!* Your sins are forgiven! Jesus entered into the darkness, the nothingness of death, and he rose triumphant for you! There is the hidden treasure! The kingdom of heaven comes to you today, in that you didn't earn it, plan it, expect it perhaps, but there it is. The kingdom of heaven comes to you today in that just as sure as I am standing here and you are sitting there, this is the moment God has decided on. He comes to you in his word. It is not my word, but his. Believe it, it's for you! He has come to you in baptism, taken you as his child. That is what he has decided to do about you. You have that hidden treasure — your ship has come in! He comes to you today in his sacrament here at his table in that bit of bread, that cup of wine, and says, "This is my body, this is my blood, and it's for you." It's like a package from home when you are far away and lonely. It reminds you to whom you belong and promises you that you will one day be back. It's here and it's for you. Eat, drink, rejoice, for here it is. God has come all the way to you! Today you have stumbled onto it! Isn't that wild? The time has come to sell out! Sell all your doubts and reservations. Sell all your attempts to hang onto the way things are. There is a new you on the way, a new kingdom under way: believe it! It will save you. Sell out, turn around. Look at God's good creation, look at what we have done to it, look into the face of starving humanity. Forget yourself, give yourself to others. They need you. They need that hidden treasure. Give it to them. Jesus entered into the nothingness of death and rose triumphant for you! *There it is!* He that has ears to hear, let him hear! Sell out!

You Have Died

COLOSSIANS 2:20–3:4

You have died, and your life is hid with Christ in God! I expect you did not reckon when, for whatever reason you bestirred yourself to show up here today, that you were going to a funeral. And you probably wondered when you saw the order of service, who has died? I've got news for you. In case you haven't heard yet — you have! I am reminded of my favorite O. M. Norlie story about the time when he was preaching a funeral sermon. As the custom was, he read the obituary before the sermon. As it happened, he had clipped it out of the local newspaper. So he read along to the end about how the deceased was survived by so many children, and "the funeral will be held tomorrow from First Lutheran Church." He stopped somewhat befuddled and said, "No, no, that's today. We're having it now!" And so it is. Your funeral is not tomorrow, or next week, or twenty or fifty years from now, it's today. We're having it now. For here stands the Word of God: "You have died!"

A shocking development! Not that you *will* die. It's already past tense: you *have* died. And there is nothing to do about that now. It's over. Nor is it that you *ought* to die, perhaps in some spiritual sense. It's not a project to be undertaken. It's an accomplished fact. It only wants announcing. And so I have to tell you.

But surely this is preposterous! Is it some kind of joke? And isn't it frivolous to do a burial service when there is no coffin? Is there not some way to escape? Perhaps it is after all only a metaphor. Perhaps we can say, "You have died, *as it were.*" Or perhaps it is only a peculiar Pauline way of

215

speaking — and you know how Paul likes to exaggerate. Maybe we can take refuge in New Testament pluralism and find a less shocking metaphor. Or perhaps we might say that Colossians is after all deutero-Pauline. Or maybe it was meant only for the Colossians. But it's no use. As Luther liked to say, "Here stands the Word of God." You have died. And there is nothing to do about that now but say it.

For what, after all, did you expect — a little artificial respiration, enough at least to get you through the day? Or did you hope, as they say in the medical profession, to have your condition upgraded from "critical" at least to "serious"? But I can't help you with that. I can only tell you the truth. And the truth is: it's over. You have died. You're through.

But what a pity to be cut down so in the prime of life, just when you thought you were getting somewhere. No doubt, so thought those early Colossians to whom these words were first addressed. They don't appear to have been bad folk. Maybe they were even accomplished religious *virtuosi* who were "getting somewhere" according to their lights, their rules and regulations: "Do not handle, do not taste, do not touch." No doubt there is little danger of that today. But we have our own foibles and dreams "according to human precepts and doctrines." Perhaps you were just getting adept at making all the obligatory noises about today's regulations about abortion, homosexuality, inclusivism, liberation, poverty, and the rights of everybody under the sun, only to have it all, good, bad, and indifferent, cut short by this imperious Word: "You have died!" What a pity to be cut down, to be brought up short by the realization that maybe God has something else in mind, to be caught in a transition of which you are not the master.

But what shall we do with you now that you have died? We can't shovel you under. There will be no committal service. Not just yet. You're still breathing and walking about. Is there any place to stand? Anything to be? Our text puts it this way: "You have died, and your life is hid with Christ in God." Yes, you are still breathing and walking about. But don't you see, that's just the miracle of it; that's the gospel. You have again been given life back, given time, set free in the one who was raised from the dead. Yes, you have died. But now, for the time being, your life is hid with Christ in God. Think of that!

So, what are you to do in the meantime? Our text has some suggestions. "If then you have been raised with Christ, seek the things that are above, where Christ is, seated at the right hand of God. Set your minds on things that are above, not on things that are on earth." Not a very popular agenda these days. You might be accused of being otherworldly or some other heinous sin. What does it mean? At the very least, it places before us a question: Should not Christians, not to say pastors and prospective pastors, have some passion for the gospel? Should they not set their sights on the eschatological vision and hope? If you have died and been raised, what else can you do? To be sure, the world will think you are probably crazy. So be it — your life is hid with Christ in God! But there is a promise. When Christ, who is our life appears, then you too will at last appear with him in glory!

Not bad for one who has died.

The Day of the Lord

2 PETER 3:8-14

The Day of the Lord shall come like a thief! I have always been tempted to think of that as a singularly inappropriate simile for the advent of our Lord! There are, after all, few things so upsetting, outrageous, and sometimes terrifying as the discovery that your home, your turf, your sphere, has been broken into, invaded, even violated by a thief. And most everyone in this evil generation has experienced it at one time or another. The Day of the Lord shall come like that? Surely there must be some mistake. Thieves come stealthily to take things away. Does not our Lord come to give? But before we rush — as is our habit these days — to take this as another instance of the ineptitude of the biblical authors in choosing their metaphors, we should note that it appears several times in the New Testament. Indeed, it is something of a favorite image for the second coming of our Lord. Surely that is no mere coincidence.

And it is not just a metaphor for the suddenness or unexpectedness of our Lord's advent. Rather, it is a reminder (not to say a warning) that he comes finally to close down the whole enterprise and to take away all that which we have so carefully hoarded, coddled, and tended. The sharp-eyed ones have always known that. The demons knew it: "What have we to do with you, O Holy One?" Satan even tried to give him this world. Imagine that! Herod suspected it and his fear drove him to slaughter the innocents at Bethlehem. He didn't want to lose his kingdom, after all! The author of our text is well aware of it, as shown in the claim that "the heavens will pass away with a loud noise, and the elements will be dissolved with fire and the earth and the works that are upon it will be burned up." And we have, of course, already been told: whoever would save his life, whoever tries to hang on to life at all costs, shall lose it. And now we are told that the second time it will be for keeps. One day it has all got to go — all of it — burned to a crisp! And there is no insurance policy to cover it!

What is that to you? The text is quite explicit: don't trade on the fact that it hasn't happened yet. "The Lord is not slow about his promise, but is forbearing toward you, not wishing any should perish, but that all should reach repentance." There is yet time, but the time is now for repentance, for detachment from all your things, yes, perhaps even to think about giving some of it away before it all gets taken away. In some small measure that is what the giving of gifts means during this season.

The day of the Lord shall come like a thief! Ponder that, and repent! Repent even now as he comes to you today in the bread and the wine. There is, you might say, even a foretaste of the divine "thievery" in this meeting as he takes from us all our reliance on our own devices and re-claims his creation: "This bread, this wine, is mine and I mean to have it back. I shall not drink of it again until I drink it anew with you in the King-dom." Ponder that and you will begin to see in the offense of this thievery that it is, after all, the gospel. For, after all, will it not be grand? Suddenly it will all be gone: the whole "works," all the bitter and the sweet fruit of our need and crazy ambition, the poverty and the riches, the fretting about the economy, the budget, the war machine, even all the hurts, the resentments and bitterness we have so carefully coddled and that in some crazy way keep us going — yes, even this lovely chapel and its magnificent organ — burned to a crisp! Won't that be grand? There is a real "Bonfire of the Van-ities" to end all bonfires! And then there will be a new heaven and a new earth in which righteousness dwells. Is that not really good news?

Yes, indeed, the day of the Lord shall come like a thief! In response, let all God's people say: "Even so, come Lord Jesus!"

Jesus Died for You

Jesus died for you. That is all he really did in the days of his flesh that is truly for you. In the end, that is all he could do. He died. He refused to do anything else. "I am the good shepherd," he said, "and the good shepherd lays down his life for the sheep." So his mission was — finally — to die. And it was — for you.

This has to be said so bluntly because too often we are tempted to think he was really doing something else, something that might seem more meaningful and profound religiously. We look at Jesus' death on the cross and we puzzle about it. We ask: "I wonder what it means?" "How could the death of Jesus be for us today? After all, it happened a long time ago." Especially when reading the Bible we think we can answer such questions by discovering some deep and eternal meaning behind the scenes that will reach through time and touch us today. Perhaps "the meaning" is that Jesus was paying God, or even Satan. Or, perhaps, it is in the offer of an exemplary heroic death for us to admire.

So, through the years we have tried to answer questions about how Jesus' death could be *for us* by means of our doctrines of the atonement. The most persistent theme, the one that has seemed most natural and logical to us, has been the idea that Jesus was "for you" because he is our substitute. Jesus does what we ought to do but can't — due to sin. We don't have enough capital to pay the debt. So our "doctrine of atonement" will say that Jesus becomes our substitute and pays a wrathful God what we owe. And since Jesus is not only man but also the Eternal Son, this payment is good for all time.

But such doctrinal explanations seem always to lead us into other puzzling problems. Questions arise that we have difficulty answering. In the first place, the idea that God is paid by the death of Jesus holds us in a false relation to God. It puts our relation on much too commercial a basis. Is God one who can be paid off, even by the death of Jesus? Furthermore, if God is paid, how can we say that God is merciful? Mercy is mercy and not payment. Our relation to God is held by the idea that God is wrathful and cannot forgive unless due payment is made. To be sure, Jesus said that he came to give his life as a "ransom" for us. But it was never said that such ransom was to be paid to God. After all, God sent Jesus to begin with. *God so loved the world that he gave his only begotten Son.*

The second problem has to do with us. How can someone else be our substitute in matters of such high moral purpose? Nobody likes to be benched for a substitute, especially in the big game! "I'll make my own way and pay my own debts. None of that cheap grace for me, thank you very much!" So we are likely to say. The claim that Jesus had to die "for you" gets brushed aside.

But the New Testament witness is persistent: Jesus died "for us," "on our behalf." That is said again and again. Translated into proclamation, it is the bold announcement that Jesus died *for you.*

How can this be? Look at it this way. Jesus, we are told, came preaching repentance and the forgiveness of sin on God's authority. In other words, God didn't have to be paid to forgive, but announced forgiveness through Jesus to begin with. But that is when the trouble starts. For we would not have it. When Jesus forgave the sins of the paralytic who had been let down through the roof, all the people were incensed. "This man is blaspheming," they said! And so it went all through his ministry. The protests grew more and more persistent. One cannot run this world on forgiveness. Finally he was crucified for it. He died for the right to say it. Even from the cross he cried, "Father forgive them, for they don't know what they are doing."

But how shall we say that this death of Jesus was *for us?* All we need to do is to look carefully at what actually happened. We do not need elaborate doctrinal theories. The fact is we killed him. We couldn't let him speak the word of forgiveness. Not here in this place. Our problem is that we live under the law. That is the way our world runs. We succumb to the temptation to regulate even our relationship to God according to law. In that sense we

221

live under the wrath of God. If we wish to live that way, God will oblige. But that is a terrible fate. It means death.

Jesus, however, comes to announce that God won't have it in the end. He comes to establish a new reality, a new relationship. So a mighty clash takes place, a "strange and marvelous strife," Luther liked to call it, in which life and death are contending. Jesus comes into "our place." He is "born of a woman, born under the law, to redeem those that are under the law." He comes to rescue us from our determination to live under the law. But that means he can only die. He cannot come into our world saying, "Come on now folks, be nice! Stop your sinning!" For that would only mean more law. There would be no end to it. He can't win this battle that way. He can't call a halt on the way up to Golgotha and escape from it all. For then there would be no end. He can only go this way to death. The on-lookers, we are told, actually taunted him to put a stop to it: "If you are the Son of God," they said, "come down from the cross." But he did not come down. Had he done that, we would be forever under the law, wrath, and death. Not even God will stop it. Jesus cries, "My God, My God, why have *you* forsaken me?"

So the only thing he can do in the end is die for us. He dies at our hands, hands resolved to go the way of the law, hands that will not give up until they have gotten him out of the way. We don't need to elaborate theories or doctrines of the atonement to see why his death is for us. We lay hands on him and put him to death. And he does not stop us. He goes his way to death without a word — like a sheep before its shearers is dumb. No one takes his part. No one. There is nothing here to imitate or emulate. His disciples betray him, deny him, forsake him, and flee. Even they provide no example for us here. In the end nothing remains even of his life to persuade us to call a halt. He is despised and rejected, "as one from whom we hide our faces" (Isa. 53:3). He dies for us. That is all he can do in the end.

But it was not the end. God vindicates the crucified Jesus by raising him from the dead. Had Jesus remained in the tomb that would have been the sad ending to our story. We would have been right and he wrong. He would remain in the bonds of death and we — supposedly — in life. But now the tables are turned. He is raised. He is right and we wrong; he is alive and we are dead. So now, he alone gives us life, life triumphant over the law, sin, and death that threatens always to consume us.

Jesus died to give us this gift. Jesus died for you.

Not the Well, but the Sick

MATTHEW 9:10-13

The theme for this day in the Week of Prayer for Christian Unity is the openness of the church. Our gospel lesson is appropriate in a double sense. On the one hand it reveals the basis for the unity and openness of the church; on the other it discloses the reason for our disunity, our closedness.

The basis for the unity and openness of the church is given in the fact that this man Jesus, sent from God, eats with tax collectors and sinners. The table is open. All are one before him. No conditions are set. Why then the disunity of the church? The reason is quite simply the same: the fact that Jesus eats with *tax collectors and sinners*. For how, in this world, shall we cope with that? How shall we proceed with matters of Christian unity when the basis for our unity is at the same time the reason for our disunity?

We should make no mistake about this question. It is directed to us as well. Jesus himself puts the answer to this question squarely: "Those who are well need not a physician, but those who are sick." What did he mean? Are we the ones who are sick? Who, then, are the well? Who are the righteous? Are there such? Are there any sick that do not need what he came to give? Much energy has been expended debating this issue. Most of it, no doubt, has been wasted. For the point, surely, is that we approach the table where *he* is the host, and we shall have to speak for ourselves. He decides whom he will invite. Yet once again, today, Jesus comes to eat with tax collectors and sinners. He came not to call the righteous, but sinners. Think on these things!